FIRST ARMY

EIGHTH ARMY

HERALDRY IN WAR

By the Same Writer

BADGES ON BATTLEDRESS: Post-War Formation Signs

Heraldry in War

FORMATION BADGES
1939—1945

Collected and Illustrated
by
LIEUT.-COLONEL HOWARD N. COLE,
O.B.E., T.D.

Revised and Enlarged Edition

The Naval & Military Press Ltd

Published and © by the
The Naval & Military Press

Unit 10 Ridgewood Industrial Park,
Uckfield, East Sussex, TN22 5QE
Tel: +44 (0) 1825 749494
Fax: +44 (0) 1825 765701

MILITARY HISTORY AT YOUR FINGERTIPS
www.naval-military-press.com
ONLINE GENEALOGY RESEARCH
www.military-genealogy.com
ONLINE MILITARY CARTOGRAPHY
www.militarymaproom.com

In reprinting in facsimile from the original, any imperfections are inevitably reproduced and the quality may fall short of modern type and cartographic standards.

CONTENTS

	page
PREFACE	xi
INDEX OF FORMATIONS	xix
HERALDRY IN WAR	1
THE BADGES	
Higher Formations	8
Home Commands	15
Overseas Commands	20
Armies	24
British Corps	30
British Armoured Divisions	39
British Infantry Divisions	46
Airborne Divisions	73
Anti-Aircraft Formations	75
County Divisions (U.K.)	83
Canadian Formations	86
Australian Formations	95
New Zealand Formations	105
South African Formations	108
Indian Formations	111
Indian State Forces	138
East and West African Formations	139
Combined Operations, Commando, and Beach Formations	143
Royal Marine Formations	146
Special Forces	150
Districts (U.K.)	153
Overseas Force and Garrison Headquarters	164
Overseas Districts and L. of C. Areas (Exclusive India and S.E.A.C.)	172
Indian and S.E.A.C. Districts and L. of C. Areas	181
Occupational Forces	190
Armoured and Tank Brigades	193
Independent Infantry Brigades and Brigade Groups	201
Miscellaneous Badges	211
Royal Artillery	214
Royal Engineers	218
Royal Signals	222
Royal Armoured Corps	223

	page
Royal Army Service Corps	224
Training Establishments and Administrative Units	229
Home Guard Units	231
American Formations	233
Allied Contingents and Formations (exclusive U.S.A.)	242
Belgium	242
Czechoslovakia	245
France	245
Greece	247
Netherlands	247
Poland	250
Yugoslavia	255
Italy (Co-belligerent Formations)	256

APPENDICES

I. List of Abbreviations	269
II. Arm of Service Strips	271
III. Vehicle Arm of Service Markings	273
IV. Descriptive Index of Badges	275

ILLUSTRATIONS

	page
How the Badges were worn	5
Types of Badges	257
Positioning of the Formation Badge	258
The "Anchor Inn" sign	259
30 Corps' Boar at Nienburg, Germany	259
30 Corps Badge as Directional Sign in Germany	260
50th Divisional Badge as Directional Sign in Normandy	260
53rd (Welsh) Division Badge as vehicle marking	261
Allied Forces vehicle marking in North-West Europe	261
A "Sign Shop" in the Western Desert	262
Formation Badges used on Greeting Cards	263
A Christmas Card of Formation Badges	264
Formation Badges on Orders of Service	265
Badges of the Eighth Army at Supply Depot, Tobruk	266
The Library, Sandhurst	267
Formation Badges at the Army Pageant "Drums"	268

COLOUR PLATES

BADGES OF

First Army: Eighth Army . . . . . *Frontispiece*

Facing Page

S.H.A.E.F.; H.Q. 21st Army Group; H.Q. 15th Army Group; A.L.F.S.E.A.; S.E.A.C.; G.H.Q. Home Forces . . . 1

Second Army; Fourteenth Army; Tenth Army; First Canadian Army; Airborne Divisions; 5 Corps 2

Guards Armoured Division; 3rd Division; 5th Division; 15th (Scottish) Division; 51st (Highland) Division; 43rd (Wessex) Division 3

8 Corps; 12 Corps; 79th Armoured Division; 52nd (Lowland) Division; 56th (London) Division; 78th Division . . . 6

8th Armoured Brigade; 27th Armoured Brigade; 6th (Guards) Tank Brigade; 32nd (Guards) Independent Brigade Group; 24th (Guards) Independent Brigade Group; London District . 7

In hoc signo vinces

In this sign shalt thou conquer

Words of Constantine's Vision, from Eusebius' "Life of Constantine"
i, 28

To

PAULINE

whose badge was a
Red Cross

PREFACE

IN no way does this book aspire to being a complete authority, or a complete catalogue, of all the formation badges worn during the Second World War. It is still early days to attempt a complete survey. The object in writing up the descriptions which follow, drawing the illustrations, and giving brief details, in some cases, of the service of the formations which carried the badges, is to place on record, while still fresh in one's mind, as much information as can be gleaned from my own collection and from scraps of information jotted down at intervals since I began to interest myself in the Army's "heraldry" of the war years.

It was in 1941 that this came about. I was, at the time, a G.S.O.2 in a Staff Duties branch of the War Office. One of my functions was to deal with the equipment of the Maritime Anti-Aircraft Artillery. These gunners were then putting up a magnificent show in the Battle of the Atlantic and around the "seven seas." The menace of the German long-range, convoy-seeking bombers, in addition to the surface raiders and submarines, was such that 40-mm. Bofors light anti-aircraft equipments were diverted from the Army to protect the Merchant Navy in their maintenance of our Atlantic life line, and our troops and supply convoys, which were perforce making the long voyages round the Cape. The gun detachments, volunteers from Anti-Aircraft Command, went to sea in the tankers, troopships and merchantmen—often a single Bofors and detachment to each craft, the men forming part of home and overseas based Maritime A.A. Regiments and Batteries.

It was decided that the time had come for these sea-going soldier gunners to have some distinguishing badge of their own. I was talking this over with my opposite number at the Maritime A.A. Headquarters, then in Cockspur Street, and made a few suggestions, offering to make some rough sketches. He agreed, and that evening I set to work, producing four ideas :—

(a) Drake's *Golden Hind* in full sail.
(b) A Mariner's Compass.
(c) Britannia.
   Each of these with the Gunners' motto " Ubique " on a scroll incorporated in the design.
(d) A Naval fouled anchor in red, with a white rope, on a black ground, with the initial letters " A.A." in white, one " A " on either side of the anchor.

The last design was subsequently accepted, mainly due, I understood, to the simplicity in reproduction as opposed to the other rather ambitious designs. I well remember first seeing the finished article on the sleeves of two Maritime gunners and hoping that they were not too critical of their new badge !

Shortly afterwards I went out on the big Home Forces Exercise " Bumper," as an observer, and soon found that a knowledge of formation badges was essential in keeping touch with troop movements during mobile operations. Details were available at the Information Room, and my rough notes on that occasion formed the basis of those which have grown into this book. The collecting of badges soon followed. I had moved to Northern Command as an S.O.R.E. when I started to collect specimens of the formations in the area, and this collection steadily grew. By the end of last year I had secured some two hundred and fifty, each one, with but few exceptions, being the gift of an individual. I would like to name them all and acknowledge their help and my appreciation of their additions to the collection. This, however, I have done personally. I hope that any of them who chance to see this book will recall the incident which led to the inclusion of their badge in the following pages. It is from these specimens that I have drawn the line illustrations for the book. Others were drawn from rough sketches made at odd times ; the 116th Independent Infantry Brigade was sketched last summer by the bridge at Wesel on the Rhine ; British Troops in Norway at a Transit Camp ; the 36th Division at Waterloo Station, and so on. In some cases it is admitted that they deviate slightly in detail from the " sealed patterns," or technically, from the heraldic aspect, are not quite correct. This can be accounted for by the fact that some have been drawn from stencilled designs on vehicles or from locally manufactured badges, or from my own hurried sketches made some time ago.

The conventional heraldic tinctures introduced early in the seventeenth century for use in engravings and drawings in line have, I regret, not been adhered to in the black and white illustrations which are confined to outline, black, and with but few exceptions, a single tint, and so careful reference has been made throughout, in the text, to the actual colours of the designs.

The brief histories of the formations, too, have been compiled from accumulated notes and a few references to current records, and are not complete in every case, and in a number of instances have perforce been omitted and reference confined to an illustration and description of the badge. This is particularly so in the case of the Independent Infantry Brigades and Brigade Groups. I have not attempted to include regimental badges. Many regiments adopted a special badge or sign. This was more especially so in the case of former Yeomanry regiments and Infantry battalions which were converted into Gunner units or other arms. A study of these would have enlarged these pages considerably, and records are not immediately available to allow full research, so I have confined the book to formations from Brigades upwards, with the exception of some miscellaneous badges which have become well known.

This, admittedly, is the main object of the book, but wherever possible supplementary information regarding the formation's activities and service has been included.

It is still difficult to obtain further details and material and so I cannot hope to have included all the formation badges that have been worn during the war. I should therefore be most grateful to any readers who know of any badge not included if they would care to help by sending me details (together with a specimen or a rough sketch) c/o the Publishers. Acknowledgment will be gladly made, for it is my intention eventually to make this book complete in giving details of every badge which has been worn.

HOWARD N. COLE.

ALDERSHOT,
May, 1946.

PREFACE TO THE SECOND EDITION

THIS record was originally intended only to cover formation badges worn during the war years, but I have now included several badges which were introduced during 1946. Chief among these is the War Office badge, and others include Malaya Command and H.Q. Land Forces, Hong Kong, together with certain new or altered badges adopted by formations since the cessation of hostilities.

In this second edition I have included details regarding some of the badges worn by our American allies. In North-Western Europe I met a number of officers and men of the Ninth U.S. Army and the Staff of S.H.A.E.F. Among them were those who gave me the first American shoulder insignia for my collection and I now acknowledge them with the inclusion of a special chapter on U.S. Army Insignia. I have also added to my references to the badges worn by our Belgian, Dutch and Polish allies, and have dealt briefly with unit signs and vehicle markings—badges which were not always worn by personnel, but were nevertheless accepted as distinguishing badges.

It has been pointed out to me that in some cases my illustrations of the badges depict the subject facing in the opposite direction to that in which they were normally seen. When badges were used as vehicle markings a standard pattern was used, and the subject adopted where applicable, always faced in one direction. This gave the lead to the, in most cases, correct assumption of the sealed pattern but there are a number of instances of the badges, when worn on the sleeve, being manufactured in pairs so that the subject automatically faced forward. When producing the illustrations I sometimes only had one of a pair from which to copy, and the specimen may have been facing left for wear on a left sleeve, when the badge was more familiar with the subject facing to the right. This is mainly the case with badges which depicted animals and birds.

Although the first edition of this book was published in June last year, my work as Author had been completed some months before that date. Six months have passed since publication, and during that period I have been reaping what I had sown in the early days of the preparation of this work, when, to complete the picture I had made numerous inquiries to obtain further particulars and confirm certain detail. Not all the answers came quickly, as it necessitated considerable research and world-wide correspondence, but they have now all been received, and consequently I have been able to make some additions and certain corrections to the original text, and in some cases to my illustrations. In addition, I have received a wide response to the request in the last paragraph of the Preface to the first edition and I must take this opportunity of thanking the many who have written to me, for their help and interest in preparing this second edition. I am indebted to my friends, in the War Office, the India Office and the Imperial War Museum, and to Brigadier W. D. Robertson, D.S.O., Capt. P. B. Fox, M.B.E., and Mr. Arthur Kipling, for their valued assistance and to the following who have provided me with additional badges and information :—

Major-General A. H. J. Snelling, C.B., C.B.E. ; Brigadier G. B. S. Hindley, O.B.E. ; Brigadier T. H. Boss ; Lieut.-Colonel A. Bigwood ; Lieut.-Colonel R. M. Grazebrook, O.B.E., M.C. (The Gloucestershire Regiment) ; Lieut.-Colonel H. C. McHugh, R.A.S.C. (Indian Army Public Relations) ; Lieut.-Colonel J. F. Thoburn, M.C., R.A.S.C. ; Lieut.-Colonel C. H. S. Howkins, K.R.R.C. ; Lieut.-Colonel S. M. Walsh, A.M.I.Mech.E., R.A.S.C. ; Lieut.-Colonel D. I. Watson ; Lieut.-Colonel W. H. Mackenzie, M.B.E., T.D., R.E. ; Major L. M. Dale, D.S.O., M.C. ; Major T. J. Edwards, M.B.E., F.R.Hist.S. ; Major E. J. Herbert ; Major H. F. Jackson, M.B.E., T.D. ; Major A. L. King-Harman, R.A. ; Major H. P. E. Pereira (The Worcestershire Regiment) ; Major J. E. Walliker ; Major A. L. Whittle ; Capt. G. E. F. Arnold, R.A. (T.A.) ; Capt. B. J. Britain, R.A. ; Capt. F. J. W. Baggs, R.A.O.C. ; Capt. A. A. Goatman ; Capt. K. A. Hall ; Capt. H. V. Sawyer, R.A. ; Capt. F. Tapp (United States Army) ; Capt. F. E. White ; Capt. T. M. Wedderburn ; Capt. H. M. Hitsman (of Canadian Military H.Q.) ; Lieut. R. Unett, K.R.R.C. ; Rev. P. Burrow, M.B.E. ; O./Cadet Andrew Poklikowski (Polish Army) ; C. Allison, Esq. ; W. H. H. Bayne, Esq. ; W. E. Bass, Esq. ; S. D. Barfoot, Esq., B.Sc. ; A. F. A. Carlisle, Esq. ; H. C. Cardew Rendle, Esq. ; W. Clark, Esq. (late R.E.) ; Patrick A. Corbett, Esq. ; E. S. Castiglione, Esq. ; H. Ellis Tomlinson, Esq. ; Peter Haswell, Esq. ; R. B. Howorth, Esq. ; G. Bradshaw, Esq. ; D. A. Green, Esq. ; D. D. Hall, Esq. ; Hugh W. B. Mackintosh, Esq. ; E. MacDonald, Esq. ; I. W. Rooke, Esq. ; R. F. Pearsall, Esq. ; R. Stern, Esq. ; C. T. Swarby, Esq. ; E. M. Wagner, Esq. ; T. White, Esq. ; A. H. Williams, Esq. ; Cpl. S. Wilson.

I must not let these acknowledgements pass without also referring to the assistance given by the Composing Room Overseer, and Mr. R. A. Wood, of Messrs. Gale & Polden, and thanking them for their interest in the production of this book.

HOWARD N. COLE.

ALDERSHOT,
December, 1946.

PREFACE TO THE THIRD EDITION

OVER four years have passed since "VJ Day", and I have found that the considerable interest which existed in the fascinating study of the formation badges worn during the war years has not in any way diminished. In fact, now that one has settled down to regard the war in retrospect, this interest is on the increase. One is now able to refer to records, war diaries, regimental histories and official archives to check in detail and establish identification.

One is now able to contact individuals with first-hand knowledge, and one's research has been generally simplified. I feel, now, that my task is almost completed; when this book was first published, in June, 1946, it was, I admit now, early days to have attempted to record the full story of the formation badges of the 1939-45 War and the stories of the formations and units which bore them. In fact, as I wrote at the time, the book did not in any way aspire to be a complete authority or a complete catalogue of all the badges which had been worn. I can, however, now that four years have passed by, say with some confidence that I do feel that this edition approaches its objective.

As the months have gone by I have carried out further research and have entered into correspondence with collectors, serving and ex-officers and N.C.Os., with commanders of formations, Regimental Depots, Libraries and Museums. The result of this has gone into this revised and enlarged edition and leads one to feel that I have neared completion in making this book a really comprehensive record of formation badges of the last war—at least, as far as British, Dominion and Indian formations are concerned.

Once again I place on record my thanks and appreciation of the help afforded to me by the many who have assisted in providing information which has gone into this book, I thank them for their interest and their assistance. Particularly I wish to record my appreciation of the help received from Colonel R. S. M.

Calder, and to Lieut.-Colonel O. G. W. White, D.S.O., of The Dorsetshire Regiment, and Brigadier W. E. H. Condon, O.B.E., of the Combined Inter-Services Historical Section of India Command, who gave me additional details concerning the Indian Army formations and the British Commonwealth Occupation Force, Japan, Colonel D. N. W. D. Irven, for the information regarding the badges of the East African formations ; Colonel G. W. M. Grover, O.B.E., R.M. (Retd.), for his help in providing me with information regarding the badges worn by the Royal Marines ; Lieut. Richard Maurice, of the 4eme Commando (French Colonial Army) for particulars of French Army badges, and to Captain A. Telders, of the Royal Netherlands Army, for details of Dutch badges, and to the following who sent me specimen badges and/or drawings of badges and additional information :—

Major-General N. Clowes, C.B.E., D.S.O., M.C., A.D.C. ; General Sir Douglas Gracey, K.C.I.E., C.B., C.B.E., M.C. (late G.O.C. 20th Indian Division) ; Major-General C. W. Palin, M.C. (Jaipur State Forces) ; Major-General C. G. Woolner, C.B., M.C. (late G.O.C. 81st West African Division) ; Brigadier J. Hunt (New South Wales) ; Brigadier J. St. C. Holbrook, C.B.E., M.C. ; Brigadier R. H. Perry, C.B.E., M.C. ; Colonel A. S. N. Corbett, O.B.E.; Lieut.-Colonel W. H. Alwyn, R.E. ; Lieut.-Colonel D. G. Birkett, R.A. ; Lieut.-Colonel D. C. Cameron, R.E. ; Lieut.-Colonel R. Chandler ; Lieut.-Colonel E. A. Cook ; Lieut.-Colonel J. F. Conolly, D.S.O. ; Lieut.-Colonel G. W. Noakes ; Lieut.-Colonel V. L. Misselbrook, O.B.E. ; Lieut.-Colonel J. A. Macrae ; Lieut.-Colonel G. L. Payne, R.A.O.C. ; Lieut.-Colonel D. N. Nicol ; Major W. A. C. Anderson, D.S.O. ; Major P. G. Braganza ; Major C. H. F. Croaker ; Major I. J. D. Hewinson Hamilton ; Major P. Henslow ; Major R. F. Kennedy, D.L.I. ; Major R. J. Ghey ; Major T. S. Martin ; Major J. F. Stephen, R.A. ; Major W. A. Simmons (Bahawalpur State Forces) ; Major H. C. Wilson ; Major H. L. Settle, M.Sc., M.D., D.Ph. ; Captain J. Hodgson ; Captain L. R. Nayak ; Captain W. J. Reader ; Captain J. Miseroy (The Essex Regiment) ; Captain F. P. Raymond ; Lieut. O. Labbett (The Devonshire Regiment) ; Dr. J. Michael ; A. F. Flatow, Esq. ; Rowland Bowen, Esq. ; W. Y. Carman, Esq. ; P. W. Montague-Smith, Esq. ; Cpl G. Campbell ; L./Cpl. F. Jinks.

HOWARD N. COLE.

ALDERSHOT,
December, 1949.

INDEX OF FORMATIONS

HIGHER FORMATIONS.
	page
Supreme Headquarters, Allied Expeditionary Force (S.H.A.E.F.)	8
Supreme Allied Command, South-East Asia (S.A.C.S.E.A.)	11
G.H.Q. Home Forces	9
G.H.Q. India	10
G.H.Q. Middle East Forces	9
Allied Force Headquarters (A.F.H.Q.)	10
Allied Land Forces, South-East Asia (A.L.F.S.E.A.)	12
H.Q. Central Mediterranean Force	11
H.Q. 11th Army Group	12
H.Q. 15th Army Group	13
H.Q. 21st Army Group	14
Canadian Military Headquarters (C.M.H.Q.)	86

HOME COMMANDS (U.K.).
Northern Command	15
Western Command	17
Southern Command	17
Eastern Command	15
South-Eastern Command	16
Scottish Command	16
Anti-Aircraft Command	75

OVERSEAS COMMANDS.
India Command (Supreme Headquarters, India)	20
Eastern Command (India)	21
Central Command (India)	20
Northern Command (India)	21
Ceylon Army Command	21
Malta Command	22
Persia and Iraq Command (P.A.I.C.)	22
West Africa Command	23
East Africa Command	23
Malaya Command	23

ARMIES.
First Army	24
Second Army	25
Eighth Army	25
Ninth Army	26
Tenth Army	27
Twelfth Army	28
Fourteenth Army	29

	page
First Canadian Army	86
First Australian Army	96
Second Australian Army	96
North-Western Army (India)	111
Southern Army (India)	111

CORPS.

1 Corps (and 1 Corps District—B.A.O.R.)	30
2 Corps	30
3 Corps	31
4 Corps	32
5 Corps	32
7 Corps	33
8 Corps (and 8 Corps District—B.A.O.R.)	33
9 Corps (and 9 Corps District—U.K.)	34
10 Corps	35
11 Corps	35
12 Corps	36
13 Corps	36
25 Corps	37
30 Corps (and 30 Corps District—B.A.O.R.)	37
1 Anti-Aircraft Corps	76
2 Anti-Aircraft Corps	76
3 Anti-Aircraft Corps	77
1 Canadian Corps	88
2 Canadian Corps	88
1 Australian Corps	97
2 Australian Corps	97
3 Australian Corps	97
15 Indian Corps	111
21 Indian Corps	112
33 Indian Corps	112
34 Indian Corps	113

BRITISH ARMOURED DIVISIONS.

Guards Armoured Division	39
1st Armoured Division	40
2nd Armoured Division	41
6th Armoured Division	41
7th Armoured Division	42
8th Armoured Division	43
9th Armoured Division	43
10th Armoured Division	44
11th Armoured Division	44
42nd Armoured Division	45
79th Armoured Division	45

BRITISH INFANTRY DIVISIONS.

1st Division	46
2nd Division	47
3rd Division	47
4th Division	48
5th Division	49
6th Division	50
8th Division	51
9th (Scottish) Division	51
12th Division	52
13th Division	52
15th (Scottish) Division	53
18th Division	54
23rd Division	54

	page
36th Division	55
38th (Welsh) Division	56
40th Division	56
42nd (East Lancashire) Division	57
43rd (Wessex) Division	57
44th (Home Counties) Division	58
45th (Wessex) Division	59
46th (North Midland) Division	59
47th (London) Division	60
48th (South Midland) Division	61
49th (West Riding) Division	62
50th (Northumbrian) Division	63
51st (Highland) Division	64
52nd (Lowland) Division (Mountain Division)	65
53rd (Welsh) Division	66
54th (East Anglian) Division	66
55th (West Lancashire) Division	67
56th (London) Division	68
59th Division	68
61st Division	69
66th Division	69
70th Division	70
76th Division	70
77th Division	71
78th Division	71
80th Division	72

AIRBORNE DIVISIONS.

1st Airborne Division	73
6th Airborne Division	74

ANTI-AIRCRAFT FORMATIONS.

Anti-Aircraft Command	75
1 A.A. Corps	76
2 A.A. Corps	76
3 A.A. Corps	77
1st A.A. Division	77
2nd A.A. Division	78
3rd A.A. Division	78
4th A.A. Division	79
5th A.A. Division	79
6th A.A. Division	80
7th A.A. Division	80
8th A.A. Division	80
9th A.A. Division	81
10th A.A. Division	81
11th A.A. Division	82
12th A.A. Division	82

COUNTY DIVISIONS.

Durham and North Riding County Division	83
Dorset County Division	83
Devon and Cornwall County Division	84
Hampshire County Division	84
Essex County Division	84
Lincolnshire County Division	85
Yorkshire County Division	85

CANADIAN FORMATIONS.

Canadian Military H.Q. (U.K.)	86
First Canadian Army	86

	page
1st Canadian Corps	88
2nd Canadian Corps	88
1st Canadian Division	89
2nd Canadian Division	90
3rd Canadian Division	91
4th Canadian Armoured Division	91
5th Canadian Armoured Division	91
1st Canadian Armoured Brigade	92
2nd Canadian Armoured Brigade	92
1st Canadian A.G.R.A.	93
2nd Canadian A.G.R.A.	93
Canadian Army Pacific Force	93
Canadian Corps District (U.K.)	159

AUSTRALIAN FORMATIONS.

H.Q. Australian Imperial Forces, M.E.F.	95
First Australian Army	96
Second Australian Army	96
1 Australian Corps	97
2 Australian Corps	97
3 Australian Corps	97
1st Australian Armoured Division	97
2nd Australian Armoured Division	98
3rd Australian Armoured Division	98
1st Australian Motor Division	98
1st Australian Division	99
2nd Australian Division	99
3rd Australian Division	99
4th Australian Division	100
5th Australian Division	100
6th Australian Division	100
7th Australian Division	101
8th Australian Division	102
9th Australian Division	102
11th Australian Division	103
12th Australian Division	103
3rd Australian Army Tank Brigade	103
4th Australian Armoured Brigade	104
34th Australian Infantry Brigade	104
Australian Imperial Forces Base Area, M.E.F.	96

NEW ZEALAND FORMATIONS.

H.Q. New Zealand Expeditionary Force	105
1st New Zealand Division	105
2nd New Zealand Division	105
3rd New Zealand Division	106
4th New Zealand Division	106
5th New Zealand Division	107
6th New Zealand Division	107
4th New Zealand Armoured Brigade	107

SOUTH AFRICAN DIVISIONS.

1st South African Division	108
2nd South African Division	109
3rd South African Division	109
6th South African Armoured Division	110

INDIAN FORMATIONS.

Southern Army (India)	111
North-Western Army (India)	111
15th Indian Corps	111

	page
21 Indian Corps	112
33 Indian Corps	113
34 Indian Corps	113
2nd Indian Division	114
3rd Indian Division	114
4th Indian Division	115
5th Indian Division	116
6th Indian Division	117
7th Indian Division	117
8th Indian Division	118
9th Indian Division	119
10th Indian Division	120
11th Indian Division	120
12th Indian Division	121
14th Indian Division	121
17th Indian Division	122
19th Indian Division	123
20th Indian Division	123
21st Indian Division	124
23rd Indian Division	124
25th Indian Division	125
26th Indian Division	125
39th Indian Division	126
31st Indian Armoured Division	126
42nd Indian Armoured Division	127
44th Indian Armoured Division	127
44th Indian Airborne Division	128
2nd Indian Armoured Brigade	128
3rd Indian Armoured Brigade	128
3rd Indian Motor Brigade	129
50th Indian Tank Brigade	129
38th Indian Infantry Brigade	131
43rd Indian Lorried Infantry Brigade	132
52nd Indian Infantry Brigade	132
60th Indian Infantry Brigade	133
72nd Indian Infantry Brigade	133
109th Indian Infantry Brigade	134
116th Indian Infantry Brigade	134
150th Indian Infantry Brigade	134
155th Indian Infantry Brigade	135
251st Indian Tank Brigade	130
254th Indian Tank Brigade	130
255th Indian Tank Brigade	131
268th Indian Infantry Brigade	135
Lushai Brigade	136
Indian Contingent in U.K.	136
Indian Units, B.C.O.F.	137
Military Adviser-in-Chief—Indian State Forces	137

INDIAN STATE FORCES.

	page
Cooch Behar State Forces	138
Jaipur State Forces	138
Bahawalpur State Forces	138

EAST AND WEST AFRICAN FORMATIONS.

	page
H.Q. East African Expeditionary Force	139
West African Expeditionary Force	139
11th (African) Division	140
12th (African) Division	140
11th (East African) Division	141
81st (West African) Division	142

	page
82nd (West African) Division	142
22nd (East African) Brigade	141
28th (East African) Brigade	141

COMBINED OPERATIONS, COMMANDO AND BEACH FORMATIONS.

Combined Operations Headquarters (C.O.H.Q.)	143
Beach Groups (British)	144
Beach Groups (Indian)	144
22nd Beach Brigade	145
Commando Brigades	145
No. 1 Commando	145
No. 2 Commando	145
H.Q. Special Service Brigade	146

ROYAL MARINE FORMATIONS AND UNITS.

Mobile Naval Base Defence Organization (M.N.B.D.O.)	146
Royal Marine Division	147
116th (Royal Marine) Infantry Brigade	147
117th (Royal Marine) Infantry Brigade	148
Amphibian Support Regiment, Royal Marines	148
Royal Marine Siege Regiment	149
Royal Marine Engineers	149
R.M. Training Centre	149

HOME DISTRICTS (U.K.).

Aldershot and Hants District	157
Central Midland District	161
East Anglian District	160
East Central District	161
East Kent District	158
East Riding and Lincs District	155
East Scotland District	161
Essex and Suffolk District	160
Hants and Dorset District	157
Home Counties District	158
Lancs and Border District	156
London District	153
Midland West District	155
Norfolk and Cambridge District	160
North Highland District	162
North Kent and Surrey District	159
North Midland District	154
North Riding District	154
North Wales District	155
North-Western District	156
Northumbrian District	153
Salisbury Plain District	157
South Midland District	158
South Wales District	155
South-Western District	158
Sussex District	159
West Lancashire District	156
West Riding District	154
West Scotland District	161
Canadian Corps District	159
2 Corps District	160
Northern Ireland District	162
British Troops in Northern Ireland	163
Orkney and Shetland Defences	163
Force 135 (Channel Islands Liberation Force)	151

OVERSEAS FORCE AND GARRISON HEADQUARTERS.	page
Malta Field Defences	164
Gibraltar Garrison	164
Iceland Force	165
Faeroe Islands Force	165
British Troops in Norway	169
British Troops in Egypt	169
New Guinea Force	166
Dodecanese Force	166
H.Q. British Troops in the Low Countries	168
H.Q. Palestine and Transjordan	166
H.Q. Land Forces, Greece	168
H.Q. British Forces in Greece	168
H.Q. Sudan and Eritrea	167
H.Q. British Troops in Aden	167
H.Q. British Troops in Iraq	167
H.Q. British Troops in Siam	170
H.Q. Land Forces, Hong Kong	168
Land Forces Adriatic (L.F.A.)	170
Transjordan Frontier Force	171
Arab Legion	171

SPECIAL FORCES.

"V" Force	150
"R" Force	150
Force 281 (Dodecanese Force)	166
Force 135 (Channel Islands Liberation Force)	151
First Special Service Force	151
G.R.E.F. (General Reserve Engineering Force)	152

OVERSEAS DISTRICTS AND L. OF C. AREAS.

H.Q. 21st Army Group (G.H.Q. and L. of C. Troops)	172
H.Q. L. of C. 21st Army Group	172
H.Q. L. of C. British Troops in North Africa	173
Netherlands District	173
Cyrenaica District	174
Tripolitania District	174
Cyprus District	176
North Levant District	176
Iraq Base and L. of C. Area	176
No. 15 Area, M.E.F.	175
No. 16 Area, M.E.F.	175
No. 17 Area, M.E.F.	175
No. 18 Area, M.E.F.	175
No. 21 Area, M.E.F.	177
No. 88 Area, M.E.F.	177
No. 1 District, C.M.F.	177
No. 2 District, C.M.F.	178
No. 3 District, C.M.F.	178
No. 56 Area, C.M.F.	179
South Caribbean Area	179
North Caribbean Area	179
Gold Coast Area	179
Nigeria Area	180
Gambia Area	180
Sierra Leone Area	180

INDIAN AND S.E.A.C. DISTRICTS AND L. OF C. AREAS.

H.Q. L. of C., S.E.A.C.	188
101st (Bihar and Orissa) L. of C. Area	181
105th (Madras) L. of C. Area	181

	page
106th L. of C. Area	182
107th L. of C. Area	182
108th (Bombay) L. of C. Area	182
109th (Bangalore) L. of C. Area	183
110th (Poona) L. of C. Area	183
202nd (Assam) L. of C. Area	183
303rd (Bengal) L. of C. Area	183
404th (East Bengal) L. of C. Area	184
505th L. of C. District	184
253rd L. of C. Sub-Area	184
254th L. of C. Sub-Area	185
Peshawar District	185
Sind District	185
Lahore District	186
Delhi District	185
Rawalpindi District	185
Nagpur District	186
Kohat District	186
United Provinces Area	187
Baluchistan District	187
Waziristan District	186
Madras Defended Port Area	187
Madras Fortress Area	187
North Ceylon Administrative Area	187
Colombo Sub-Area	188
Trincomalee Fortress Area	188
South Burma District	188
No. 2 Area, S.E.A.C. (Singapore)	189

OCCUPATION FORCES.

British Commonwealth Occupation Force (Japan)	192
H.Q. British Army of the Rhine	190
H.Q. British Troops in Austria	190
British Troops in Berlin	190
Control Commission for Germany	191
Allied Control Commission for Austria	191

ARMOURED AND TANK BRIGADES.

1st Armoured Brigade Group	193
2nd Armoured Brigade	193
4th Armoured Brigade	193
6th Guards Tank Brigade	194
7th Armoured Brigade	194
8th Armoured Brigade	195
9th Armoured Brigade	195
16th Armoured Brigade	196
20th Armoured Brigade	196
21st Army Tank Brigade	196
22nd Armoured Brigade	196
23rd Armoured Brigade	197
25th Armoured Engineer Brigade	197
23rd Army Tank Brigade	200
24th Army Tank Brigade	200
25th Army Tank Brigade	200
27th Armoured Brigade	198
31st Tank Brigade	200
32nd Army Tank Brigade	198
36th Tank Brigade	200
33rd Armoured Brigade	198
34th Armoured Brigade	199
35th Armoured Brigade	198

INDEPENDENT INFANTRY BRIGADES AND BRIGADE GROUPS.

	page
1st Independent Guards Brigade Group	201
5th Infantry Brigade	201
24th Independent Guards Brigade Group	201
29th Independent Brigade Group	202
31st Independent Brigade Group	202
32nd Independent Guards Brigade	202
33rd Guards Brigade	203
36th Independent Infantry Brigade	203
37th Independent Brigade Group	203
38th Infantry Brigade	203
56th Independent Infantry Brigade	204
61st Independent Infantry Brigade	204
70th Independent Infantry Brigade	204
71st Independent Infantry Brigade	205
72nd Independent Infantry Brigade	205
73rd Independent Infantry Brigade	205
115th Independent Infantry Brigade	205
116th (Royal Marine) Infantry Brigade	147
117th (Royal Marine) Infantry Brigade	148
148th Independent Infantry Brigade	206
162nd Independent Infantry Brigade	206
204th Independent Infantry Brigade	206
206th Independent Infantry Brigade	206
212th Independent Infantry Brigade	207
214th Independent Infantry Brigade	207
218th Independent Infantry Brigade	207
219th Independent Infantry Brigade	208
223rd Independent Infantry Brigade	208
231st Independent Infantry Brigade	208
301st Infantry Brigade	209
303rd Infantry Brigade	209
304th Independent Infantry Brigade	210
Jewish Brigade Group	210

MISCELLANEOUS BADGES.

G.H.Q. Liaison Regiment	211
Political Warfare Executive, M.E.F.	213
British Military H.Q., Balkans	212
Army Film and Photographic Service	211
Indian Field Broadcasting Units	212
Hong Kong Service Badge	94

ROYAL ARTILLERY BADGES.

Newfoundland Units, R.A.	214
A.A. and Coast Defence Units, R.A. (C.M.F.)	214
Maritime A.A. Artillery	215
Coast Artillery Units	214
1 Corps Artillery	216
1st Division, R.A.	216
6th Army Group, R.A.	216
Heavy A.A. Brigade, Malta	217
H.Q., R.A., and Mobile Artillery, Malta	217
R.A. Units, Gibraltar Garrison	217

ROYAL ENGINEER BADGES.

R.E. Depot	218
Transportation Training Centre R.E.	218
Tunnelling Companies, R.E.	218
Chemical Warfare Groups, R.E.	218
Airfield Construction Groups	219

	page
1st Corps Troops Engineers	220
8th Army Troops Engineers	220
8th G.H.Q. Troops Engineers	219
42nd Armoured Engineer Regiment	221
Madras Sappers and Miners	221

ROYAL SIGNALS BADGES.

Air Formation Signals	222
Indian Air Formation Signals	222
1st Divisional Signals	222

ROYAL ARMOURED CORPS BADGES.

R.A.C. Training Centre, B.A.O.R.	223
No. 1 Armoured Replacement Group, C.M.F.	223
Royal Armoured Corps Depot (India)	229

ROYAL ARMY SERVICE CORPS BADGES.

Air Despatch Group, R.A.S.C.	224
War Department Fleet	224
Pack Transport Group, C.M.F.	225

R.A.S.C. Unit Badges.

No. 14 C.R.A.S.C.	226
840 General Transport Company	226
277 Armoured Divisional Transport Company	226
236 Bridge Company	226
534 Tank Transporter Company	227
558 Water Tank Company	227
234 Petrol Depot	227
No. 9 Military Petrol Filling Centre	227
No. 36 Detail Issue Depot	228
No. 25 Field Bakery	228

TRAINING ESTABLISHMENTS AND ADMINISTRATIVE UNITS.

British Reinforcement Training Centre (India)	229
B.A.O.R. Training Centre	229
G.H.Q. 2nd Echelon, C.M.F.	230
163rd Infantry O.C.T.U.	230
Special Training Centre, Lochailort	230
U.D.F. Repatriation Unit	110

HOME GUARDS UNITS.

Lincolnshire Home Guard	231
8th Bn. Cornwall Home Guard	231
9th Bn. Cornwall Home Guard	232
12th Bn. Cornwall Home Guard	232

AMERICAN FORMATIONS.

European Theatre of Operations	233
Persian Gulf Service Command	233
U.S. Army Forces in the Middle East	234
12th Army Group	234
First American Army	234
Third American Army	234
Fifth American Army	235
Ninth American Army	235
XVIII Airborne Corps	235

	page
17th Airborne Division	236
82nd Airborne Division	236
101st Airborne Division	236
1st Division	237
2nd Division	237
3rd Division	237
5th Division	237
28th Division	238
29th Division	238
34th Division	238
42nd Division	238
45th Division	239
66th Division	239
75th Division	239
85th Division	239
87th Division	240
American Armoured Divisions	240
Tank Destroyer Units	240
Army Service Forces	241
U.S. Army Air Forces	241
Eighth U.S. Air Force	241
Ninth U.S. Air Force	242

ALLIED CONTINGENTS AND FORMATIONS.

Belgium.

1st Independent Belgian Brigade Group	242
2nd Independent Belgian Brigade Group	243
4th Belgian Infantry Brigade	243
5th Belgian Infantry Brigade	243
6th Belgian Infantry Brigade	244
Belgian Congo Brigade	244
Belgian Army Infantry School	244

Czechoslovakia.

Czech Independent Armoured Brigade Group	245

France.

Free French Forces	245
1st French Army	246
1st Division	246
4th Moroccan Division	246

Greece.

1st Greek Independent Brigade	247
2nd Greek Independent Brigade	247
3rd (Greek) Mountain Brigade	247

The Netherlands.

Royal Netherlands Brigade	247
1st Netherlands Division	248
2nd Netherlands Division	248
Royal Netherlands Army (Garrison Troops) (Overseas)	249
Royal Netherlands Army (Garrison Troops) (Holland)	249

Poland.   *page*
H.Q. Polish Armies in the Middle East 250
Polish L. of C. Units 250
1st Polish Corps 250
2nd Polish Corps 251
Polish Army Corps 251
1st Polish Armoured Division 252
2nd Polish Armoured Division 252
4th Polish (Grenadier) Armoured Division 252
3rd Carpathian Division 253
5th (Kresowa) Infantry Division 253
7th Polish Division 253
Polish Parachute Brigade 253
6th (Lwow) Polish Infantry Brigade 254
7th Polish Infantry Brigade 254
2nd Polish Army Tank Brigade 254
2nd Polish Armoured Brigade 254
16th Polish Armoured Brigade 255

Yugoslavia.
Royal Yugoslav Forces 255

Italy.
Friuli Group 256
Cremona Group 256
Folgore Group 256

xxx

HERALDRY IN WAR

FORMATION badges or signs had their origin in the 1914-18 war. In 1914 all vehicles and directional signs disclosed unit identities by inscriptions "in clear." When these were removed to prevent identification by the enemy, enabling them to ascertain the composition of our force, it soon became apparent that there was a necessity for some form of distinguishing mark or sign to facilitate recognition of Corps and Divisional vehicles and personnel.

The adoption of formation signs therefore fulfilled the dual purpose of providing an easily recognizable mark for each formation, at the same time introducing a security measure in preventing the disclosure to the enemy of the identity of the formation opposing them on any sector of the front.

The choice of signs was left to each formation and this soon led to a wider meaning. It built up the *esprit de corps* of the Corps and Divisions. The 1914 Army as a whole had, to a very great extent, always thought on a regimental basis; the formation of which a battalion formed part served only as the operational command, and was not regarded as a unit with traditions and its own *esprit de corps*. Men spoke of serving with the Buffs or the Dorsets and not of the 5th or the 12th Division. Formation *esprit de corps* had to some degree been built up during the South African War by the introduction of the Guards and Highland Brigades of Lord Roberts's Force, but between the wars tours of duty only brought the Regular Army into Divisions for training and administration during their tour in any particular garrison. For example, a battalion stationed in the Aldershot Command automatically formed part of the 1st or 2nd Divisions, but on moving, say, to Colchester, became part of the 4th Division.

The Territorial Force was more closely knit into a Divisional pattern and the T.F. formations had a pre-1914 Territorial designation. These designations were retained after the allotment of Divisional numbers and continued when the Territorial Army was re-formed in 1921—*e.g.*, the 42nd (East Lancashire) Division, the 48th (South Midland) Division, the 53rd (Welsh) Division, etc.

The adoption of the formation sign did much to foster *esprit de corps* and men came to feel proud of their badge.

Signs between 1914 and 1918 were limited mainly to Armies, Corps and Divisions. Many became famous and have taken a rightful place in the records of our national military history. There is a collection of them in the Imperial War Museum; they served as illustrations in numerous books; and in the late twenties a whole series of cigarette

S.H.A.E.F.

H.Q. 21st ARMY GROUP

H.Q. 15th ARMY GROUP

ALLIED LAND FORCES
SOUTH-EAST ASIA

SOUTH-EAST ASIA
COMMAND

G.H.Q. HOME FORCES

cards was published giving a picture, a description of each design, and a brief history of the formation.

Among the best-remembered are the red fox of General Sir Hubert Gough's Fifth Army; the eye of the Guards Division; the double-three domino of the 33rd Division; the 36th (Ulster) Division's red hand; the "HD" of the 51st (Highland) Division; Wat Tyler's dagger of the 56th (London) Division; the 62nd (West Riding) Division's pelican; the anchor of the 63rd (Royal Naval) Division; and the symbolic broken spur of the 74th Division, which was composed of regiments of dismounted Yeomanry.

Divisional signs were discontinued by the Regular Army after the 1914-18 war, although a number of Territorial Army Divisions retained their distinguishing badge; all ranks continuing to wear their woven formation signs on their service dress. Among these were the 47th (2nd London) Division (until disbanded in 1935); the 49th (West Riding) Division; 51st (Highland), 52nd (Lowland) and 55th (West Lancs) Divisions.

"Divisional Signs" were reintroduced early in 1940, but instructions were given in December the following year for them to be described as "Formation Badges." It was ruled that the signs were to be worn by all ranks of Command Headquarters, Corps, Divisions, Independent Brigade Groups and Independent Infantry Brigades. Designs were chosen and approved by the Commanders concerned and the War Office notified. It was not long before the coloured cloth patches and woven badges on battledress sleeves became familiar to the Army and, by sight, to the general public. More strongly than before was the security aspect of the badges considered; even more necessary it became to guard the secret of the signs; no disclosure of our order of battle could be permitted. Lists of signs were "Security" documents, and the Army took this in its stride in its application of "Security." Formations embarking for overseas removed their badges from uniforms, and painted over those on the unit transport before leaving their mobilization centres for ports of embarkation. The only exception to this rule was when 21st Army Group embarked for the invasion of the Continent, when the troops went straight into battle from their concentration areas in England.

Signs became more widely used. In the period following the evacuation from Dunkirk, when the Army stood on guard around our own coastlines, signs, hitherto confined to Corps and Divisions, were adopted by Home Commands, Districts and by Independent Brigades, in accordance with War Office Instructions.

The signs chosen fell broadly into six categories. These can be classified as the "Heraldic," the "Symbolic or Emblematic," the "Territorial or Geographical," the "National," the "Animal," and the "Geometric," there being a link between the "National" and "Territorial" and the "Animal"; *e.g.*, the rhinoceros of the 11th (East African) Division, the panther of 34 (Indian) Corps, the oyster catcher of Faeroe Islands Force, etc. There is another link between the "Animal" and the "Symbolic," this more especially in the case of Armoured Divisional signs; for example, the charging

2

SECOND ARMY

FOURTEENTH ARMY

TENTH ARMY

FIRST CANADIAN ARMY

AIRBORNE DIVISIONS

5 CORPS

rhino of the 1st Armoured Division, the charging bull of the 11th, the bull's head of the 79th. The "Heraldic" linked with the "National"; e.g., the lion of the 15th (Scottish) Division, the St. David's cross of the 38th (Welsh), and the St. Andrew's cross of the 52nd (Lowland) Division; but more especially was this the case in the "Territorial" signs of Districts of the Home Commands, which in many cases were adapted from the arms of the counties they covered; e.g., St. Oswald shield of Northumbria (Northumbrian District); the heraldic Scottish lion (all Districts of Scottish Command); the dragon of Wales (South Wales District); Essex and Suffolk; and Norfolk and Cambridge District. The "Geometric" class of sign was chosen mainly for its simplicity, but some had a link with the formation. In the case of 10 Corps, the circle above an oblong was a "10" on its side; the 15 (Indian) Corps had a design made up of three Roman "Vs"; 3rd Division had a triangle surrounded by three others; whilst 4th Division had a circle, its fourth quarter displaced.

A few formations continued to wear the same sign as was used in the 1914-18 war. The Guards Armoured Division bore the eye of the Great War Guards Division; the 51st (Highland) Division retained its famous "HD"; the 55th, their red rose of Lancaster; whilst the 42nd (East Lancs) and 52nd (Lowland) had but slight variations of their 1914-18 sign.

Signs were widely used, exceeding the original intention of a distinguishing badge for personnel and vehicles. Routes allotted to formations during operations were signposted by the Military Police, often by means of a directional arrow and a stencilled formation sign on a board. Billets and stores and captured equipment were similarly marked, a point in favour of the " Geometrical " sign, the simplicity of which made it possible to be used by the meanest of artists. The routes of the 50th and 53rd Divisions could easily be followed through France and Belgium by the two " Ts " or the " W " hastily painted or chalked on the walls of farms and villages.

In Army welfare the badges played their part. On the L. of C. of 21st Army Group one frequently saw signs in use in Corps Admin. and Rest areas above the entrances to the formation welfare institutions. There was the "Spearhead Club" of 1 Corps; "The Crusader Club"—the charging knight of 8 Corps; and "The Bocage"—the three trees of 12 Corps; whilst in Germany, after the cessation of hostilities, 30 Corps made good use of their boar badge. One frequently saw hanging above a village *Gasthaus* a typically British inn sign. "The Pig at Rest" depicted the boar comfortably seated in an armchair. The "Boar at Anchor" by the Steinhudermer Lake in Hanover was another. At Nienburg the 30 Corps badge was perpetuated above the entrance to the *Rathaus*—the work of a stonemason who transformed the stone Nazi eagle into a boar—and also by a statue of the famous boar. It was in December, 1945, that Lieut.-General Sir Brian Horrocks performed his last public duty as Commander of 30 Corps in unveiling this memorial outside the Corps Headquarters. The boar rests on a stone plinth on which are carved the formation badges of the Divisions which composed the Corps and also the battles n which the formations had participated. It has now

GUARDS ARMOURED DIVISION

3RD INFANTRY DIVISION

5TH INFANTRY DIVISION

15TH (SCOTTISH) INFANTRY DIVISION

51ST (HIGHLAND) INFANTRY DIVISION

43RD (WESSEX) INFANTRY DIVISION

been moved from Nienburg to Luneburg, where it stands outside the British barracks.

On all vehicles, formation badges were stencilled in colour on the forward and rear mudguards or on the tailboard of lorries and trucks; on jeeps the badge appeared on the body below the windscreen on the driving side. The formation signs linked with the conventional arm of service vehicle marking, to enable one to see at a glance that, for instance, it was a staff car of H.Q. 8 Corps or a 3-tonner of 49th Division, R.A.S.C. The arm of service markings (given in detail in Appendix III) were painted squares: red and blue halves for the Gunners, black for formation H.Qs., red and green diagonals for the R.A.S.C., light blue for the Sappers, etc.

On uniform, signs were worn on the sleeves of uniforms except on greatcoats; in battledress, one inch below the regimental or corps shoulder title, and immediately above the arm of service strip. These narrow strips, introduced in the autumn of 1940, gave a quick identification of the wearer's arm of the service when wearing steel helmet and with no cap or other dintinguishing badges. These simple two-inch strips were of coloured cloth: red for infantry, blue and red for Gunners and Sappers, yellow and red for the Royal Armoured Corps, blue and yellow for the R.A.S.C., and so on. (The full list is given in Appendix II.) Infantry battalions wore one, two or three red strips one below the other to indicate the brigade to which they belonged.

It has been ruled when the badges were introduced in 1940 that they were not to be made of metal in view of the shortage of material, and so the formation badges were either woven or were stencilled in paint on cloth. As austerity progressed, the latter type became more familiar. Others were of "local" manufacture. Some of these, for example, worn by the Eighth Army, were made up "on the ground" by Italian civilians; and in some cases were made by the troops themselves.

In North Africa and other "tropical kit" areas, the formation signs were often worn affixed to the sleeves of K.D. jackets by means of press studs to facilitate laundering, or were worn stitched on to khaki drill "slip on" epaulettes for wear on the shoulders of K.D. shirts. In East and West Africa and in S.E.A.C. the badges were worn either stitched to the side of the pugaree or on the turn-up of the felt bush hat.

A number of collections of formation badges have already been made; undoubtedly they will ultimately find a place of honour in the Imperial War Museum alongside those of the 1914-18 war. Formations have become sign-minded. Some units have adopted the Divisional badge on notepaper and other stationery in preference to that of their own regiment or corps. Corps and Divisional signs were the motif of many of 1945's army Christmas cards. Continental shopkeepers, with an eye to business, soon produced brooches of the badges of the British Liberation Army—embroidered handkerchiefs, too. By the end of September, 1944, it was possible to buy in Brussels an enamel brooch of 21st Army Group or Second Army, and others soon followed. Brussels had by that time become very badge conscious. Our formation badges were greatly sought after as souvenirs,

HOW THE BADGES WERE WORN

In South-East Asia Command and in India*–In the Middle East—In Home Forces and in North-Western Europe.

S.E.A.C.

B.L.A.

M.E.F.

---

* Only the formations and units of the Indian Expeditionary Force (which was formed in March, 1943, and became the 33rd Indian Corps in October of that year). These formations were the 2nd and 36th Divisions. All other formations and units in S.E.A.C. wore their badges on the sleeve as was the case with all Indian troops, who wore the pugri or the cap, G.S., and not the bush hat as depicted in the illustration. When worn on the sleeve, the badges were often sewn on a cloth or buckram patch and affixed to the bush shirts or K.D. jackets by press studs.

and nearly half the girls and children that one saw wore the Divisional signs stitched to the sleeves of their frocks and coats.

The collecting of brass regimental cap-badges as adornments to waist-belts, so treasured by the old soldier of yore, gave way to some extent in the late war to the collection of the cloth patches of formations. The modern counterpart of the cavalry trooper's badged belt was undoubtedly the leather jerkin of the A.T.S. girl, the lining of which was covered with badges carefully stitched on in a pattern in patchwork quilt style. This method of collecting badges was also favoured by some E.N.S.A. artists, who thus recorded to whom they had given their shows.

Formation badges are a feature of the War Memorial in the English church at Batavia, Netherlands East Indies, unveiled in June, 1946, by Lieut.-General Sir Montagu Stopford, G.O.C. Allied Land Forces, South East Asia. This memorial, to the men and women of the British Commonwealth killed in Java, 1942-46, designed by Cpl. R. Roberts, R.A.S.C., and subscribed for by Service personnel, bears the badges of the 15 (Indian) Corps, the 5th, 23rd and 26th Indian Divisions, the 30th Indian Tank Brigade and the 5th Parachute Brigade.

Although not strictly a War Memorial in the accepted sense, the D Day stone on South Parade, Southsea, unveiled in 1948 by Field-Marshal Lord Montgomery, bears above the commemorative inscription the formation badge of Second Army.

The inclusion of formation badges in memorials is not, however, new to the 1939-45 war: the Divisional signs of the Scottish formations of the 1914-18 war are perpetuated in the Scottish National War Memorial in Edinburgh Castle, which was opened in 1927. There, on the exterior wall of the shrine erected to the undying memory of those Scots who fell in the Great War, are carved the badges of the 9th (Scottish) and 15th (Scottish) Divisions—two of the earliest formations of Kitchener's Army—the New Army Divisions, and the 51st (Highland) and 52nd (Lowland) Territorial Divisions, whilst the famous "broken spur" badge of the 74th Division is incorporated in the memorial to the Scottish Yeomanry.

At the junction of Hospital Hill, Knollys Road and Queen's Avenue, Aldershot, the 1914-18 War Memorial to the 2nd Division stands on a high grass bank overlooking the road. The Divisional sign is carved on the rear panel of the base of the stone cross and, in addition, the Memorial stands on a base which depicts the sign; this was a black oval with a large central eight-pointed red star flanked by a white eight-pointed star on either side. The two white stars stood for the 2nd Division, and the red star for the 1 Corps—"The Second Division of the First Corps."

The base of the Memorial at Aldershot is rarely seen except by those who go to the top of the mound to see the oval design reproduced in flint, the smaller stars in white stone, and the central red star, upon which the Memorial cross stands, in red brick.

Undoubtedly the formation badges of 1939-45 will in time find their honoured place on the memorials to those who fell in the second Great War, for the soldier of to-day is proud to identify himself with

8 CORPS

12 CORPS

79TH ARMOURED DIVISION

52ND (LOWLAND) INFANTRY DIVISION

56TH (LONDON) INFANTRY DIVISION

78TH INFANTRY DIVISION

the formation with which he served and with its symbol—the Formation badge.

The display of formation badges emblazoned on banners carried in the grand finale of " Drums," the Army Pageant held at the Royal Albert Hall in May, 1946, is an indication of the association of the now familiar badges with future Army pageantry. The formation badge has come to stay in days of peace, and may in the future be, to the Corps and Divisions, the equivalent of the Regimental Colours of battalions. What better than a Divisional " Colour," the formation badge embroidered thereon, inscribed with the formation's own battle honours ?

There is no doubt that the formation badges have their undisputed place among the records of the military history recently completed, and will always be remembered by those who wore them during its making.

8TH ARMOURED BRIGADE

27TH ARMOURED BRIGADE

6TH (GUARDS) TANK BRIGADE

32ND (GUARDS) INDEPENDENT BRIGADE GROUP

24TH (GUARDS) INDEPENDENT BRIGADE GROUP

LONDON DISTRICT

THE BADGES

★

HIGHER FORMATIONS

SUPREME HEADQUARTERS ALLIED EXPEDITIONARY FORCE (S.H.A.E.F.).

The now well-known emblem of SHAEF was worn on the left sleeve only, by all ranks—American, British and Allied—on the staff of General Eisenhower's Headquarters in England, in France (at Versailles and Reims), and finally in Germany (at Frankfurt).

The official description of the badge was given as: The shield-shaped cloth patch, with a black background, representing the darkness of Nazi oppression, bears the crusader's sword of liberation, with the red flames of avenging justice leaping from its hilt. Above the sword is a rainbow, emblematic of hope, containing all the colours of which Allied flags are composed. The heraldic field of blue above the rainbow is emblematic of peace and tranquillity for the enslaved peoples of Europe—the objective of the United Nations.

G.H.Q. HOME FORCES.

A heraldic winged lion, woven in gold within a gold border set upon a circular background of red and blue, was the badge of G.H.Q. Home Forces which commanded all formations and units in the United Kingdom, other than those of Anti-Aircraft Command and War Office training establishments—*i.e.*, I.T.Cs. and P.T.Cs. Training Regiments and Depots and Schools of Instruction.

G.H.Q. MIDDLE EAST.*

A brown or gold camel on a black square background was the badge of G.H.Q. Middle East, although yellow paint instead of gold was inevitably used for vehicle marking. Located in Cairo, G.H.Q. M.E.F. (Middle East Forces) provided the main operational and administrative headquarters for all our forces in Egypt (B.T.E.), Palestine, Syria, Iraq, Persia, Cyprus, Aden, the Sudan, Eritrea, Cyrenaica, Tripolitania, and the Dodecanese.

---

* G.H.Q., M.E.F., was redesignated Middle East Land Forces (M.E.L.F.) in 1946.

G.H.Q. INDIA.

A five-pointed yellow star set in the centre of a shield, of which the top half was red and the lower dark blue, was the sign adopted by G.H.Q. India; blue and red being G.H.Q. colours and the star emblematic of the Star of India.

ALLIED FORCE HEADQUARTERS (A.F.H.Q.).

The distinguishing badge of A.F.H.Q. established in Algiers during the North African campaign in 1942 was a saxe blue circle surrounded by a red border, the letters " A.F." in white in the centre of the circle. This Headquarters was in command of all American and British formations in Morocco, Algiers, and Tunisia, and was composed of a mixed U.S. and British staff. After the defeat of the Axis forces in North Africa and Sicily, A.F.H.Q. moved to Italy and was established at Caserta.

H.Q. CENTRAL MEDITERRANEAN FORCE.

This Headquarters was formed upon the disbandment of Allied Force H.Q. in Italy. It then became the Operational and Administrative Headquarters for all British forces in Italy and the Mediterranean area. Its badge was the (black) torch of freedom with three red flames against a white background the lower portion of which had three thick wavy blue bands to denote the Mediterranean (similar to the badge of 15th Army Group). The design was set in a shield with a black border. It was said that the badge was chosen to commemorate Operation "Torch"—the code name for the allied operations which carried the war against the Axis into the Western Mediterranean in November, 1942.

SUPREME ALLIED COMMAND, SOUTH-EAST ASIA (S.A.C.S.E.A.).

The Headquarters staff of Admiral Lord Louis Mountbatten, the Supreme Commander, South-East Asia, wore as their badge a blue phoenix rising from red flames on a white circular background within a blue border, emblematic of Allied might rising from the ashes of the Japanese-occupied territories of Burma, Malaya, China, the East Indies and South Pacific.

ALLIED LAND FORCES, SOUTH-EAST ASIA (A.L.F.S.E.A.).

A.L.F.S.E.A's. badge was a white shield; on it a red crusader's cross. Behind the shield the wings of victory in yellow or gold and a crusader's sword in white; the whole set on a background of light blue, with a dark blue base. The badge was emblematic of the wings of victory carrying the crusader's sword and shield across the seas to the liberation of enemy-occupied territories and the defeat of Japan.

11th ARMY GROUP.

This formation, which became on 1st January, 1945, H.Q. Allied Land Forces, South East Asia, had as its badge a yellow sampan sailing on a dark blue sea, with a red sky. The blue and red—Army colours—being evenly divided as the background. The badge illustrated was that used as a vehicle marking.

11th Army Group was formed in Delhi in October, 1943, under the command of General Sir George Giffard, G.C.B., D.S.O., A.D.C. An advance H.Q. was set up in Delhi whilst Main H.Q. was established at Barrakpore. Main H.Q. and most of Advance H.Q. was later moved to Kandy, and it was here that it was redesignated A.L.F.S.E.A.

HEADQUARTERS 15th ARMY GROUP.

15th Army Group was formed for the invasion of Italy and controlled the two operations in that invasion carried out by the Seventh American and Eighth British Armies; 7 plus 8 equals 15, and this was the reason for the choice of the number for this Army Group. The Formation badge, a white shield set on a red square, on it three wavy blue lines, was sponsored by Field-Marshal Lord Alexander when 15th Army Group H.Q. evolved into H.Q. Allied Armies in Italy. In January, 1945, H.Q. A.A.I. was abolished and 15th Army Group constituted. This was a mixed American and British formation, composed of the Fifth (U.S.) and Eighth (British) Armies under the command of General Mark W. Clark. Its mixed troops were of many nationalities, American, British, Brazilian, Indian, South African, New Zealand, Polish, Palestinian and Italian. The formation H.Q. took over the A.A.I. badge. It was this formation that pierced the Gothic Line, and during the winter of 1944-45 formed up across Italy from the flats of the Senio River across the Apennines to the Gulf of Genoa. Its task for the spring campaign was the destruction of some thirty enemy divisions in the north of Italy. 15th Army Group's attack was launched in the Bologna area in April, 1945, and its drive into the Po Valley commenced. By 2nd May the whole country had been overrun, from the French border to Trieste and northwards to the Brenner. On 4th May the German forces laid down their arms, and General Clark accepted the formal surrender of the German Commander-in-Chief of all German troops in Northern Italy and the southern Austrian provinces.

HEADQUARTERS 21st ARMY GROUP.

The familiar sign of Field-Marshal Viscount Montgomery's Headquarters first appeared in September, 1943. The badge worn on both arms of the battledress blouse or service jacket by all members of the H.Q. Staff of 21st Army Group was two crusaders' swords in gold, "in saltire" (*i.e.*, crossed diagonally), on a blue cross on a red shield. The badge was also worn by G.H.Q. 2nd Echelon, 21st Army Group.

It was 21st Army Group which carried out the invasion of Europe in June, 1944, fighting its way from the Normandy beaches to the banks of the Elbe, its Commander accepting the surrender of the German Army at Luneburg Heath on 6th June, 1945. When H.Q. 21st Army Group became, in August, 1945, H.Q. British Army of the Rhine, the sign continued to be worn by the staff of the British H.Q. in Germany.*

★ ★ ★ ★ ★

---

* See also British Army of the Rhine, page 190.

HOME COMMANDS
(United Kingdom)

NORTHERN COMMAND (U.K.).

A green apple on a small dark blue diamond was the badge of Northern Command, which had its Headquarters in York. The sign was chosen during the time that the former Adjutant-General (General Sir Ronald F. Adam, Bart., G.C.B., D.S.O., O.B.E.), was G.O.C., and, like the badge of 3 Corps, Northern Command's sign was adopted for its association with the name of its Commander—*i.e.*, Adam's apple.

EASTERN COMMAND (U.K.).

Eastern Command's coastline stretched from the Wash to the Thames, and a similar motif to the South-Eastern Command sign was adopted. On a black square, a white bulldog stood on guard. Eastern Command's war-time H.Q. was at Luton, and its territory covered East Anglia and the Central Midland Counties. Eastern Command has now reverted to its pre-war boundaries and includes Kent, Surrey and Sussex.

SCOTTISH COMMAND.

The heraldic lion rampant of Scotland woven in gold on a scarlet background with a central horizontal black band, the colours of a Command H.Q. brassard, was the badge of H.Q. Scottish Command at Edinburgh. Units of the Command other than the H.Q. Staff had the same badge, but with a plain red background.

SOUTH-EASTERN COMMAND (U.K.).

This Command came into existence during the war, and was formed for operational and administrative purposes from the Aldershot Command and that part of the pre-war Eastern Command which lay south of the Thames. The Headquarters was at Reigate, and the distinguishing badge of the Command was a tiger's head, the tiger roaring defiance, symbolic of the fact that the Command's coastline of Kent and Sussex faced the German-held French Channel coast. South-Eastern Command ceased to exist at the end of 1944, its territory being divided between Eastern and Southern Commands.

WESTERN COMMAND (U.K.).

The yellow cross of St. David of Wales, with the red rose of Lancaster superimposed on the centre of the cross, within a red circle on a black background, was the distinguishing sign of Western Command, which has its Headquarters at Chester, and its boundaries embracing the whole of Wales and the bordering North-Western and North-Midland Counties.

SOUTHERN COMMAND (U.K.).

A conventional representation of the constellation of the Southern Cross set on a shield formed the basis of the Southern Command sign. The colouring of the shield, forming a background to the five stars, varied according to the arm of the service of the unit of the wearer. In the case of Command Headquarters, the colouring of the shield was the red and black horizontal bars of a Command H.Q. pennant and brassard. There were eighteen variations of this Command's badge, according to the regimental or Corps colours of the different arms of the service. For example, the Royal Artillery's shield was halved, the right being dark blue, and the left half red; the Sappers had a red shield divided by a dark blue diagonal strip; the R.E.M.E. shield had three vertical bars of blue, yellow and red; that of the R.A.S.C. was half yellow, half dark blue. In all cases the pattern of the stars of the Southern Cross was superimposed.

The eighteen variations of the badge of Southern Command were as follows:—

Unit (Arm of Service).	Shield.	Stars.
Command Headquarters	RED, with central horizontal BLACK bar.	WHITE.
Royal Artillery	Divided vertically. Left half RED, right half BLUE.	WHITE.
Royal Engineers	RED, divided by BLUE diagonal bar top left to bottom right.	WHITE.
Royal Signals	Divided vertically. Left half DARK BLUE, right half WHITE.	WHITE on DARK BLUE. DARK BLUE on WHITE.
Royal Armoured Corps	Divided vertically. Left half RED, right half YELLOW.	RED on YELLOW. YELLOW on RED.
Infantry	RED.	WHITE.
Royal Army Medical Corps	MAROON.	WHITE.
Royal Army Service Corps	Divided vertically. Left half DARK BLUE, right half YELLOW.	YELLOW ON DARK BLUE. DARK BLUE on YELLOW.
Royal Army Ordnance Corps	RED with central vertical BLACK bar.	WHITE.
Royal Electrical and Mechanical Engineers	Divided in three vertical bars. Left, RED; Centre, YELLOW; Right, DARK BLUE.	DARK BLUE on centre bar. WHITE on side bars.
Corps of Royal Military Police	Divided vertically. Left RED, right BLACK.	WHITE.
Royal Army Dental Corps	Divided vertically. Left GREEN, right WHITE.	WHITE ON GREEN. GREEN ON WHITE.
Royal Army Pay Corps	YELLOW.	BLUE.

Unit (Arm of Service).	Shield.	Stars.
Royal Army Educational Corps	CAMBRIDGE BLUE.	WHITE.
Royal Pioneer Corps ...	Divided vertically. Left GREEN, right RED.	WHITE.
Intelligence Corps	GREEN.	WHITE.
Army Physical Training Corps	BLACK.	RED.
Women's Royal Army Corps	DARK BROWN with narrow GREEN edging.	BEECH BROWN.

The command vehicle marking differed from the badges worn on uniform, inasmuch as the marking was a rectangle, divided in horizontal bars of red, black and red, and with the addition of a fifth star on the central black band immediately below the middle star of the central row of three.

Southern Command Vehicle Marking.

OVERSEAS COMMANDS

INDIA COMMAND.
SUPREME HEADQUARTERS, INDIA.

The badge of India Command was a shield divided into three vertical bars, of dark blue, red and light blue, the colours of the Royal Navy, the Army and the R.A.F.; on each bar being the badge of the service—the crest of the Royal Indian Navy; the lion and crown and crossed swords of the Army; and the crown and albatross of the R.A.F. is superimposed on a circle bearing the motto, "Per Ardua ad Astra," and surmounted by a crown. The badges were in yellow, and the crowns in red and yellow.

This was a unique Command as it embodied under one head all three services. The badge was worn by those staffs under the Commander-in-Chief which dealt with the H.Qs. of all three services in New Delhi. After the partition of India in 1947, the badge was worn by the staff of Supreme Headquarters, India.

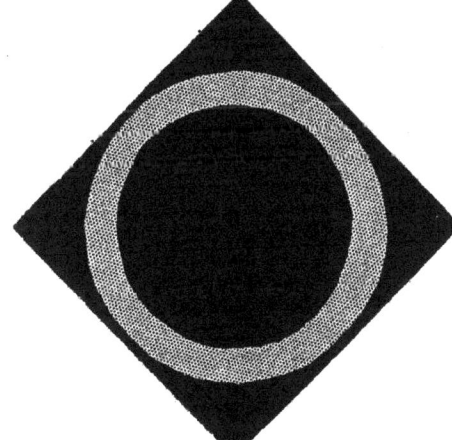

CENTRAL COMMAND (INDIA).

A red circle, set within a black equal-sided diamond, was the sign adopted by the Central Command in India.

EASTERN COMMAND (INDIA).

The truncated heraldic head of a horse in white on a square black background was the badge of India's Eastern Command.* Eastern Command was the successor to Eastern Army, and was the H.Q. responsible for the operations in the Arakan and elsewhere in Burma until the formation of the Fourteenth Army in November, 1943.

The design of the badge stressed the horse's mane, thereby connecting the badge with the name of the formation commander, General Sir Mosley Mayne, K.C.B., C.B.E., D.S.O., A.D.C.

NORTHERN COMMAND (INDIA).

The symbolic compass North Point, as used in cartography, in white set on a red shield divided by a black band, was the badge of this Indian Command.

CEYLON ARMY COMMAND.

Superimposed on a background of Command colours, red, black and red, an elephant's head in yellow was the badge of Ceylon Army Command.

---

* See also 21 Indian Corps, page 112.

PERSIA AND IRAQ COMMAND.

Generally known by the accepted abbreviations "PAIF" or "Paiforce" or "PAIC" (Persia and Iraq Command), this force comprised the Tenth Army and its bases and L. of C., extending, as its designation proclaimed, over Persia and Iraq. It conducted the operations which quelled the Iraqi rebellion of 1941, and those which expelled the Axis agents from Persia. Its badge, a red elephant's head with white tusks, on a royal blue oblong, was, it was said, chosen in view of the fact that the first G.O.C. was General (now Field-Marshal) Sir Henry Maitland Wilson, G.C.B., D.S.O., M.C., universally known by his popular nick-name, "Jumbo."* On the disbandment of "Paiforce" the badge continued to be worn by H.Q. British troops in Iraq.

MALTA COMMAND.

A white Maltese cross set on a shield of command colours, red, black and red, was the badge of Malta Command, the senior military formation of the " George Cross Island."†

---
* See also Ninth Army, page 26, and British Troops in Iraq, page 167.
† See also Malta, page 164, and 231st Infantry Brigade, page 208.

WEST AFRICA COMMAND.

This Command covered the West African Colonies—Nigeria, Gold Coast, Gambia, and Sierra Leone. The Command's badge was a West African palm tree in black set on a white rectangular background.

EAST AFRICA COMMAND.

This Command covered Kenya, Tanganyika, British Somaliland, Abyssinia and Italian Somaliland. Its badge was two crossed *pangas* set on a green background.

Its badge was originally two crossed *pangas* (machetes) set on a green background. This was subsequently changed to a scarlet circle, surmounted by a black ring. Within the circle a pair of *pangas* crossed, left over right, each with a silver blade and black handle. When used on vehicles the badge was 8 inches in diameter. The black border was ½ inch in width and the *pangas* 6½ inches long.

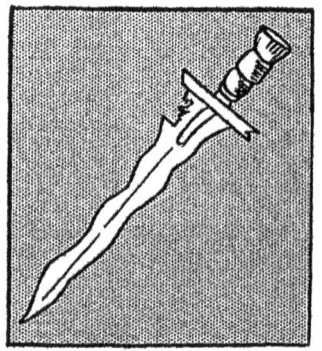

MALAYA COMMAND.

This Command, re-established after the liberation of Malaya, adopted as its badge a kris, the native Malayan dagger with a wavy shaped blade, in yellow set on a green background.

THE ARMIES

FIRST ARMY.

The distinguishing badge of the First Army, commanded by Lieut.-General Sir Kenneth Anderson, K.C.B., M.C., worn throughout the campaign in Tunisia, was the red cross of St. George on a white shield, a crusader's sword superimposed on the upright of the cross. The First Army landed in North Africa in November, 1942, and commanded the British formations which cleared Algeria of the Nazi occupying forces, and holding them during the winter of 1942-43 until the final battles in Tunisia which led to the capitulation of von Arnim and the entire German force in North Africa. First Army was composed of the 5 and 9 Corps.

The following description of the First Army badge* was given in the Programme of the First Army Thanksgiving Service held in Tunisia for the victory granted to the Allies in North Africa :—

"*The Shield*: Representing our country—our home set in the midst of the sea, a sure and safe refuge—a land, shaped like a shield, which has stood us in good stead all through the long pages of our history. The base of our strength to-day. 'Breathes there a man with soul so dead, who never to himself hath said, "This is my own, my native land"?'"

"*The Crusader's Cross*: The symbol by which all men shall know the ideals and principles for which we stand, no sacrifice being too great in the cause of freedom. For nothing can be higher than the hope expressed by that symbol—persecution, oppression and terror banished, and replaced by Christian peace and toleration. No one can doubt the intention of those who serve and follow The Cross."

"*The Drawn Sword*: Long ago a Christian soldier gave us an example of the cause for which the sword should be drawn. This example we of First Army endeavour to follow. St. George drew his sword and destroyed a dragon which had enslaved a nation. We endeavour to destroy a dragon which has arisen in Europe which would enslave the whole world. We cannot sheathe our sword until our task be thoroughly finished."

---

* In the Programme the Badge was referred to as the "First Army Sign."

SECOND ARMY.

The Second Army, formed in England in the summer of 1943, adopted a similar sign to that of the First Army, a blue cross being substituted for the red. Second Army was raised for the invasion of Europe, and went ashore in Normandy on D Day, 6th June, 1944, forming part of the 21st Army Group. Under the command of Lieut.-General Sir Miles Dempsey, K.C.B., K.B.E., D.S.O., M.C., Second Army saw much hard fighting in the establishment of the beachhead, at Caen, and in the break-out which culminated in the German defeat at Falaise. Then followed the drive across France, the crossing of the Seine and the Somme, the liberation of Brussels, and the sweep up to the banks of the Maas, which was held during the winter of 1944-45. The spring of 1945 saw Second Army engaged in the clearance of the enemy between the Maas and the Rhine, and on 24th March, 1945, it was 12 and 30 Corps of Second Army which forced the northern crossing of the Rhine. Then followed the drive across North-West Germany—Munster, Osnabruck, Bremen and Hamburg—and to the banks of the Elbe, which ended in the surrender of the last remaining German armed forces.

EIGHTH ARMY.

The existence of the Eighth Army became known when in November, 1941, General Sir Alan G. Cunningham, K.C.B., D.S.O., M.C., was appointed to its command at the opening of General Sir Claude Auchinleck's offensive in the Western Desert. The Eighth was formed from the original Army of the Nile, and included the 13 and 30 British Corps with South African, Australian, New Zealand and Indian formations. It was engaged in much hard fighting in the Desert against the combined forces of the Italians and Rommel's Afrika Korps throughout 1942, which culminated in the withdrawal to the defensive line at the gateway to Egypt. It was at this time that Lieut.-General (later Field-Marshal Viscount) Montgomery was appointed to its command and directed its efforts into the great victory of El Alamein in October, 1942. Under his inspiring leadership the Eighth swept on across Cyrenaica and Tripolitania to the Mareth Line and thence northward into Tunisia to the final defeat of the Axis forces in North Africa. "The achievements of the Eighth Army," said Mr. Churchill in an address at Tripoli in February, 1943, "will gleam and glow in the annals of history." The Eighth next saw action in the invasion of Sicily, and then into Italy where, under command of the 15th Army Group, they fought their way northwards across the Sangro, the Volturno, through the Gothic and Adolf Hitler Defence lines and finally in the swift, decisive Po Valley campaign which culminated in the surrender of the German forces in Northern Italy.

The Eighth Army H.Q. and Army Troops wore as their badge the now famous golden crusader's cross on a white shield set on a dark blue background. The badge was later adopted by H.Q. British Troops in Austria (B.T.A.).*

NINTH ARMY.

The Ninth Army was formed in the Middle East at the end of 1941. It was raised in The Levant, as the Headquarters for all forces which might have been used in that area against a German thrust which it was anticipated might follow further enemy successes at the time in Southern Russia.

The badge of the Ninth Army, which was commanded by General (now Field-Marshal) Sir Henry Maitland Wilson, G.C.B., D.S.O., M.C., was a charging elephant, on its back a castle, from which flew the red and black flag of an Army commander. The design was in red on a black circular background, the elephant, as in the case of the Paiforce badge, associating with the formation the nickname of its commander—"Jumbo."

The badge on the disbandment of H.Q. Ninth Army, was subsequently adopted by North Levant District.†

---

* See British Troops in Austria, page 190.
† See North Levant District, page 176.

TENTH ARMY.

The Tenth Army was raised in Iraq and formed the major part of "Paiforce" (Persia and Iraq force). It was composed of British and Indian troops and was actively engaged in quelling the Iraqi rebellion in 1941 and in the operations against the Axis elements in Persia. The main task of the Tenth Army was the maintenance of the lines of communication to Russia from the Persian Gulf to the Caspian and the protection of the South Persian and Iraq oilfields. Its badge was a golden Assyrian lion with human head set on a black background. A variation of this colouring was a white lion on a pale blue background.

★ ★ ★ ★ ★

TWELFTH ARMY.

Twelfth Army H.Q. was first formed in the Middle East, and was a H.Q. set up for the planning of operations in the Mediterranean. Its badge was then a black performing seal on a yellow background, balancing upon its nose a globe showing the Eastern Hemisphere.

The Twelfth Army was re-formed in Burma on 28th May, 1945, and, under the command of Lieut.-General Sir Montagu Stopford, K.B.E., C.B., D.S.O., M.C., took part in the final operations against the Japanese which led to the liberation of Burma. It was responsible for the final clearance of the Japanese from Burma after the capture of Rangoon. The formation was disbanded on 1st January, 1946, and the Corps and Divisions under its command were incorporated in the Burma Command. Its badge was a Burmese dragon, the *chinthe* (pagoda custodian) in white and gold superimposed on a background of two red and one, central, black horizontal bar above the Roman figures "XII" in white.

FOURTEENTH ARMY.

A red shield, with a narrow white inner border, the centre divided by a black horizontal band, on which the Roman figures "XIV" were inscribed in white, set across a white sword, hilt uppermost, was the badge of the hard-fighting Fourteenth Army, commanded by General Sir William Slim, G.B.E., K.C.B., D.S.O., M.C. This Army, which was disbanded on 31st December, 1945, was formed in November, 1943, and was the largest single army of the war. In its time it held the longest battle line, from the Bay of Bengal to the borders of India and China, and fought through some of the most difficult country in the world from Manipur to Rangoon. At one time its strength was nearly a million. It was grouped into three corps, the 4 and the 15 and 33 Indian Corps. A fourth corps, the 34, was formed for the invasion of Malaya, but Fourteenth Army never, in fact, commanded more than three corps, for when 34 Corps was raised, 4 and 33 Indian Corps were under command of the Twelfth Army. The Fourteenth Army's great victories in the Arakan, at Imphal, Kohima, Kennedy Peak, Mandalay, and Meiktila, led to the defeat of the Japanese and the liberation of Burma and Malaya. Fourteenth Army was withdrawn to India in June, 1945, to prepare for the invasion of Malaya. The H.Q. followed 34 Indian Corps to Malaya in September, 1945. The following divisions served with the Fourteenth Army: the 2nd and 36th British Divisions, the 3rd (The Chindits), 5th, 7th, 17th, 19th, 20th, 23rd, 25th and 26th Indian Divisions, the 11th East African and the 81st and 82nd West African Divisions.

The design of the Fourteenth Army badge was submitted anonymously in a competition open to all ranks for the choice of badge—when it was chosen, it was disclosed that the artist was none other than the Army Commander, General Sir William Slim.

★ ★ ★ ★ ★

BRITISH CORPS

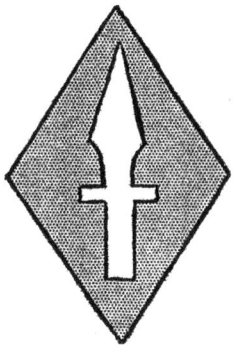

1 CORPS.

A white spearhead on a scarlet diamond was the badge of 1 Corps.* The Corps formed part of the B.E.F., proceeding overseas in September, 1939, to France. It was among the formations withdrawn from Dunkirk in May, 1940. The Corps badge was adopted whilst the formation was part of the B.E.F., and was symbolic of the selection of this Corps as an assault formation. 1 Corps landed in Normandy on D Day, 6th June, 1944, and fought across France, Belgium and Southern Holland. The formation formed the first static district of occupied Germany, taking over the control and administration of the Rhine Province and Westphalia in the final stages of the campaign.

2 CORPS.

2 Corps formed part of the B.E.F.: landing in France in October, 1939, and in April, 1940, it moved forward into Belgium to meet the German invasion. The Corps returned to England via Dunkirk when the B.E.F. was withdrawn from the Continent. The formation badge

---

* 1 Corps Troops Engineers wore the white spearhead on a background of R.E. Colours, see page 220, and the Corps Artillery wore the spearhead on a diamond of R.A. colours, see page 216.

1 Corps badge was incorporated in that of one of the Belgian formations which served under its command—the 6th Brigade, see page 244.

was said to have been chosen as an association with the name of its commander, Lieut.-General Sir Alan Brooke (now Field-Marshal Viscount Alanbrooke, G.C.B., D.S.O.) and was originally three dark wavy blue bands on a white oblong, symbolizing a brook. The red fish, a leaping salmon, was added to give the badge a more "watery" effect, and the badge was bordered by a narrow red line.

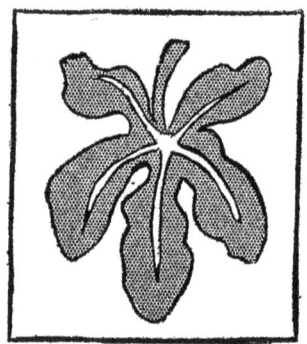

3 CORPS.

3 Corps, comprising the 42nd (East Lancs), 44th (Home Counties) and 51st (Highland) Divisions, joined the B.E.F. in France in March, 1940, and (less the 51st Division) took part in the operations leading to the withdrawal to and evacuation from Dunkirk. The Corps badge was adopted while the formation was in Northern Ireland. This badge, a green fig leaf on a white background, was chosen for its association with the name of the Corps Commander, Lieut.-General Sir Ronald Adam (later G.O.C. Northern Command and Adjutant-General to the Forces). In 1943 the Corps embarked for Persia. Moving later to Syria and Egypt, it subsequently served in Italy and Greece, where the Corps H.Q. became H.Q. Land Forces, Greece.*

---

* See also H.Q. Land Forces, Greece and British Forces in Greece, page 168.

4 CORPS.

A black elephant on a red background was the badge of this British formation of the Fourteenth Army. The Corps was moved from Iraq to India in the spring of 1942, and from then onwards was actively engaged in operations against the Japanese, firstly under command of Eastern Army (India) and then with the Fourteenth Army. The Corps saw much hard fighting in the liberation of Burma. It established the Irrawaddy bridgehead and, moving across country, drove the Japanese from Meiktila. The Corps was in the van of the Fourteenth Army in its drive to Mandalay and Rangoon.* Finally, the Corps came under command of Twelfth Army.

5 CORPS.

5 Corps formed part of the N.W.E.F. in Norway in 1940. The formation badge, a Viking ship, was subsequently chosen to commemorate the Corps' service in Scandinavia. 5 Corps joined First Army, from Home Forces, in North Africa in 1942, taking part in the operations which led to the final defeat of the Axis forces in Tunisia and the surrender of von Arnim, commander of the Axis forces in Africa, to the Corps Commander, at Cap Bon. 5 Corps next saw service in Sicily and Italy, where it advanced northwards in the

---

* See also 253 L. of C. Sub-Area, page 184.

Adriatic sector. As part of 15th Army Group, and composed of the 56th, 78th, 2nd (New Zealand) and 8th (Indian) Divisions, a Commando and two Armoured Brigades, 5 Corps, under command of the Eighth Army, took part in the final operations in the Po Valley which culminated in the surrender of the German armies in Italy.

The badge depicted the Viking ship and sail in white; on the sail a cross in red picked out in black, the design on a black background.

7 CORPS.*

7 Corps was formed in the U.K. in the summer of 1940, and, under the command of the Canadian, Lieut.-General McNaughton, was composed of the 1st Armoured Division, the 1st Canadian Division, and the 2nd New Zealand Division. The Corps was formed for an anti-invasion operational role on the South Coast of England during the Battle of Britain. With the defeat of the Luftwaffe and the German reluctance to venture across the Channel, the emergency passed and the need for this formation ceased to exist, and 7 Corps was disbanded on Christmas Day, 1940.

First Eighth Corps Badge.

Second Eighth Corps Badge.

8 CORPS.

8 Corps has had two badges. As 8 Corps District (covering the counties of Devon, Cornwall and Somerset) of Southern Command in 1940-42, the badge of a black (Francolin) partridge on a white oval was worn. In February, 1943, H.Q. 8 Corps moved to Scotch Corner, near Darlington, in Northern Command. The 9th and 42nd Armoured Divisions were placed under command and a new badge was adopted, the original badge being retained by the newly formed South-Western District which was raised to take over the former 8 Corps area in South-West England.† 8 Corps' second badge was appropriate to the formation's new role, an armoured corps. It was a charging knight in armour in white on a scarlet square. 8 Corps

---

* So far as the author has been able to trace, 7 Corps never had a formation badge.

† See also South-Western District, page 158.

formed part of 21st Army Group, landing in Normandy in June, 1944. With the 7th and 11th Armoured Divisions under command it took part in the operations from the beachhead to the Elbe, moving into Schleswig-Holstein on the final defeat of the German armies, where it formed 8 Corps administrative district of the British Army of the Rhine, with its H.Q. at Plon.

First Ninth Corps Badge worn in U.K.

Second Ninth Corps Badge adopted in North Africa.

9 CORPS.

A black "Kilkenny" cat, back arched in defiance, on an orange square was the first badge of 9 Corps. It was said that the badge was adopted as a play on the "9" and the traditional nine lives of a cat, but it had been chosen by the corps commander whose home was in Kilkenny. As 9 Corps District of Northern Command, the Corps area covered the counties of Northumberland, Durham, and the North Riding of Yorkshire, until mobilized in 1942 for service in North Africa.

On mobilization it was decided to change the badge, and the black cat was removed from all vehicles and personnel for security reasons before embarkation. The new badge selected in April, 1943, in North Africa was a trumpet. The idea behind its adoption came from the biblical motto—"If the trumpet make an uncertain sound who shall prepare for battle ?"

"I give you this sign," wrote Lieut.-General J. T. Crocker, the Corps Commander, in his order notifying its adoption, " as a trumpet call to duty, the highest of all military virtues, confident that you will all, with me, strive to live up to its great ideal."

The Corps served in Algeria and Tunisia with the First Army. It was disbanded after the capture of Tunis and the conclusion of the North African campaign.

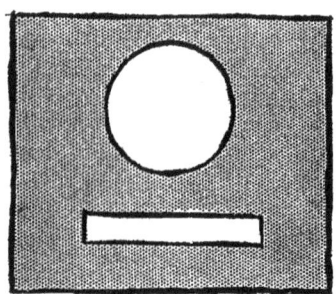

10 CORPS.

The official designation of the 10 Corps badge was "A green square, with a white rectangle in the bottom portion, and a white ball in the upper portion," but the Corps badge has been worn on a red background, and also on a green semi-circular background. This was one of the Western Desert formations. Composed of the 50th (Northumbrian) and 4th (Indian) Divisions at El Alamein, the Corps pushed forward with the Eighth Army into Cyrenaica and Tripolitania and broke through the Mareth Line defences on into Tunisia to the defeat of Afrika Korps. 10 Corps then formed part of British forces in Italy, and under command of the Eighth Army took part in the final operations in the Po Valley which led to the German capitulation in Northern Italy, in May, 1945.

11 CORPS.

A black and white chequered Martello tower was the badge of 11 Corps. This Corps formed part of Home Forces, and did not serve overseas, being disbanded in U.K. It was popularly accepted that the badge was chosen as symbolic of the number of " pill-boxes " and strong points constructed by the Corps along the East Coast whilst fulfilling its anti-invasion role in 1940 and 1941.

12 CORPS.

12 Corps, formed in Home Forces, was until 1944 located in South-Eastern Command. Its badge, familiar in Kent and Surrey, was three trees—foliage green and black trunks—an oak, an ash and a thorn, set in a white oval frame on a black background. The three trees were chosen to link with the name of the commander, Major-General (now Lieut.-General) Sir A. F. A. N. Thorne, K.C.B., C.M.G., D.S.O., and "the Oak, the Ash, and the Thorn" in "Puck of Pook's Hill," for it was in the Pook's Hill country that the Corps was raised. 12 Corps formed part of 21st Army Group for the invasion of Europe, and fought its way as part of Second Army through France, Belgium and Holland, across the Rhine, where it was one of the two assault corps, and in the sweep through North-West Germany, Hamburg falling to 12 Corps in the final operations before VE Day.

13 CORPS.

A leaping red gazelle in a white circle on a red diamond, with a narrow white border, was the formation badge adopted in the Western Desert by H.Q. 13 Corps. The badge was later changed to a red gazelle on a white circle on a red diamond with a narrow white border. The formation was part of the Eighth Army in the hard fighting in the Western Desert in the winter of 1941-42 and, with the 4th (Indian) and 2nd (New Zealand) Divisions and a tank brigade under command, fought the battle of the Omars. The Corps took part in the battle of El Alamein and the advance through Libya to Tunis. It was 13 Corps which landed in Sicily and fought at Catania and cleared the Axis forces from the island. On 3rd September, 1943, the Corps, then composed of the 5th British and 1st Canadian Divisions, landed on the toe of Italy. The Corps remained in Italy throughout the remainder of the war and, with the 6th Armoured and 10th (Indian) Divisions under command, took part in the final operations in the Po Valley which brought about the German surrender on 4th May, 1945.

25 CORPS.

Formerly the badge of the H.Q. of the British Troops in Cyprus,* the badge was taken on by 25 Corps. It was a Cyprus lion, as appeared in the Coat of Arms of Richard Cœur de Lion, in red on a yellow background.

30 CORPS.

Another badge adopted in the Middle East was that of 30 Corps, a black charging boar set in a white circle on a square black background. The 30th was one of the Western Desert formations, where it distinguished itself in the drive to Tobruk in November, 1941,

---
* See also Cyprus District, page 176.

and the battle of the Omars. The Corps formed part of the Eighth Army at El Alamein, where it was composed of the 50th (Northumbrian), 51st (Highland) and the 7th (Armoured) Divisions. Early in 1944 the formation was withdrawn from the Mediterranean and returned to U.K. to join 21st Army Group. Landing in Normandy, the Corps, under the command of Lieut.-General Sir Brian Horrocks, K.B.E., C.B., D.S.O., M.C., fought across France, Belgium and Southern Holland to the Rhine. It was one of the assault formations in the Rhine crossing and drove deep into Germany in the final operations. 30 Corps became one of the Corps Districts of the British Army of the Rhine, covering the Province of Hanover, with its H.Q. at Nienburg.

[*Reproduced by permission of H.Q. B.A.O.R.*

The 1945 Christmas Card of 30 Corps District, depicting on the shields of the Knights in Armour the badges of formations then forming part of the Corps District, the 5th, 43rd and 51st Divisions, the 1st Canadian Division, the 8th Armoured Brigade, and the 1st Polish Armoured Division.

BRITISH ARMOURED DIVISIONS*

THE GUARDS ARMOURED DIVISION.

This formation was composed of regiments and battalions of the Household Brigade. The well-known badge worn by the Guards Division in the 1914-18 war was reintroduced for use by the Guards Armoured Division. The sign, designed by the late Major Sir Eric Avery, Bt., M.C. (who commanded the Guards Divisional M.T. Company in the first B.E.F.), was a white eye, on a blue shield, with a red border, the present badge being selected from a number of designs painted on some of the Division's vehicles by the late Rex Whistler.

The Guards Armoured Division was formed in September, 1941, and it formed part of 21st Army Group for the invasion of Europe. As part of 8 Corps it landed in Normandy in June, 1944, took part in the hard fighting at Caen and Falaise and the dash to the Somme on the break out of the beachhead. It was the first formation to enter Brussels on its liberation in September, 1944, and then took part in the operations which cleared the area from the Meuse to the Rhine. Crossing the Rhine under the command of 12 Corps, the Division fought its way across Germany to Bremen and Cuxhaven, accepting the surrender of the latter port shortly before VE Day. From the north of Germany the Division was moved back to the Rhineland, where the Guards Division had been in occupation in 1918-19. The Division were converted to an Infantry Division in June, 1945. On the 10th of that month the formation paraded for the last time with its armour, and Field-Marshal Montgomery attended the ceremonial parade held to mark the occasion at Rothenburg. Redesignated the Guards Division, the formation then formed part of the British Army of the Rhine.

---

* See also Canadian Armoured Divisions, page 91, Australian Armoured Divisions, page 97, South African Armoured Division, page 110, Indian Armoured Divisions, pages 126 and 127.

1st Armoured Division original and final badge.

1st ARMOURED DIVISION.

A charging rhinoceros in white on a black oval background was the badge of the 1st Armoured Division. The Division joined the B.E.F. in 1940 as part of the forces on the L. of C. in the fighting which took place around the Somme and the Seine. Back in U.K. it formed part of the 7 Corps in South-East England. In 1941 the Division sailed for the Middle East and formed part of the British force in the Western Desert and was engaged in the fighting which halted Rommel's Afrika Korps' drive to Egypt. The Division formed part of the Eighth Army at El Alamein and in the advance across Libya to the Mareth Line, and into Tunisia in the spring of 1943, and was composed of the 2nd Armoured Brigade (The Bays ; 9th Lancers ; 10th Royal Hussars ; and the Yorkshire Dragoons) and the 7th Motor Brigade (2nd and 7th Bns. R.B. and 2nd Bn. K.R.R.C.). The Division subsequently took part in the operations in Italy (when a new badge was adopted, the "charging rhino"), but after the breakthrough of the Gothic Line, the formation was broken up. Its original badge continued to be worn by the 2nd Armoured Brigade* and in July, 1946, when the 6th Armoured Division was redesignated 1st Armoured, the Division wore the "mailed fist" badge of the 6th Armoured Division.†

1st Armoured Division badge as worn in Italy, 1943-44.

---

* See also 2nd Armoured Brigade, page 193.
† See 6th Armoured Division, page 41.

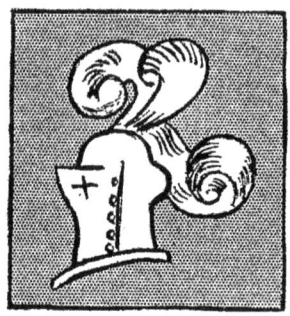

2nd ARMOURED DIVISION.

A knight's helmet in white on a red background was this formation's badge. This was one of the Western Desert formations which took part in the early fighting against the Axis forces in Libya. The Division was formed in U.K. and embarked for the Middle East in November, 1940. At the time of its departure it was the only fully equipped armoured formation in Home Forces, but it was a critical time in the Middle East and this bold move paid a good " dividend."

6th ARMOURED DIVISION.

A clenched mailed gauntlet in white, on a square black background, was this Division's badge. The formation served in the B.N.A.F. with the First Army during the campaign in Tunisia in 1942-43, and it was this Division which linked up with the advancing Eighth Army in the coastal sector of Tunisia in the final round up and defeat of von Arnim's broken Axis forces. The 6th Armoured served through the Italian campaign, and as part of the Eighth Army took part in the 15th Army Group's operations in the Po Valley in the spring of 1945. The Division's dash to Gorizia in the last days of the campaign saw the crumbling of the final German resistance in Northern Italy. The Division was subsequently renumbered and became the 1st Armoured Division.

First style badge.   *Second style badge.*

7th ARMOURED DIVISION.

The 7th Armoured Division, the famous " Desert Rats," was the first formation to go into the Western Desert at the outbreak of war with Italy. It was in the sands and barren wastes of Libya that the Division earned its title, thanks to its " scurrying and biting " activities, and the adoption of the jerboa (the desert rat) as its badge —a red rat in a white circle on a red square. This form was later changed to a red rat, picked out in white, on a black background. The Division formed part of Field-Marshal Lord Wavell's original desert force, which became the Army of the Nile. It took part in the first offensive against Graziani's forces which rolled the Italians back beyond Benghazi in 1941. Throughout all the desert operations, in General Sir Claude Auchinleck's offensive, and with the Eighth Army under General Montgomery, the Division was to the forefront of the battle—at Sidi Barrani, the Battle of the Omars, Gazala; it took part in the battle of El Alamein, the advance through Libya, and in the final battles in Tunisia which brought the British Armies in North Africa to their goal. The Division was withdrawn from the Mediterranean early in 1944 to participate in the invasion of Europe with 21st Army Group, and it landed in Normandy in June. It was in action at Caen and Falaise and in the operations in France, Belgium and Holland which culminated in the assault on the Rhine and the drive into Germany. It was the 7th Armoured Division which formed the bulk of the British force which entered Berlin, taking part in the Victory march before the " Big Three " in the heart of the fallen capital, a fitting end to the long, hard-fought road from the Western Desert, where the " Desert Rats " first went into action.

8th ARMOURED DIVISION.

Raised in England in 1940, this formation embarked for the Middle East in 1942. It did not, however, go into action as a complete division, although within a few weeks of disembarking in Egypt one brigade took part in the Eighth Army's hard-fought withdrawal to El Alamein. Not long after the Division was broken up on the reorganization and redistribution of units and equipment in the M.E.F.

The formation badge was taken from the familiar traffic light signals—the word " GO " in black on a green circle within a black square.

The Divisional motto being " No stop ; No caution ; Go on." The badge of the 8th Armoured Division continued to be borne after the disbandment of the Division by the R.A.S.C. Company of the 24th Armoured Brigade. The Company later became the 334 Corps Troops Company, R.A.S.C., and carried this badge as its vehicle marking in Sicily and Italy with the 13 Corps.

9th ARMOURED DIVISION.

This war-formed Armoured Division was raised in the U.K. in 1941, adopting as its formation badge the head of a giant panda. The Division formed part of Home Forces, and was disbanded at the end of 1944, when most of its personnel joined 21st Army Group.

The badge was said to have been adopted as a pun on the German "Panzer" Divisions.

10th ARMOURED DIVISION.

A fox's mask in red on a black (or yellow) circle was this formation's badge. The Division was raised in the Middle East and made up mainly of mechanized units of the original Cavalry Division, including the Yeomanry cavalry that were dispatched to Egypt and Palestine early in 1940. The Division formed part of the Eighth Army at El Alamein, and in the advance across Libya to Tripoli, the Mareth Line and Tunisia.

11th ARMOURED DIVISION.

Formed in England during the build-up of our armoured forces in 1941, the 11th Armoured Division adopted the badge of a charging black bull with red horns, eyes and hooves, on a yellow oblong background. As one of the armoured formations of 21st Army Group, with the fitting Divisional motto, "Taurus Pursuant," the Division, forming part of 8 Corps, took part in the heavy fighting around Caen, the break out of the Normandy beachhead, the operations in France, Belgium and Holland which followed, and finally in the sweep across Germany to the Elbe which ended with the German surrender in May, 1945.

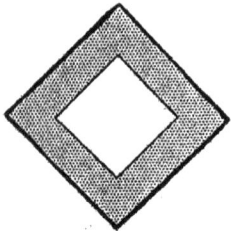

42nd ARMOURED DIVISION.*

This Armoured Division was formed in 1941 by the conversion of the 42nd (East Lancashire) Division. It formed part of Home Forces, and continued to wear the badge of the East Lancs Division, an equal-sided white diamond within a larger red diamond. The formation was disbanded in 1943.

79th ARMOURED DIVISION.

A bull's head with black and white markings; red and brown nostrils and red-tipped horns on a yellow background set on an inverted equilateral triangle to form the "V" for Victory, within a narrow black border was the badge of the 79th Armoured Division, which was commanded by Major-General Sir P. C. S. Hobart, K.B.E., C.B., D.S.O., M.C.

The Division was formed in England in October, 1942. It was reorganized in April the following year and converted to a specially equipped assault formation, its armoured units being equipped with " Flails " (for minefield clearance), " Crocodiles " (flame throwers), "Buffaloes" (amphibious carriers), "Kangaroos" (for the armoured

---

* See also 42nd (East Lancashire) Division, page 57 and 42nd Armoured Engineer Regiment, page 221.

lift of infantry), and many special assault devices. The Division included the 1st Assault Brigade Royal Engineers, later redesignated the Armoured R.E., made up of three regiments equipped with A.Vs.R.E. (Armoured Vehicles R.E.), and specially designed assault bridging and demolition stores. The formation formed part of 21st Army Group and had a distinguished record in the fighting from D Day to VE Day, taking part in the assault actions of the Normandy landing; at Caumont, Villers Bocage, Caen, Tilly and Falaise; at Boulogne and Calais; at the mouth of the Scheldt; at Breskens and on the Island of Walcheren; at Roermond and in the Siegfried Line at Geilenkirchen; the Rhine crossing; the Ruhr pocket, and on through North-West Germany.

★ ★ ★ ★ ★

BRITISH INFANTRY DIVISIONS

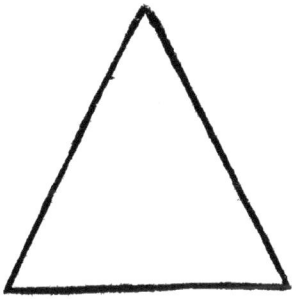

1st DIVISION.

A white triangle was the formation badge of the 1st (Regular) Division. It formed part of the original B.E.F. and embarked for France in September, 1939, as part of 1 Corps. It saw much hard fighting in the 1940 operations in Flanders and in the evacuation from Dunkirk. In 1942 the Division joined the First Army in B.N.A.F. (British North Africa Force) and took part in the campaign in Tunisia, thence to Italy, as one of the formations of C.M.F. (Central Mediterranean Force).

The triangular badge on the sleeve was often improvised out of ordnance flannelette, whilst the Divisional Artillery* wore the white triangle in the centre of an evenly divided red and blue diamond, and the Divisional Signals* the white triangle on a dark blue diamond.

Prior to 1939 the only corps more or less permanently in existence was 1 Corps at Aldershot. The badge of the Corps was a spearhead† —the spearhead of the B.E.F. both in 1914 and 1940. The 1st Division therefore took the tip of the spearhead as its badge.

---

* See 1st Div. R.A., page 216 and 1st Div. Signals, page 222.
† See 1 Corps, page 30.

2nd DIVISION.

Two white keys, crossed, on a black square was the badge adopted by the 2nd Division. It was chosen in 1940 by the G.O.C., Lieut.-General Sir H. Charles Lloyd, K.C.B., D.S.O., M.C.

The badge was an appropriate choice, for in the earliest days of the history of British arms, it was the practice in time of need for two armies to be raised, one in the South of England by the Archbishop of Canterbury, and the other in the North by the Archbishop of York. The northern army carried on its shield and banners the crossed keys taken from the coat of arms of the Archbishop of York.

This was a pre-war Regular division and it formed part of the 1939 B.E.F., serving in France and Belgium until the withdrawal from Dunkirk in May, 1940.

The Division left England for India in 1942. After nearly two years' training in India it was hurriedly moved to Dimapur on the borders of India and Burma in March, 1944. It subsequently became one of the two British divisions with the Fourteenth Army in the victorious campaign which drove the Japanese from Burma.

The Division returned to India in June, 1945, and was moved to Malaya at the end of that year. One brigade of the Division (the 5th) formed part of the British Commonwealth Occupation Force in Japan.*

3rd DIVISION.

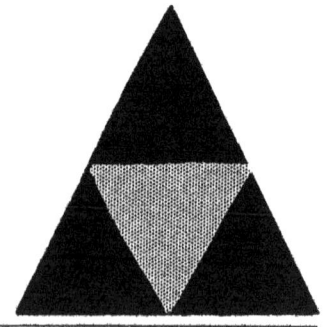

Another Regular Army division which served with the B.E.F. and took part in the heavy fighting in holding the Dunkirk perimeter during the evacuation in May, 1940. The Assault Division of Second Army, the 3rd Division landed on the Normandy beaches on the 6th of June, 1944. As part of 1 Corps it took part in the estab-

---

* See 5th Infantry Brigade, page 201.

lishment of and the subsequent break out of the beachhead and the operations in North-Western Europe culminating in VE Day in May, 1945. In the autumn of that year the Division was withdrawn from the British Army of the Rhine and embarked for the Middle East.

3rd Division's badge was a red triangle surrounded by three black ones, the whole forming an equilateral triangle.

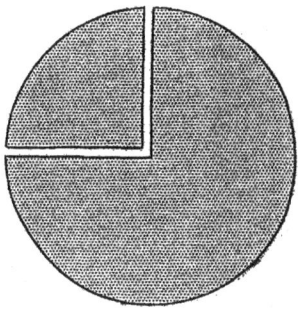

4th DIVISION.

This Regular Division first adopted as its badge the fourth quadrant of a circle in red, but this was later changed to a red circle, with one quadrant displaced, set in a white square. It formed part of the B.E.F., arriving in France as part of 2 Corps in October, 1939. In the evacuation in 1940 it held the west flank of the Dunkirk perimeter. The Division later saw service in North Africa with First Army and with the Central Mediterranean Force in Italy and in Greece.

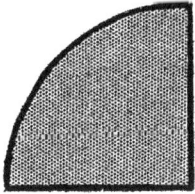

First pattern badge.

Badge as worn until 1946.

New pattern badge adopted in B.A.O.R. 1946.

5th DIVISION.

This Division undoubtedly holds the record of the most travelled formation of the war. A Regular Division located pre-war in Northern Command in the Catterick area, it joined the B.E.F. in France in 1939. In the spring of 1940 one Brigade (the 15th) was withdrawn to participate in the operations in Norway with the N.W.E.F. The remaining two brigades took part in the battles in Belgium and North-Western France which led up to the evacuation from Dunkirk. These brigades, under the command of Major-General Franklyn, together with two brigades of the 50th (Northumbrian) Division and the 1st Army Tank Brigade, became " Frankforce " and were allotted a special role on the flank of the withdrawing B.E.F. In U.K. again, the Division served in Home Forces in England and Northern Ireland until mobilized in 1942 for further service overseas. The formation took part in the occupation of Madagascar, and thence to India.

The next move was to " Paiforce," where it formed part of the garrisons of Persia and Iraq. In 1943 the 5th moved to Egypt and joined the M.E.F. In July of that year it embarked for Sicily, and in September went to Italy. It took part in the Anzio landing the following year, and in July, 1944, was withdrawn from A.A.I. and moved to Palestine. February, 1945, saw the Division back in Italy, but only for a short period, for in March it joined 21st Army Group in Belgium in time to move forward and participate in the final stages of the war in Germany. The Division now forms part of the British Army of the Rhine.

The Divisional sign was, during the war, a white "Y" for Yorkshire to denote its pre-war association with Northern Command. Set on a khaki background, this badge was changed in 1946 and became a white "Y" on a black circular background.

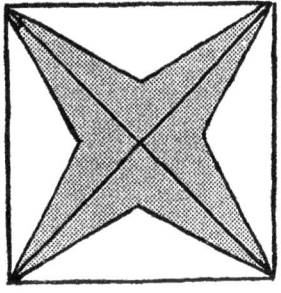

6th DIVISION.*

A red four-pointed star set in a white square was this formation's badge. A Regular Division, it was formed in Egypt in February, 1941, under the command of Major-General (later Lieut.-General) J. F. Evetts from regular army units serving in the Middle East. The Division saw action soon afterwards in the Western Desert. The Division established the Bagush " Box," East of Mersa Matruh. In June, 1941, the Divisional H.Q., was hastily moved to Palestine to take command of the 5th Indian Infantry Brigade (detached from the 4th Indian Division) and other troops then moving into Syria against the Vichy Forces. Other Brigades moved up from the Western Desert came under command of the Division which then came under command of 1 Australian Corps with the 7th Australian Division. At the conclusion of hostilities in Syria 6th Division was composed of the 14th, 16th and 23rd Infantry Brigades with certain Australian gunner and sapper units under command.

The Division's next move was to Tobruk in relief of the 9th Australian Division. The relief of the Tobruk garrison was completed by sea in October, 1941, and on the 10th of that month, the 6th Division was redesignated the 70th Division. This was a security measure designed to deceive the enemy and to prevent the change-over in Tobruk becoming known. The Divisional Transport was left in Syria with the 6th Australian Division which for a while used the 6th Division's red star badge.

Inside Tobruk the Division, then commanded by Major-General (now Lieut.-General Sir Ronald) Scobie, had some 25,000 troops under command, including one Australian Battalion (the 2nd/13th) the Polish Carpathian Brigade, the 11th Czech Battalion and the 32nd Anti-Tank Regiment. On breaking out of Tobruk in November, 1941, and joining up with Eighth Army troops the Division was withdrawn from the Western Desert to Palestine, from where it was transferred to India Command.

---

* See also 70th Division, page 70.

8th DIVISION.

This was a Regular Division, formed from two infantry brigades in Palestine in 1938, and commanded by Major-General A. R. Goodwin Austen. It remained in Palestine on the outbreak of war and was engaged in internal security duties until February, 1940, when it was broken up. The Divisional H.Q. was disbanded in Egypt on the 26th February, 1940. Its badge was a red cross on a blue shield.

9th (SCOTTISH) DIVISION.

This second-line Territorial Army Division was raised in 1939 when the Territorial Army was doubled. It was the duplicate Division of the 51st (Highland) Division. It was disbanded at the end of 1940, when the greater part of the formation joined the re-formed 51st Division to fill the gaps created by the loss of the 152nd and 153rd Infantry Brigades after their gallant stand at St. Valery-en-Caux.

The sign of the 9th (Scottish) Division was a silver thistle set on a dark blue background within a silver circular border, the same badge as borne by the 9th (Scottish) Division during the 1914-18 war.

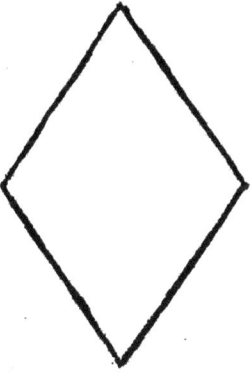

12th DIVISION.

This was a second-line Territorial Army Division, the duplicate formation of the 44th (Home Counties) Division. It was formed in 1939. It joined the B.E.F. in 1940, under the command of Major-General R. L. Petre. The Division, less the 36th Brigade, took part in the hard fighting following the German break-through to the Channel ports, going into action on the lower reaches of the River Somme and in Northern Normandy under the command of Brigadier R. J. P. Wyatt. Part of the Division joined up with the 51st Division and fought with that formation up to St. Valery. Major-General Petre had been cut off from his Division during the German armoured thrust, and collected together an emergency force known as "Petreforce," to protect the flank of the B.E.F. from Arras and along the Canal du Nord. The 12th Division had as its badge a white diamond. The Division was subsequently disbanded on the reorganization of the forces in the United Kingdom.

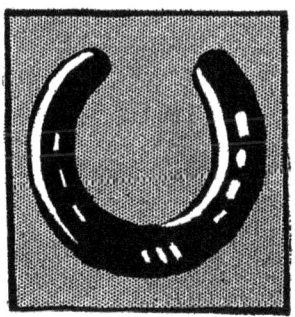

13th DIVISION.

Raised in Greece during the winter of 1945-46 from the British element of the 4th Indian Division when that formation returned to India, the 13th Division adopted as its badge the Divisional sign borne by the 13th Division in the 1914-18 war—a black horseshoe, picked out in white, set on a square red background. The 13th Division has therefore had a close association with Indian Formations in two wars. In the late war, the British battalions and Divisional troops came from the 4th Indian Division; whilst in the Great War the 13th (Western) Division, composed of new army units, formed part of the Mesopotamian Expeditionary Force, where it served with the Third Army Corps and was the only British Division in that force serving with the 14th, 15th, 17th and 18th Indian Divisions.

It was said that the horseshoe for luck was chosen as the Divisional sign to offset any bad luck which, to the superstitious, may have followed the allotment of " 13 " as the Divisional number.

15th (SCOTTISH) DIVISION.

This second-line Territorial Army Division was formed in the summer of 1939 as the duplicate of the 52nd (Lowland) Division (T.A.). As its formation badge, the Division adopted the Scottish heraldic lion rampant, set in a yellow circle with a white border, on a black square.

As part of Home Forces, the Division manned the coastal area of Northumberland in an anti-invasion role as part of 9th Corps District (later Northumbrian District) until placed under command of 21st Army Group in the autumn of 1943. Landing in Normandy in June, 1944, the Division played its part in the establishment and subsequent break out of the beachhead, the crossing of the Orne, and the sweep across France and Belgium to the Maas. It took part in the operations which drove the enemy from the west bank of the Rhine, the crossing in March, 1945, and the drive across Westphalia and Hanover to the Elbe.

18th DIVISION.

This second-line Territorial Army Division, duplicate of the 54th (East Anglian) Division, was composed of Territorials from Essex, Norfolk, Suffolk and Cambridgeshire. Under the command of the late Major-General Beckwith-Smith, of the Welsh Guards (who died in a Japanese prisoner-of-war camp), the Division was dispatched from the U.K. to India in the autumn of 1941. Early in 1942 it was hurriedly dispatched to Malaya, disembarking at Singapore a few days before the fall of the city in February, 1942. The Divisional badge was the conventional sign of a windmill, to denote its association with East Anglia, in black, set on an orange background.

23rd DIVISION.

A Tudor rose in white, set on a blue (sometimes green) background, was the sign of the 23rd Division which joined the B.E.F. in France in 1940. It was located on the L. of C. when the German penetration into France threatened to cut off the main B.E.F. from its reserves and bases. The Division was allotted part of the line of the Canal du Nord and the Scarpe and formed part of the hastily formed force under Major-General Mason McFarlane (then D.M.I. at G.H.Q. B.E.F.) which was known as " MacForce." The formation was evacuated to the U.K. with the bulk of the B.E.F., but was subsequently disbanded.

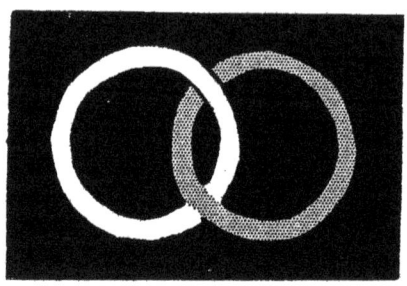

36th DIVISION.

The Division was originally an Indian Division, although two of its brigades were composed entirely of troops from U.K. The Division was formed early in 1943 as the Army component of the Combined Training Centre in India. At this time the Division wore the badge subsequently adopted by the 33 Indian Corps. In 1943 the 29th and 72nd British Brigades were allotted to the formation, but all the other units were Indian. At this time the Division came under command of the Indian Expeditionary Force and adopted a badge of its own, which was two interlocked circles, one red, one white, set on a black rectangle. The badge thereby incorporated the badges of two of the brigades—the 29th, a white circle, and the 72nd, a red circle.* The Division, under the command of Major-General F. W. Festing, D.S.O., took part in the operations on the Arakan front in 1944 in support of the 5th Indian Division in the jungle-covered hill country in the area of the Ngakyedauk Pass.

In May, 1944, the Division was withdrawn from the Arakan and after a short rest near Shillong in Assam, moved to Ledo, the terminus of the Burma Road, where the formation came under command of General Stillwell's Chinese-American Army, and saw much of the hard fighting in the Myitkyina and Mogaung areas. In January, 1945, the Division crossed the Irrawaddy and advanced into the Shan States, and came under command of the 14th Army during the final operations which broke the last Japanese resistance in Burma. After the capture of the Myitkyina and Mogaung airfields in December, 1944, the 26th Indian Brigade was flown from India to join the Division. Later this Indian brigade was replaced by the 26th British Brigade, and thereby the formation became the 36th British Division. In June, 1945, the Division returned to India and was disbanded.

---

* See pages 202 and 133.

38th (WELSH) DIVISION.

Formed in the summer of 1939 as a second-line Territorial Army Division, duplicate of the 53rd (Welsh) Division (T.A.), the 38th was composed of Territorial Battalions of the Welch Regiment, The Royal Welch Fusiliers and Welsh Border regiments. The formation adopted as its sign the yellow cross of St. David of Wales, set on a black shield on a khaki background. The Division formed part of Home Forces.

40th DIVISION.

This Division was raised in Sicily in the autumn of 1943 and was made up of Overseas Garrison battalions and L. of C. units. The formation was raised to add to the order of battle in Sicily at the time that the 50th and 51st Divisions were withdrawn from the Mediterranean to return to U.K. to join 21st Army Group. Initially the 40th Division was composed only of three battalions, the 30th Battalions of the Royal Norfolk Regiment, the Somerset Light Infantry and the Green Howards; each battalion assumed the role of a brigade, the Commanding Officers flying a Brigadier's pennant and the Adjutants signing correspondence as " Brigade-Major."

The formation badges, made up " on the ground," were an acorn cut out of brown cloth stitched on to a white linen square.

It is interesting to note the association of this badge with the Divisional sign of the 40th Division in the 1914-18 war. This formation sign was a bantam cock, on it a white diamond, within the diamond was an oak leaf and an acorn which was added on G.H.Q. authority to commemorate the capture of Bourlon Wood.

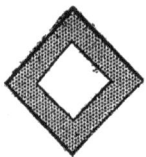

42nd (EAST LANCASHIRE) DIVISION.*

A first-line Territorial Army Division, this formation was made up of Territorials from Manchester and the East Lancashire towns. The Division formed part of the B.E.F. in France in 1940 and took part in the advance into Belgium and the hard fighting which culminated in the withdrawal to and evacuation from Dunkirk. In 1941, whilst under the command of Home Forces, the formation was converted to an Armoured Division and the sub-title "East Lancashire" was dropped. The Division did not, however, serve overseas as a formation, and it was disbanded in 1943. The Divisional Engineers remained as a formation and became the 42nd Assault Regiment, Royal Engineers (later designated the 42nd Armoured Engineer Regiment), and formed part of the Armoured Engineer Brigade of the 79th Armoured Division.†

Following the precedent of the 1914-18 war, when the 42nd (East Lancs) Division wore as their sign a red and white diamond, the formation badge adopted in 1940 by the Division was a small white diamond superimposed on a larger red diamond. This was one of the smallest of the formation signs, being nine-tenths of an inch in diameter.

43rd (WESSEX) DIVISION.

This first-line Territorial Army Division was composed of the T.A. Battalions of the Devon, the Wiltshire, the Hampshire and the Dorset Regiments and the Somerset and Duke of Cornwall's Light Infantry. As its badge it adopted the ancient emblem of the Kings of Wessex, the heraldic wyvern in gold set on a dark blue square.

---

* See also 42nd Armoured Division, page 45.
† See also 42nd Armoured Engineer Regiment, page 221.

The Division formed part of Home Forces as part of 12 Corps and as such in 1943 joined 21st Army Group for the invasion of Europe. It landed in Normandy in June, 1944, and took part in the operations which led to the establishment of the beachhead, which was followed by the hard fighting at Falaise, the crossing of the Seine, and the sweep across France and Belgium. It formed part of the force which forced the Rhine crossing in March, 1945, and took part in the final drive across Germany which led to the surrender of the German armies in May of that year.

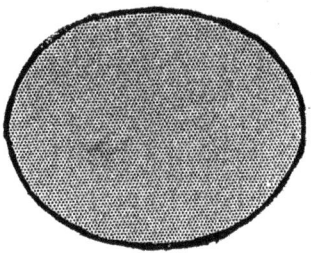

44th (HOME COUNTIES) DIVISION.

This first-line Territorial Army Division was made up of T.A. units of Kent, Surrey and Sussex and the County of London. A scarlet horizontal oval was the formation sign when used as a vehicle marking; the red oval sometimes had a narrow white border. The 44th formed part of the B.E.F. in 1940, taking part in the defence of Cassel and the withdrawal to and evacuation from the Dunkirk beaches. Dispatched to the Middle East via the Cape in 1942, it took part in the operations in the Western Desert and was part of the Eighth Army at El Alamein, but was subsequently disbanded on the reorganization of our forces in the M.E.F.

★ ★ ★ ★ ★

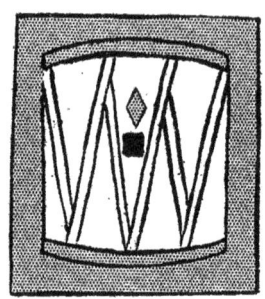

45th (WESSEX) DIVISION.

Drake's drum was appropriately chosen as the formation badge of this second-line Territorial Army Division which was formed as the duplicate division of the 43rd (Wessex) on the doubling up of the Territorial Army in 1939. Like the 43rd it was composed of T.A. units of the south-western counties. It formed part of Home Forces, serving in Northern Ireland and in England in an anti-invasion role. The Division subsequently became a training formation.

The colours of the badge were: A yellow drum, red bands top and bottom, white cords, and with a small red diamond and dark blue square in the centre. The drum was set on a khaki background.

46th (NORTH MIDLAND) DIVISION.

A tree, the Sherwood Forest oak, set on a black square was adopted by the 46th Division—an apt badge for this Territorial Army Division composed of Territorials of the north-midland counties. The tree had a brown trunk and green foliage and was picked out with a narrow white border.

The 46th Division (T.A.) had ceased to exist in 1936 when a number of its original infantry battalions were converted into Anti-Aircraft Brigades R.A. and A.A. Battalions R.E. in the reorganization of the Territorial Army to meet the increasing commitments of A.D.G.B. (Air Defence of Great Britain). The Division was, however, re-formed three years later when duplicate formations of the existing T.A. field force formations were raised.

The three infantry brigades and the Divisional Engineers joined the B.E.F. in the spring of 1940 for duty on the L. of C., one brigade in the Nantes area and two near Rennes. One brigade subsequently joined the main body of the B.E.F. and was among the last to leave the Dunkirk beaches; the rest of the Division was evacuated from the Normandy and Brittany ports after the fall of France.

The Division formed part of Home Forces until the opening of the North African Campaign in Algeria and Tunisia, when it joined First Army and took part in the operations which led to the final defeat of the Axis forces at Cap Bon. The Division next saw action in Italy, where, on 9th September, 1943, it was among the first troops ashore in the Anglo-American landings at Salerno under command of the 5th American Army. It subsequently took part in the crossing of the Volturno and the Garigliano. The Division was withdrawn to the Middle East for four months to train and rest, but returned to Italy to take part in the attack which broke through the Gothic Line and drove northwards. In November, 1944, one brigade (the 139th) flew to Greece, two battalions going to Athens, the other to Salonika. In February, 1945, the two remaining brigades of the Division joined them from Italy. The Division returned to Italy in April and formed part of the Eighth Army in 15th Army Group for the final operations in the Po Valley which culminated in the capitulation of the German forces. The 46th then crossed the Alps to form part of the British Army of Occupation in Austria.

47th (LONDON) DIVISION.

One of the original first-line Territorial Army Divisions, this formation did not exist between 1936 and 1939. Prior to 1936 there had been two T.A. Divisions in London, the 56th (1st London) and the 47th (2nd London); the latter made up of County of London

Territorials. The heavy calls on the Territorial Army for A.A. Brigades R.A. and A.A. Battalions R.E. to meet the needs of the 1st Anti-Aircraft Division made it necessary to reduce the London Divisions to one; the 56th, being the senior, remained. The 47th was, however, re-formed in 1939, when the Territorial Army was doubled. During the war it formed part of Home Forces, latterly as a training formation. The appropriate divisional badge was two red bells with a red bow (Bow bells of London) on a dark blue background.

48th (SOUTH MIDLAND) DIVISION.

The badge adopted by the 48th Division was a blue macaw set on a red diamond within a dark blue oval. This first-line Territorial Army Division was made up of Territorials from Gloucestershire, Berkshire, Buckinghamshire, Worcestershire and Warwickshire. This was the first line T.A. Division to join the B.E.F. in January, 1940, and took part in the operations in France and Belgium until the evacuation from Dunkirk in May, 1940. The 48th Division did not serve overseas again as a formation. For the remainder of the war it formed part of Home Forces, filling, in the latter years, the role of a training formation, which was adopted in 1942.

The Divisional badge was adopted in 1940. At the time the Division's H.Q. was in an old Elizabethan house at Littlecote, on the River Kennet, two miles west of Hungerford. In the hall was a macaw in its cage. When the G.O.C., Major-General (later Lieut.-General Sir) Andrew Thorne first entered the house the bird called out " Good luck—Good luck." This was taken as an omen, and, when a formation badge was selected, the macaw was chosen to commemorate the incident. It was set on a red diamond background to link the badge of the Division with that of the 1914-18 War when the sign was a white diamond.

First pattern Badge adopted in Iceland.

49th (WEST RIDING) DIVISION.

This first-line Territorial Division was recruited in the East and West Ridings of Yorkshire. It first saw active service in 1940, with the North-Western Expeditionary Force in Norway. It did not remain long in the United Kingdom after the withdrawal from Norway, and later in the year embarked for Iceland to form the main part of our force which held that Atlantic base. The Division spent over two years in the garrisons Reykjavik, Akureyri, and Halfurdurfjord. The formation's original sign was the white rose of Yorkshire, which had been the Divisional sign during the 1914-18 war and was worn between the wars, but whilst in Iceland the now familiar badge of the polar bear on a black background was adopted.* The design depicted a polar bear with its head pointed downwards as if looking into the water; this was afterwards changed, the head of the bear looking upwards, head thrown back in defiance. On its return to the United Kingdom in 1943 the Division formed part of the force destined for the invasion of Europe and, as part of 21st Army Group, landed in Normandy in June, 1944. It took part in the operations in France, Belgium and Southern Holland, and in the latter stages of the campaign was under the command of 1st Canadian Army in the final liberation of the Netherlands.

Second pattern badge as worn in North-Western Europe.

---

* See also Iceland Force, page 165.

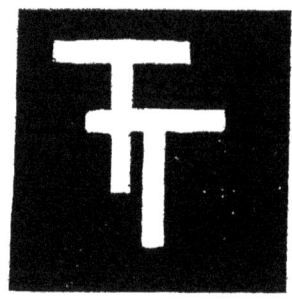

50th (NORTHUMBRIAN) DIVISION.

Composed of Territorials recruited from Northumberland and Durham, this was a first-line Territorial Army Division, and saw active service in France and Belgium in 1940 as the 50th (Motor) Division under the command of Major-General Le Q. Martel, seeing much hard fighting in May, 1940, prior to the withdrawal of the B.E.F. to the U.K. In 1941 the Division embarked for the Middle East and joined our forces in the Western Desert, where it took part in the operations in Libya in General Auchinleck's offensive, at the Battle of Knightsbridge and the Omars. The Division formed part of 30 Corps at El Alamein and took part in the victorious advance through Cyrenaica and Tripolitania. It participated in the invasion of Sicily and was heavily engaged in the fighting at Catania. The 50th was among the formations withdrawn from the Mediterranean early in 1944 and returned to England to join the 21st Army Group. It took part in the Normandy landings in June, 1944, and the hard-fought battles around Caen which led to the establishment of the beach-head, and in the battles of the Falaise Gap and the crossing of the Seine. The Division was withdrawn from operations in the late autumn of 1944 and returned to England with the exception of the Divisional Engineers, who remained in B.L.A. as G.H.Q. Troops Engineers. Part of the 50th were, however, destined to proceed overseas for a fourth time, as the H.Q. and some Divisional troops formed the nucleus of the British force which went to Norway in May, 1945.

The Divisional badge was two capital " Ts " (for the Tyne and Tees) in red on a black square.

51st (HIGHLAND) DIVISION.

This first-line Territorial Army Division was composed of the T.A. Battalions of all the Highland Regiments. It joined the B.E.F. in France in January, 1940, as part of the 3 Corps, moving up to the Belgian frontier and in March taking over a sector from the French Army.

The Division was detached from the British zone in April and moved to the Saar front, where they took over a sector of the forward defences of the Maginot Line in the *Ligne de contact*. The 51st were in the Saar when the German attack broke upon the Netherlands and Belgium, and the Division was moved up from the French zone at the time that the German motorized columns were pouring into the gap where they had broken through to the Channel ports. The 51st came up to the attack on the south of the German line of advance, going into action at Abbeville and on the Bresle. The Division saw much hard fighting, sustaining heavy casualties as they moved through Normandy to stem the tide of the enemy advance : one brigade was detached from the Division to form part of " Arc force " in the defence of Le Havre and was finally evacuated from that port ; the two remaining brigades (the 152nd and 153rd) being cut off and trapped, their backs to the sea, above the cliffs of St. Valery-en-Caux. It was not possible for them to be taken off by sea, and with ammunition almost spent, suffering severe casualties, and hemmed in by superior enemy forces, the remains of the Division were forced to capitulate.

The 51st Division was re-formed in U.K., with its original remaining brigade as the nucleus. The Division moved overseas in 1942 to the Middle East and went into action at El Alamein with the Eighth Army, pushing on into Cyrenaica on the heels of the retreating Axis forces. On into Tripolitania through the Mareth Line, the pipes of the Highland Division were heard in Tunisia as the 51st moved forward to the final defeat of the Afrika Korps and their scattered Italian allies.

The Division took part in the invasion of Sicily in July, 1943, and the landings in Italy in August. The formation was withdrawn from the Mediterranean later in the year and returned to U.K. to join 21st Army Group for the invasion of Europe. June, 1944, saw the Highland Division in the Normandy beachhead. It took part in the break out and the hard fighting at Falaise, in the dash across France to the Seine and on to the liberation of Belgium, the fighting which drove the enemy back across the Rhine, and in the final advance through Germany to the Elbe.

The 51st wore as their badge the Divisional sign of the Highland Division of the 1914-18 war: the letters " HD " in red joined together within a red circle on a blue background.

52nd (LOWLAND) DIVISION (MOUNTAIN DIVISION).

Recruited from the Lowlands of Scotland, this was a first-line Territorial Army Division. The 52nd embarked for France in June, 1940, during the critical days following Dunkirk, and landed at Brest, Cherbourg and St. Malo. It formed part of the covering force for the withdrawal from the lines of communication immediately prior to the fall of France. Whilst forming part of Home Forces, the formation was allotted the role of a mountain division and was specially equipped and trained as such. It did not, however, operate in this role and joined 21st Army Group on the Continent in October, 1944, taking part in the operations along the Maas, the Rhine crossing, and the drive into Germany. The formation sign was a modified version of that worn by the Division in the 1914-18 war. That sign was composed of the cross of St. Andrew on a blue shield, a thistle superimposed on the cross, the shield being set in the angle of a black " L " (for Lowland) on a khaki background. The " L " and the thistle were dispensed with in the new badge, the white cross of St. Andrew on a blue shield only being worn. The word " Mountain " in white on a blue ground on a separate scroll worn beneath the shield was added when the formation adopted this special role.

G

53rd (WELSH) DIVISION.

A first-line Territorial Army Division composed of Territorial Battalions of the Welch Regiment, Royal Welch Fusiliers, K.S.L.I., and the purely Territorial Regiments of Monmouthshire and Herefordshire. Mobilized in South Wales in 1939, the Division moved to Northern Ireland in 1940, where it remained until 1942. It then moved to South-Eastern Command and later became part of 21st Army Group. Landing in Normandy in the early days of the invasion of Europe, the Division saw much hard fighting at Caen and Falaise, in the Ardennes, in the Reichswald Forest; took part in the crossing of the Rhine and the sweep across Germany. The Divisional badge was a red " W," the base of the letter resting on a horizontal bar. On the Divisional transport this " W " was shown on a green background, but when worn on uniform the sign had a khaki background. It was said that the " W " stood for Wales, and was also symbolic of the firm base of the attack (the horizontal), the spearhead of the attack (the centre inverted " V " of the " W "), and the outflanking movements (the side members of the letter). It was also said that the badge was symbolic of a Bardic crown, and again that it represented the traditional tall hat of the women of Wales.

54th (EAST ANGLIAN) DIVISION.

A first-line Territorial Division made up of T.A. units from Norfolk, Suffolk, Cambridgeshire, Herts and Essex. The formation did not serve overseas as a Division, although it was absorbed into the

L. of C. of 21st Army Group. The Divisional badge was a small red circle, the monogram " JP " in blue in the centre. These were the initials of the Divisional Commander (Major-General J. H. T. Priestman, C.B.E., D.S.O., M.C.). One brigade of the formation (the 162nd) remained as an independent infantry brigade within 21st Army Group and retained the former Divisional sign as their badge.*

55th (WEST LANCASHIRE) DIVISION.

The red rose of Lancaster, the Divisional sign adopted by West Lancs Division in 1916, was retained by the 55th Division, a first-line Territorial Army formation, composed of Territorials from Liverpool and West Lancashire, between the wars, and continued as the formation badge during World War II. The rose depicted in the badge has five petals inside and five outside; the leaves are arranged five on each side of the stem, thereby repeating the Divisional number " 55." The Divisional vehicle marking did not include the stem and the leaves, and was confined to the Lancashire rose. In the arm badge the rose was red, with green stem and leaves set on a khaki circular background. The 55th did not serve overseas; it formed part of Home Forces, latterly in a training role.

---

* See also 162nd Independent Infantry Brigade, page 206.

56th (LONDON) DIVISION.

The badge of this London Division was a black cat set on a red background. It was "Dick Whittington's cat," as well as being a lucky black cat, and the badge was chosen by its original Commander, Major-General Sir Claude Liardet (the first T.A. Officer to command a Division). The 56th formed part of Home Forces until 1942, when it embarked for the Middle East and joined the forces which garrisoned Palestine, Syria and Iraq. The Division joined the Central Mediterranean Force in 1943 and took part in the landings at Salerno and Anzio and the advance through Italy, being well to the fore in the crossing of the Garigliano. As part of the Eighth Army, the 56th took part in the Po Valley campaign, forging through the Argenta Gap, winning the bridgehead over the Reno, and sweeping north-east to the liberation of Venice at the end of the 15th Army Group's victorious campaign in Northern Italy.

59th DIVISION.

This second-line Territorial Army formation, duplicate division of the 46th (North Midland) Division, was composed mainly of Staffordshire Territorials, and appropriately selected as its badge one depicting pit-head gear in red, against a black slag-heap on a blue background.

The Division served in Northern Ireland and England as part of Home Forces, and joined 21st Army Group for the invasion of Europe. After taking part in the fighting which established the beach-head and the capture of Caen, the Division ceased to exist as a Field Force formation, the personnel going as reinforcements to other formations of Second Army. The Divisional Engineers remained as G.H.Q. Troops Engineers.

61st DIVISION.

This was the duplicate (second-line) Territorial Army Division of the 48th (South Midland) Division. Raised in 1939 to 1945, it formed part of Home Forces. Its badge was a red diamond on a blue background. The Division moved to Northern Ireland in July, 1940, being distributed over the counties of Londonderry and Antrim. It later moved to Armagh, Tyrone and Fermanagh. It returned to England in 1943 and was mobilized for service in North-Western Europe, but it was subsequently stood down and became a training and drafting Division in Home Forces. The Division was then earmarked for service in the Far East, but due to the collapse of Japan it was not required and was disbanded in 1946.

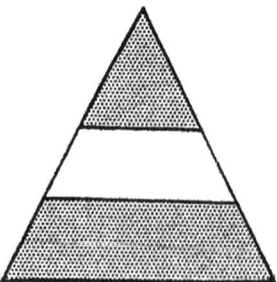

66th DIVISION

This was a second line T.A. Division, raised in 1939 as the duplicate Division of the 42nd (East Lancashire) Division (T.A.), and was known as the 66th (Lancs and Border) Division. The Division was only in existence for a short time, for it was disbanded in the spring of 1940. The divisional badge was never issued, but the design adopted was a light blue equilateral triangle divided by a central horizontal yellow band, the same design as the divisional sign of the 66th Division in the 1914-18 war.

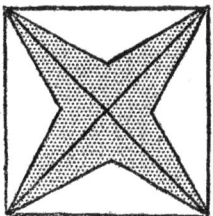

70th DIVISION.*

Originally designated the 6th Division, this formation was renumbered 70th whilst forming part of the Middle East Forces in the Western Desert. It formed the garrison at Tobruk in 1941, and in November of that year made the sortie which linked up with the 1st South African and 7th Indian Brigades during General Auchinleck's offensive. On the relief of Tobruk the Division was withdrawn from the M.E.F. and dispatched to India to meet the threat of the Japanese invasion. Whilst in India Command the formation was reorganized and formed the British element of the 3rd Indian Division (The Chindits). The 70th Division retained the 6th Division's badge when it was renumbered—a red four-pointed star on a white background.

76th DIVISION.

This was a war-formed Division, on a special establishment, forming part of Home Forces, and allotted a training role. Its badge was a Norfolk wherry in full sail, in red, on a black background, the design linking the Division's associations with East Anglia.

---

* See also 6th Division, page 50.

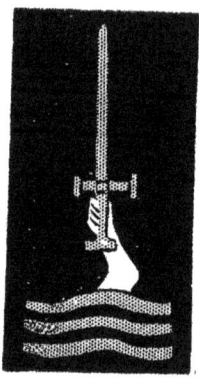

77th DIVISION.

This was also a war-formed formation with a similar role to that of the 76th Division. It was composed mainly of battalions of West Country county regiments, and adopted as its badge King Arthur's Excalibur, held aloft from the water. The colours of the badge were: red sword; white arm; and three wavy blue lines to represent the water; the design was on a black background.

78th DIVISION.

This was a war-formed Division which was raised in Scotland in preparation for the North African Expedition, and landed with " Blade Force " at Algiers on 8th November, 1942. The Division had its first main clash with the enemy at Tebourba. As part of the First Army the Division saw much hard fighting, holding the line along the borders of Algeria and Tunisia during the winter of 1942-43, clinging on to Medjez el Bab, and the fierce fighting at Fort MacGregor and Longstop Hill. It took part in the final operations in Tunisia culminating in the surrender of the Axis forces at Cap Bon.

Landing in Sicily on 25th July, 1943, the Division fought at Cantanuova, Adrano, Bronte, and Randazzo. Operations in Sicily were concluded on 15th August, and the following month saw the Division in Italy fighting up to Larino with the Eighth Army. The 78th were later withdrawn to Egypt, but only for a short time, for the winter saw the Division back in action again in the Apennines. As part of the Eighth Army in 15th Army Group the Division took part in the forcing of the Argenta Gap into Northern Italy, and in the final round-up of the broken German Army reached Austria, where the Division became part of the Army of Occupation. The badge of the 78th Division was a yellow battle-axe on a black square or circular background.

80th DIVISION.

This was a war-formed Division. Under command of Home Forces it was located in Western Command, and had a training and draft-finding role. The latter function was said to be the reason for the Divisional badge, a liner steaming across the high seas. The ship was red; the sea and smoke from the funnel in light blue; the whole design on a yellow background within a light blue border.

★ ★ ★ ★ ★

THE AIRBORNE DIVISIONS

The well-known badge of Bellerophon astride a Pegasus in pale blue on a dark maroon background is worn by all Airborne troops, and there were no separate badges to distinguish between the units of the 1st and 6th Airborne Divisions. Below the badge on a separate maroon strip is the word "Airborne," in pale blue. The word "India," also in pale blue, is incorporated in the badge, below the hooves of Pegasus, when worn by Indian airborne troops. It was in November, 1941, that Major-General Sir F. A. M. Browning, K.B.E., C.B., D.S.O., was appointed G.O.C. and the Airborne Forces began to take shape with the formation of the 1st Parachute Brigade. This was the result of the hard work of experiment and development which had commenced in the summer of 1940. February, 1941, had seen the first British airborne action. On the 10th of that month the first British parachutists to drop on enemy territory landed in Italy near Monte Volture with the object of destroying the aqueduct water supply of the Province of Apulia. This was followed by the successful airborne action at Bruneval, near Le Havre.

From these beginnings the airborne forces grew, and by May, 1943, two airborne divisions had been formed in the U.K.

1st AIRBORNE DIVISION.

The 1st Airborne Division first went into action in North Africa in 1942 when, in support of the British First Army landings, the 1st Parachute Brigade were allotted the task of capturing and securing the airfield at Bone; this was successfully accomplished. A second landing was effected at Souk el Arba. Their initial task complete, the formation fought as an infantry division during the winter of 1942-43 when the First Army was holding on to the scattered line from Cap Serrat to Medjez el Bab, Bou Arada and Fondouk. With the collapse and final surrender of the Axis forces in Tunisia, preparations went ahead for the invasion of Southern Europe. The 1st Airborne Division took part in the invasion of Sicily in July, 1943: first glider-borne troops landed on the 9th and 10th, and three days later Paratroops were dropped in the vicinity of Syracuse. The Division also took part in the invasion of the Italian mainland, landing at Taranto and pushing forward to the capture of Castellaneta, the Air Landing Brigade occupying Foggia. With the progress of the invasion more men became available, the Airborne Troops were relieved in their forward positions, the Division was withdrawn and returned to U.K.

The formation's next action was in Holland. It was the 1st Airborne which won undying fame at Arnhem during those days, the 17th to 25th September, 1944, when, under command of Major-General R. E. Urquhart, C.B., D.S.O., the Division landed in Holland to establish a bridgehead north of the Waal in an attempt to force the end of the war in Europe by a left hook sweep by 21st Army Group into the heart of Germany through the bridgehead established by the airborne troops. The final objective was not achieved, but it was estimated that the operation was eighty-five per cent. successful and the efforts of the Division had not been in vain.

The formation was withdrawn to England. In May, 1945, it went overseas again, landing in Norway, where the Division formed part of the British liberating forces.

6th AIRBORNE DIVISION.

While the 1st Airborne Division was in North Africa, Sicily and Italy, the 6th Airborne Division, which had been formed in May, 1943, was training and being equipped to play an important role in the invasion of North-Western Europe. The first parachutists of the Division landed in Normandy soon after midnight of the 5th/6th June, 1944, with the object of seizing the crossings over the River Orne and the Caen canal near Benouville, thereby being in a position to help 1 Corps in the protection of the left flank of the British sector. In the hard fighting that followed the Division distinguished itself in the establishment of the bridgehead. When in August the order was given for a general advance, the Division swept northeast to Le Havre and crossed the Seine to Honfleur. The Division was withdrawn to U.K. early in 1945, to prepare for its second airborne action.

This was the assault of the Rhine in March, the Division landing on the eastern banks of the river whilst Second Army made the land assault. The Division then took part in the sweep across Germany, which was halted only by the surrender of the German armies after British troops had reached the Elbe and Schleswig-Holstein. The Division remained in Germany until the autumn of 1945, when it was moved to the Middle East. The 5th Parachute Brigade left the Division earlier. In July, 1945, it was dispatched to India to take part in the operations for the recapture of Malaya as part of 34 Corps. This Brigade was one of the first to land in Singapore at the conclusion of operations.

ANTI-AIRCRAFT FORMATIONS

ANTI-AIRCRAFT COMMAND.

The black bow and arrow, aimed upwards, set on a scarlet square was the familiar badge of Anti-Aircraft Command. Originally the badge was worn only by the staff of General Sir Frederick Pile's Headquarters, but in 1943 it was universally adopted for use by all formations and units of A.D.G.B. (Air Defence of Great Britain), including the Home Guard batteries, and the use of separate signs (as previously worn by the three A.A. Corps and twelve Divisions) was discontinued.

The A.A. badge was symbolic of defence against air attack, but its choice was influenced by the crest, of which the sign was a reproduction, which by coincidence appeared above the entrance of "Glenthorn," at Stanmore, the house taken over as the Command's Headquarters.

ANTI-AIRCRAFT CORPS AND DIVISIONS

The distinguishing badges of the Anti-Aircraft Corps and Divisions were withdrawn in 1943, when all A.A. formations adopted the A.A. Command badge.*

1 ANTI-AIRCRAFT CORPS.

This A.A. Corps covered the South of England and adopted as its badge a red eagle in flight, an arrow through its breast, set on a bright blue background.

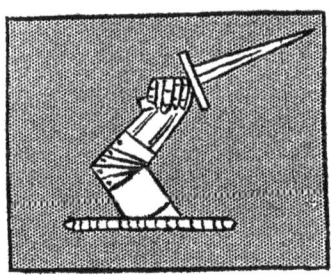

2 ANTI-AIRCRAFT CORPS.

A mailed fist, clasping a dagger, in blue on a red oblong background was the badge of 2 A.A. Corps, which covered the Midlands and North of England.

* See H.Q. Anti-Aircraft Command, page 75.

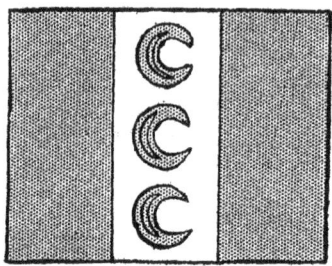

3 ANTI-AIRCRAFT CORPS.

With its H.Q. located in Edinburgh, this Corps area was in Scotand, its badge was the Corps Headquarters brassard colours of red, white, red. On the white centre of the background were three " Cs " in red.

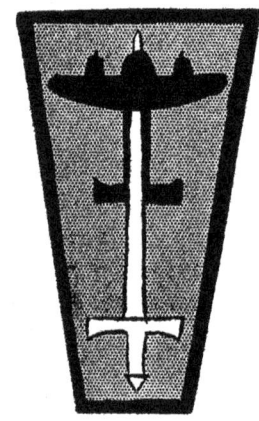

1st ANTI-AIRCRAFT DIVISION.

This was the first Anti-Aircraft operational formation and was raised in 1935. Composed originally of Territorials drawn from London and the Home Counties, it became in 1938 a purely London T.A. formation. The Divisional badge subsequently chosen was a Heinkel, in black, pierced by a sword in red, on a light blue background within a black border. The badge had a distinctive shape—an inverted isosceles triangle, the angle at the apex being squared off. The sword in the badge was taken from the arms of the City of London.

An earlier pattern of the badge had a plain khaki background.

2nd ANTI-AIRCRAFT DIVISION.

This was the second Anti-Aircraft formation to be raised. It was formed in 1936 and was composed of Territorial Army A.A. Units located in the Midlands and North of England. Its badge was a red witch on her broomstick in flight, set on a dark blue background.

The badge was chosen to be symbolic of the formation's motto " We sweep the skies."

Badges in these colours were usually embroidered but the badge was also used with the red witch, broom and clouds stencilled in red on a plain khaki background.

3rd ANTI-AIRCRAFT DIVISION.

A pre-war Territorial Army Anti-Aircraft formation located in Scotland and with the majority of units of Scottish origin, this Division adopted as its badge a white thistle, on a blue square background, the letter "A" set on either side of the Scottish emblem.

4th ANTI-AIRCRAFT DIVISION.

This was also a Territorial Army Anti-Aircraft formation, located in the North-Western Counties. Its badge was a red inverted equilateral triangle ; on it in pale blue were three buckles. An alternative to this badge was a single buckle in red stencilled on a plain khaki background. The buckles of this formation badge were one of the charges in the Commander's coat of arms.

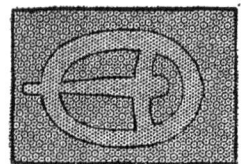

First Design

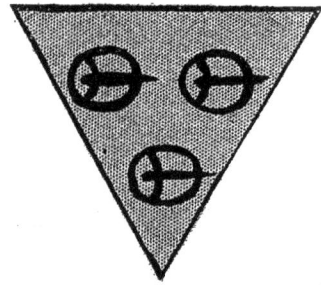

Second Design

5th ANTI-AIRCRAFT DIVISION.

This Territorial Army Anti-Aircraft Division was raised in 1938 and was composed of T.A. A.A. Brigades R.A., and A.A. Battalions R.E. drawn from the Home Counties, the South and West of England, plus a few units from the County of London. The Divisional Headquarters were at Reading, and the badge was a falling Heinkel in black, nose downwards, five red flames rising upwards from the wings and fuselage, the whole on a khaki background.

6th ANTI-AIRCRAFT DIVISION.

A black and white target, with a red arrow piercing the bull, was the 6th A.A. Division's badge. The Division's operational area covered the Thames Estuary, Essex and North Kent.

7th ANTI-AIRCRAFT DIVISION.

Located in the North-Eastern Counties with its H.Q. in Gosforth, Newcastle, the sword and scales of the seventh sign of the zodiac in red on a blue background distinguished the units of the 7th A.A. Division.

8th ANTI-AIRCRAFT DIVISION.

The 8th A.A. Division's badge was a distinctive silhouette, in black, of a German bomber, nose downwards, a red eight-pointed star superimposed on the fuselage, indicating a shell burst; the whole set on a sky blue square background. The Division was located in South Wales and the West of England.

9th ANTI-AIRCRAFT DIVISION.

An aircraft silhouette in red, on the back of a black cat, the tail of which, outlined in red, made the shape of a figure "9," was the badge of the 9th A.A. Division.

10th ANTI-AIRCRAFT DIVISION.

This Division's badge was the heraldic head of a lion in black, outlined in white, set on a khaki background.

The formation was located in Yorkshire.

11th ANTI-AIRCRAFT DIVISION.

A German eagle, in black and yellow, with a scarlet arrow thrust upwards through its breast, the design set on a khaki background, was the badge of the 11th A.A. Division. This formation manned the defences of the West and Central Midlands.

12th ANTI-AIRCRAFT DIVISION.

The double six domino, in dark blue and white, set on a red horizontal diamond was 12th A.A. Division's badge. The Divisional area included the South-West of Scotland, including the Clyde Estuary, and the A.A. Defences of Northern Ireland.

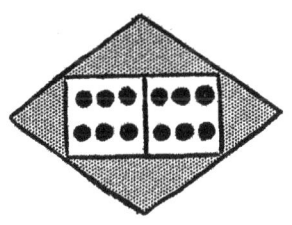

★ ★ ★ ★ ★

THE COUNTY DIVISIONS

County Divisions were raised in 1940 for an anti-invasion role, providing an operational and administrative H.Q. for the grouping of independent brigades and units into an operational formation. The County Divisions raised in coastal areas ceased to exist when replaced by Field Force formations.

DURHAM AND NORTH RIDING COUNTY DIVISION.

This Division had as its badge a pair of sheep shears in yellow, on a dark green background, the badge associating the formation with the wool industry of the North Riding of Yorkshire and the name of the Commander, Major-General P. J. Shears, C.B. The Divisional H.Q. was later re-designated Durham and North Riding Coastal Area.

DORSET COUNTY DIVISION.

Three black lions set on a circle, right half yellow, left half white, the whole on a square khaki background, was the badge of the Dorset County Division.

DEVON AND CORNWALL COUNTY DIVISION.

The arms of the Duchy of Cornwall, fifteen gold bezants on a black shield, with a gold border superimposed on the sword Excalibur, yellow hilt and white blade, set on a dark blue rectangle. was this formation's badge; it was subsequently adopted, when the formation was disbanded, by the 73rd Independent Infantry Brigade.*

ESSEX COUNTY DIVISION.

The three seaxes of the arms of the County of Essex, in white on a red shield or red square background, was this County Division's badge, which was later adopted in design, but not in colour by the 223rd Independent Infantry Brigade.†

HAMPSHIRE COUNTY DIVISION

A black Hampshire hog, set on a white rectangular or semi-circular background, was the badge adopted by the Hampshire Division in 1940.

---

* See 73rd Independent Infantry Brigade, page 205.
† See 223rd Independent Infantry Brigade, page 208.

LINCOLNSHIRE COUNTY DIVISION.

The tulip, the traditional flower of Lincolnshire, was worn by the Lincolnshire County Division in 1940 and 1941. When the formation was disbanded, the badge continued to be worn by the 212th Independent Infantry Brigade.* The badge was a red tulip with green stem and leaf set on a white rectangular background.

YORKSHIRE COUNTY DIVISION.

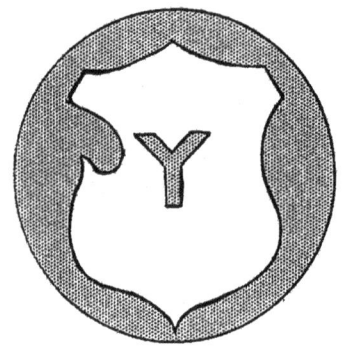

The badge of this County Division was a red "Y" on a white shield, set in a red circle.

★ ★ ★ ★ ★

---

* See 212th Independent Infantry Brigade, page 207.

THE CANADIAN FORMATIONS

CANADIAN MILITARY HEADQUARTERS (C.M.H.Q.).

The gold maple leaf of Canada set on a black circle within a golden border was the appropriate badge of C.M.H.Q. which was established in England in the autumn of 1939 to command and administer, other than operationally, all the Canadian Forces in the U.K. and the European theatres of operations. The H.Q. was located in London, in Cockspur Street, by Trafalgar Square.

FIRST CANADIAN ARMY.

The First Canadian Army was raised in England on 6th April, 1942, having under command by the end of that year the 1 and 2 Canadian Corps, comprising the 1st, 2nd and 3rd Canadian Divisions and the 4th and 5th Canadian Armoured Divisions. The

1 Canadian Corps with the 1st Canadian Division and the 5th Canadian Armoured Division left the United Kingdom in 1943 to come under command of the Eighth Army in the invasion of Sicily and Italy. First Canadian Army, with the remaining Canadian forces in the U.K., then came under command of 21st Army Group for the invasion of Europe, and the formation went ashore in Normandy in June, 1944. After the break-out from the beachhead the Canadian Army was allotted the coastal route in the sweep up the Channel coast through France and Belgium as far as the Scheldt estuary. During the winter of 1944-45 First Canadian Army was located at Tilburg in Southern Holland; it then moved forward to Grave, near Nijmegen, for the operations which drove the enemy from the Reichswald Forest and to the north bank of the Waal. Following the Rhine crossing the Canadian Army swung north and west into occupied Holland and fought westwards in the final operations which led to the capitulation of the Nazi forces and the liberation of Holland.

The First Canadian Army's sign was a scarlet horizontal diamond with a centre band of dark blue. A different badge was used for vehicle markings and directional signs. This was a yellow maple leaf superimposed on a red background with a central black bar.

Canadian Army Vehicle Marking

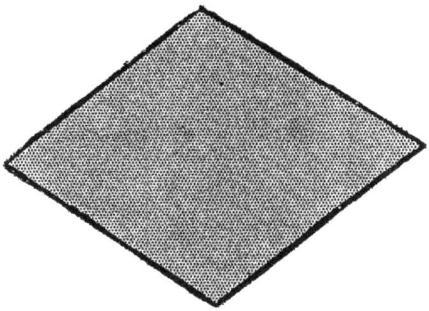

1 CANADIAN CORPS.

With the arrival in U.K. of the 2nd Canadian Division, which was completed in December, 1940, 1 Canadian Corps was formed to command the 1st and 2nd Canadian Divisions, then in England. The Corps was located in South-Eastern Command. It embarked for the Mediterranean in 1943, landing in Italy in September in command of the 1st Canadian Infantry Division and the 5th Canadian Armoured Division. The Corps took part in the hard-fought advance through Italy, including Cassino and the piercing of the Adolf Hitler line. The formation was withdrawn in March, 1945, to North-West Europe to join the 1st Canadian Army in Holland in time for the closing operations which led to the final liberation of the Netherlands. The formation badge was a scarlet horizontal diamond.

2 CANADIAN CORPS.

The 2 Canadian Corps was also raised in England when the Canadian Divisions numbered five with the arrival of the 4th Canadian Armoured Division in 1942. Forming part of 1st Canadian Army, the Corps took part in the landings in Normandy, the establishment of the beachhead, and in the general advance was allotted the coastal forward route through Dieppe and northwards along the Channel coast to the Scheldt. Throughout the winter of 1944-45 it was on the right flank of 21st Army Group and took part in the operations which drove the enemy to the east bank of the Rhine and finally from Holland in the last stages of the campaign in North-West Europe. The Corps badge was a dark blue horizontal diamond.

CANADIAN DIVISIONS

The Canadian Divisions, as in the 1914-18 war, all wore a similar sign, a rectangular cloth patch, called the "battle patch," the colour varying for each formation as follows:—

1st Division	Red.
2nd Division	Royal Blue.
3rd Division	French grey.
4th Armoured Division	Dark green.
5th Armoured Division ...	Maroon.

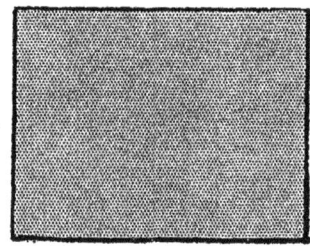

1st CANADIAN DIVISION. (*Red patch.*)

This was the first Canadian formation to proceed overseas from the Dominion. The first troops arrived in the Clyde on 17th December, 1939; there were 7,500 all ranks, the forerunners of the 335,000 Canadian troops who finally landed in the United Kingdom. The 1st Division was then commanded by Major-General (later General) A. G. L. McNaughton. In 1940 part of the Division was warned for duty in Norway, but although it moved to Scotland in preparation for embarkation to Trondhjem, the operation was cancelled. In May, 1940, the Division received orders to join the B.E.F., but following the German break-through to the Channel coast, these too were cancelled. The 1st Canadian Infantry Brigade, of the Division, finally embarked for France in June, landing in Brittany a few days before the fall of France. The Brigade had moved up from Brest to the Le Mans area, only to be evacuated a few days later. Back in England it formed part of the 7th Corps, then forming up for its anti-invasion role in South-East England. The Division subsequently formed part of 1st Canadian Corps, and the Canadian Corps District. Selected units of the Division were withdrawn in 1941 to participate in the Spitzbergen expedition, and in 1942 other units took part in the Dieppe raid.

The Division left England in June, 1943, landing in Sicily in July. In September it formed part of the invasion force which landed on the toe of Italy, and under command of the Eighth Army it distinguished itself at Ortona, in the Liri Valley and the break through the Gothic Line. In March, 1945, together with the other Canadian forces in Italy, it was withdrawn to join the First Canadian Army in North-Western Europe and took part in the final operations leading to the defeat of the German Army and the liberation of Holland.

2nd CANADIAN DIVISION. (*Royal blue patch.*)

This Division arrived in England in August and September, 1940; some units, including two infantry battalions, did not arrive until December, having served several months after leaving Canada with the British troops in Iceland. The formation was concentrated in Surrey and Sussex in the Canadian Corps District. 2nd Canadian Division formed the main part of the force which took part in the first major assault on Nazi-occupied Europe in the raid on Dieppe, distinguishing itself in the fierce fighting on the beaches and the town defences. The Division Commander, Major-General J. H. Roberts, was the military force commander during the operation. The Division returned to Europe in June, 1944, as part of First Canadian Army in 21st Army Group, and took part in the break out of the Normandy beachhead, the Falaise battle, and the sweep up the French Channel coast, taking Dieppe and the Channel ports up to the mouth of the Scheldt. Thence into Holland, taking part in the operations which drove the Germans from the area south of the Waal, and finally, in the last phases of the campaign, in the liberation of the remaining Nazi-occupied territory of Holland.

Soon after its arrival in England, the Division adopted as its formation badge a royal blue patch upon which was a gold (or yellow) letter "C," the Roman figure II in the centre of the "C." This badge was subsequently superseded by the plain royal blue "battle patch" to conform with the other Canadian divisions. The use of the "C II" badge was, however, continued to distinguish the Division's installations and welfare organizations.

3rd CANADIAN DIVISION. (*French grey patch.*)

The 3rd Division left the Dominion for England in July, 1941, and took its place in the Canadian Corps with the 1st and 2nd Divisions. Its first active service was in the invasion of the Continent in June, 1944, where it went ashore in Normandy as one of the assault divisions, winning distinction in the fierce fighting around Caen and later in the Falaise battle, the advance through France and along the Belgian Coast, and finally in the liberation of Holland following the defeat of the German occupying forces.

4th CANADIAN ARMOURED DIVISION. (*Dark green patch.*)

Arriving in the United Kingdom in the autumn of 1942, this Division also formed part of the First Canadian Army in the invasion of Europe, going ashore up the Normandy beaches, participating in the battles of the beachhead break-out, and forming the armoured spearhead of the Canadian drive that cleared the Germans from the Channel coast and from Holland.

5th CANADIAN ARMOURED DIVISION. (*Maroon patch.*)

Originally designated the 1st Canadian Armoured Division, the 5th Armoured left Canada in June, 1941, to join the Canadian forces in the United Kingdom, where it remained until the late autumn of 1943, when it embarked for the Mediterranean. The Division landed at Naples in November, 1943, and with the 1st Canadian Division formed part of the 1 Canadian Corps in the operations leading up to the assault and break through the Gothic Line. In March, 1945, the Division was withdrawn from Italy and joined the Canadian Army in Holland for the final phase of the war in North-West Europe.

1st CANADIAN ARMOURED BRIGADE.

A black horizontal diamond with a red centre band was this formation's badge. The Brigade participated in the invasion of Sicily and subsequent operations in Italy. It joined 1st Canadian Army in North-West Europe in 1945.

2nd CANADIAN ARMOURED BRIGADE.

Also a black horizontal diamond, but with a dark blue central band, was the badge of the 2nd Canadian Armoured Brigade, which formed part of the First Canadian Army in the campaign in France and Belgium and in the liberation of Holland.

The horizontal diamond badges of the 1st and 2nd Canadian Armoured Brigades, described above, were the badges worn by the personnel of the brigades. The vehicle markings were of similar colouring, but the shapes were oblong, with a yellow maple leaf in the centre.

1st CANADIAN A.G.R.A.

This Army Group R.A. formation wore a red and blue patch, the central blue band having a red zigzag line similar to that in the R.A. Regimental tie. The formation formed part of 1st Canadian Army and served in North-Western Europe.

2nd CANADIAN A.G.R.A.

This formation wore a similar badge to the 1st Canadian A.G.R.A. It is a dark blue patch with a red zigzag line.

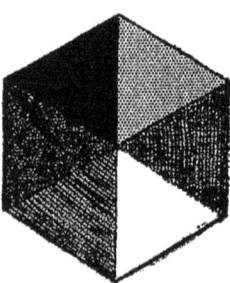

CANADIAN ARMY PACIFIC FORCE.

This formation was to have comprised one division (the 6th Canadian) and details and was made up of Canadian Army volunteers for the Japanese War. Organization of the force was proceeded with after the defeat of Germany and volunteers from the Canadian

Army overseas in Europe returned to the Dominion. The force was to have been organized on American lines and equipped in the U.S.A. Advance parties had reached Fort Knox, Kentucky, when owing to the collapse of Japan, it was decided that the force would not be completed and volunteering closed on the 15th of August, 1945. All ranks actually posted in Canada to C.A.P.F. wore a hexagon, three inches in diameter, of six equal segments, reading clockwise, red, blue, French grey, green, maroon and black; the division between the red and black segments being at the top centre. The colours were representative of the Divisions of the Canadian Army overseas except the black, which represents the independent armoured brigades.

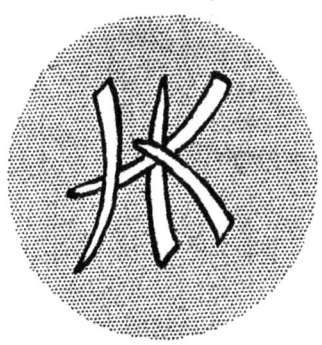

HONG KONG SERVICE BADGE

This badge was not in any sense a formation badge, although it was worn on the sleeve in the same manner. It was not issued until 1945, and was worn by all Canadian Army personnel who had served in Hong Kong in 1941, and issued to them as soon as they arrived at the reception camps in British Columbia on repatriation to the Dominion. In the Canadian Press it was called a "battle patch," and it was proudly worn by all Canadians, who were among the first of the Dominion troops to see major action in the 1939-45 war. The badge was composed of a red circle approximately two inches in diameter with, in the centre, a white embroidered Chinese style monogram "HK."

★ ★ ★ ★ ★

AUSTRALIAN FORMATIONS

Most Australian formations adopted as their badges the national animals and birds of the Commonwealth, the kookaburra, emu, parakeet, swan, kangaroo and koala bear. With few exceptions, all the Australian badges incorporated a boomerang in the design. The badges were used as divisional signs and vehicle markings; combinations of coloured patches being worn on uniforms as distinguishing marks for personnel. The coloured patches of the Australian military forces were first adopted in the 1914-18 war. Coloured flags were used to distinguish unit lines in large camps, and these were of different shapes and colours. The use of these coloured geometrical shapes was later extended and small replicas of the designs were taken into use for wear on uniforms. The small coloured patches worn on the sleeves vary in shape according to the branches of the service, and combinations of colours denote the brigades of division and battalions of brigades, etc. The Militia divisions of the Australian Army wore, between the wars, the coloured patches borne by the Australian Imperial Forces of the 1914-18 war. To distinguish units of the 1939-45 A.I.F., a narrow grey border was added to all formation and unit patches.

H.Q. AUSTRALIAN IMPERIAL FORCES M.E.F.

A badge similar to the General Service cap-badge of the Australian Commonwealth Forces was adopted by the Headquarters of the A.I.F. in the Middle East. The design was in yellow on a blue background. The badge does not, as is popularly supposed, represent the Rising Sun. It originated from the badge of the first regiment of Australian Light Horse, who served with the Imperial Forces in South Africa (1899-1902), which had been designed to represent a trophy of arms—swords and bayonets surrounding the crown.

AUSTRALIAN IMPERIAL FORCES BASE AREA M.E.F.

The Base area of the Australian Imperial Forces in the Middle East adopted as its badge a dingo above a boomerang. The design in white on a black background.

FIRST AUSTRALIAN ARMY.

First Australian Army was raised in 1942 in Melbourne under the command of Lieut.-General Sir J. D. Lavarack. From 1942 until 1944 it was located in Australia. In August, 1944, it embarked for New Guinea where the formation took over the operational and administrative responsibilities of New Guinea Force, and also the command of all Australian troops in the Solomon Islands, New Britain and Aitape. Its badge was the Swan of Western Australia in white, set above a white boomerang on a black background.

SECOND AUSTRALIAN ARMY.

Raised in October, 1942, the Second Australian Army did not serve outside the Commonwealth. It was located at Ivanhoe in Victoria, and later at Parramatta, New South Wales. Its badge was a horse set above a boomerang.

1 AUSTRALIAN CORPS.

This Corps was formed in the Middle East in April, 1940, under the command of Lieut.-General Sir Thomas Blamey. The Corps was withdrawn from M.E.F. in 1942, and took part in the operations in New Guinea.

2 AUSTRALIAN CORPS.

This formation was raised in 1943. It was later redesignated New Guinea Force* and assumed the administrative and operational responsibility for all Australian activities in New Guinea. In 1944 it was reconstituted as a Corps and relieved the XIV American Corps at Bougainville. The Corps badge was a parakeet's head above a boomerang.

3 AUSTRALIAN CORPS.

This Corps H.Q. became H.Q. Western Command, Australia, and included the Western Australia L. of C. Area. Its badge was a black and white magpie.

1st AUSTRALIAN ARMOURED DIVISION.

Raised in Australia in 1941. This formation was redesignated in 1943 the 1st Armoured Brigade Group, and saw active service in the operations at Buna, Port Moresby and Milne Bay. Its badge was an armour-clad arm and hand holding aloft a battleaxe in white on a black background.

---

* See also New Guinea Force, page 166.

2nd AUSTRALIAN ARMOURED DIVISION.

Formed in 1942 from the 2nd Australian Cavalry Division, which for a short period was designated the 2nd Australian Motor Division, this formation badge was a scorpion. The Division did not serve outside Australia.

3rd AUSTRALIAN ARMOURED DIVISION.

Formed in November, 1942, from the 1st Australian Motor Division, this formation badge was a mounted knight in armour. The Division did not serve outside the Commonwealth.

1st AUSTRALIAN CAVALRY DIVISION.
1st AUSTRALIAN MOTOR DIVISION.

The 1st Australian Cavalry Division, comprised of the famous Australian Light Horse Regiments, was reorganized in March, 1942, and redesignated the 1st Australian Motor Division. Its badge was a greyhound leaping above a boomerang. The formation later became the 3rd Australian Armoured Division. (*See above.*)

1st AUSTRALIAN DIVISION.

Formed in December, 1941, in New South Wales, this Division served in Australia. Its badge was an athlete with raised javelin set above a boomerang.

2nd AUSTRALIAN DIVISION.

This Division, raised in February, 1942, served in New South Wales and in Western Australia. The formation badge was a penguin set above a boomerang.

3rd AUSTRALIAN DIVISION.

This formation, raised in 1942, saw much hard fighting in New Guinea in the operations which culminated in the defeat of the Japanese at Salamaua and in their strongholds in the Buna area and around the Huron Gulf and the Markham Valley, and later at Bougainville in the Solomons. A koala bear and a boomerang was the Divisional badge.

4th AUSTRALIAN DIVISION.

Raised in 1943, this formation was designated York Force, and in October, 1943, assumed command of the Torres Strait area, where it remained until September, 1944. It was disbanded the following month. The formation badge was a porcupine above a boomerang.

5th AUSTRALIAN DIVISION.

This Division, which was raised in 1942 in Queensland, saw operational service the following year in New Guinea, taking part in the hard fighting at Kouriatum, Bobdubi and Salamaua. From April to September, 1944, it took part in the operations in the Alexishafen area and at Hansa Bay and Sepik River. In October, 1944, it moved to New Britain. A boar's head above a boomerang was the formation badge.

6th AUSTRALIAN DIVISION.

This Division sailed from Australia in January, 1940, to join the British Forces in the Middle East, and formed part of General (later Field-Marshal) Lord Wavell's original force which swept the Italians back from the Egyptian border in our first offensive. Bardia, Tobruk, Derna fell to the 6th Australian Division; they captured Giarubub and forced the surrender of Benghazi. The Division was withdrawn from Libya to form part of the force which was dispatched to Greece in 1941. Following the evacuation the Division moved to Crete and then back to Egypt. It also took part in the operations in Syria against the Vichy forces.

Withdrawn from the Middle East in 1942, the Division was moved to Ceylon to meet the threat of a Japanese invasion. The Division returned to Australia. It next saw service in New Guinea at Buna, Salamaua, the Danmap River, and at Wewak.

The Division's well-known badge was a white kangaroo leaping above a white boomerang, the two on a black background.

7th AUSTRALIAN DIVISION.

This Division first saw service in the Middle East in the Western Desert, one Brigade taking part in the defence of Tobruk. The Division also took part in the operations in Syria, and was then withdrawn to Australia.

The 7th Australian Division played a prominent part in the reconquest of New Guinea in the hard fighting around Finschafen and Lae, the operations in the Markham and Ramu valleys and in the Madang area and at Hansa Bay. The badge of the Division was the Australian bird the kookaburra, perched on a boomerang, set on a black background. This badge was changed when the Division was allotted an airborne role and a kookaburra in flight was adopted. Although an airborne formation, the Division participated in operations in New Guinea mainly in an infantry role. In consequence, humorists depicted the kookaburra wearing heavy boots when the sign was used as a vehicle marking.

8th AUSTRALIAN DIVISION.

This Division formed part of the Empire forces in Malaya at the time of the Japanese invasion. It arrived at Singapore in February, 1941, and on 14th January the following year, was in action against the invaders, withdrawing fighting a stubborn rear-guard action across the Johore Strait, back to Singapore and was part of the force which was forced to capitulate on Singapore Island at the fall of Malaya.

An emu above a boomerang was the formation badge.

9th AUSTRALIAN DIVISION.

This formation served in the Middle East and took part in the hard fighting in the Western Desert. It formed part of the Eighth Army at El Alamein, but was withdrawn from the M.E.F. early in 1943 and in February sailed for Australia. Here the Division was re-equipped and was moved to New Guinea, where, with the 7th Australian Division, it took part in the operations against the Japanese-held port of Finschafen, at Lae, in the Ramu and Markham valleys, and at Madang. The Division later saw service in Borneo. Its badge was a duck-billed platypus above a boomerang.

11th AUSTRALIAN DIVISION.

This Division was formed in December, 1942, at Milne Bay in New Guinea from Milne Force, and took part in the operations in the Finisterre Ranges and in New Britain. The formation badge was a palm tree.

12th AUSTRALIAN DIVISION.

Raised in 1942, this formation later became the Northern Territory force with its headquarters at Port Darwin. It did not serve outside Australia. Its badge was a water buffalo set above a boomerang.

3rd AUSTRALIAN ARMY TANK BRIGADE.

The armour clad head of a knight's charger similar to that of the British 20th Armoured Brigade was the badge of this Australian Army Tank Brigade.

4th AUSTRALIAN ARMOURED BRIGADE.

Formed in 1943 in New South Wales, this Brigade served in Queensland until the end of that year when it embarked for New Guinea and took part in the operations at Buna, Finschafen, Torokina and Wewak, and later in New Britain and Borneo. Its badge was an alligator before a palm tree set above a boomerang. The design in white on a black background.

34th AUSTRALIAN INFANTRY BRIGADE.

A badge similar to the general service cap badge of the Australian Commonwealth Forces, set above a boomerang, was the sign adopted by the 34th Infantry Brigade.

* * * * *

THE NEW ZEALAND FORMATIONS

The New Zealand Formation Badges were used for vehicle markings: personnel being distinguished by combinations of colour patches worn on battledress.

NEW ZEALAND EXPEDITIONARY FORCE.

Four red stars set on a square black background was the badge of the H.Q. of the New Zealand Expeditionary Force.

1st NEW ZEALAND DIVISION.

A battle-axe was the badge of the 1st New Zealand Division, a New Zealand Home Defence Formation.

2nd NEW ZEALAND DIVISION.

The New Zealand national emblem of the fern leaf, in white on a black circular background, was the badge adopted by the famous 2nd New Zealand Division.* The formation arrived in the United Kingdom in 1940 under the command of Lieut.-General Sir Bernard C. Freyberg, V.C., K.C.B., K.B.E., C.M.G., D.S.O., and formed part of the 7 British Corps, after Dunkirk, in its South-Eastern England operational area in

---

* This badge is now borne on the vehicles of the Royal Wiltshire Yeomanry, an honour granted to the Regiment by the New Zealand Division with which formation the Wilts Yeomanry served in the Western Desert and in Italy.

an anti-invasion role. The N.Z. Division proceeded overseas the following year to the Middle East. It saw action in the Western Desert and in Greece and Crete, and then back to the Desert, taking part in the hard fighting at Sidi Rezegh. It formed part of the Eighth Army at El Alamein and in the drive through Cyrenaica and Tripolitania to the Mareth Line and on into Tunisia to the final defeat of the Axis forces in North Africa. In Italy the Division added fresh honours to its name. It took part in the final operations of 15th Army Group in the Po Valley. It was the formation that entered Padua and captured Mestre and swept on to Trieste, where it linked up with Tito's Yugoslavian forces advancing from the east.

The Division ceased to exist early in 1946, leaving with C.M.F. only a Brigade Group, intended as New Zealand's contribution to the British Commonwealth's occupational force in Japan.

3rd NEW ZEALAND DIVISION.

This formation adopted as its badge the national bird of New Zealand, the kiwi.

The Division was held in readiness in New Zealand in 1942 against the Japanese drive in the Pacific. It later saw service in New Caledonia, and one brigade group saw action in the Solomon Islands.

4th NEW ZEALAND DIVISION.

A charging bull was the Divisional badge. The formation did not serve outside New Zealand.

5th NEW ZEALAND DIVISION.

A kea's head was adopted by the 5th New Zealand Division as its badge.

The Division formed part of New Zealand's Home Defence Force.

6th NEW ZEALAND DIVISION.

This formation was raised in 1942 in the Middle East, at the time of Rommel's threat to Egypt. It was raised from units of the N.Z.E.F. not forming part of the 2nd New Zealand Division Order of Battle, and was made up from reinforcements, Training Establishments, and L. of C. Units. The formation was later disbanded and the units reverted to their former roles or were absorbed into the 2nd New Zealand Division.

The 6th New Zealand Division adopted as its badge the kiwi, as also borne by the 3rd New Zealand Division in the Pacific.

4th NEW ZEALAND ARMOURED BRIGADE.

This Brigade was formed in New Zealand from a nucleus of the 2nd New Zealand Division which returned from the Middle East after participation in the operations in Greece and Crete. The Brigade rejoined the N.Z.E.F. in the Middle East after El Alamein, and served in the final phase of the operations in North Africa. As part of the 2nd New Zealand Division the Brigade subsequently served in the Italian campaign. The formation badge was a dragon.

SOUTH AFRICAN DIVISIONS

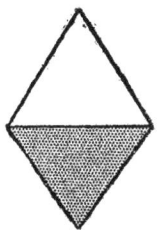

1st SOUTH AFRICAN DIVISION.

This Division was formed in Kenya in 1940 and was composed of the 2nd and 5th South African Brigades. It formed part of Lieut.-General Sir Alan Cunningham's Force which routed the Italians in Somaliland and pursued them in the operations which followed and led to the conquest of Abyssinia. It was this formation which occupied Moyale in the early stages of the advance on the road to Harar and the fall of Addis Ababa, and the final round-up of the scattered Italian Army.

The Division next saw action in the Middle East. It was part of 30 Corps with the Eighth Army in November, 1941, and took part in General Sir Claude Auchinleck's offensive. It was at El Alamein in October, 1942, and in the advance through Cyrenaica and Tripolitania, in the battles which broke the Axis forces in North Africa.

The badge of the 1st S.A. Division was a diamond. It was divided into halves, the top yellow, the lower green. The Division subsequently adopted another badge. A square, evenly divided, the top half yellow, the lower green. Superimposed on this background was the black silhouette of a white-tailed gnu, or black wildebeest, once common on the plains of the Transvaal and the Orange River Colony.

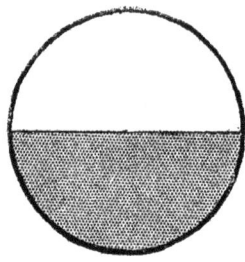

2nd SOUTH AFRICAN DIVISION.

This Division also served in the Middle East and saw much hard fighting with the Eighth Army in Libya. Two Brigades of the Division formed the major part of the garrison in Tobruk when Rommel swept forward in June, 1942, and were lost when the port fell to the superior numbers of the Afrika Korps and their Italian allies.

The Divisional badge was a divided circle, the top being yellow, the bottom division green.

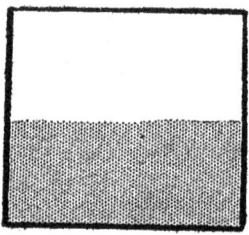

3rd SOUTH AFRICAN DIVISION.

A cloth patch equally divided; top half yellow, and lower half green, was the badge of the 3rd South African Division.

6th SOUTH AFRICAN ARMOURED DIVISION.

A green triangle with a yellow centre was the badge of the 6th South African Armoured Division. This formation formed part of the Allied Armies in Italy from May, 1944, until the end of the campaign, taking part in the battle of Cassino and the piercing of the Gothic Line. It was under command of the 15th Army Group during the final operations in the Po Valley, driving into Trevisio in the last stages of the campaign which led to the German capitulation.

U.D.F. REPATRIATION UNIT(S).

The head of a springbok in light yellow and white, picked out in black and set on a khaki background was the badge of the Repatriation Units of the Union Defence Force.

★ ★ ★ ★ ★

THE INDIAN FORMATIONS

SOUTHERN ARMY (INDIA).

The Southern Cross, four yellow stars on a square background, evenly divided into three horizontal bands of red, black and red, was the badge of India's Southern Army.

NORTH-WESTERN ARMY (INDIA).

A castle gateway, symbolic of the North-Western gateway of India, the Khyber Pass, was the badge of the North-Western Army of India. The gateway was in white set on a square background of equal red, black and red bands.

15 INDIAN CORPS.

A geometric design composed of three Roman figure "Vs"—for fifteen—in white or black on a red rectangular or circular background, was the badge of the 15 Indian Corps, which was one of the three Indian Corps of the Fourteenth Army during the hard-fought campaign for the liberation of Burma.

The Corps was engaged in prolonged and bitter fighting in the Second and Third Arakan Campaigns. In the Second Arakan Campaign, 1943-44, it inflicted the first decisive defeat that any Japanese force had ever suffered at the hands of the British, breaking for the first time the legend of Japanese invincibility in the South-East Asia theatre.

In the Third Arakan Campaign, 1944-45, which was a series of combined operations, 15 Indian Corps carried out no less than nine combined assault landings varying in size from a brigade group to a divisional operation. These operations culminated in a divisional assault on the Rangoon River which led to the capture of Rangoon itself in May, 1945. By the end of the war the Corps had been withdrawn to India to prepare for operations in Malaya, but was eventually moved to the Netherlands East Indies to command the British and Indian force in this area.

21 INDIAN CORPS

The Corps, which was one of the Middle East formations, bore as its badge the truncated heraldic head of a horse in white on a square black background, similar in design to that of Eastern Command, India.*

33 INDIAN CORPS.

The first badge of the 33 Indian Corps was a black silhouette of the head of the Duke of Wellington on a green background within a red circle. The badge was chosen by Lieut.-General A. F. P. Christison, the Corps Commander, because the operational area allocated to the formation covered much of the territory over which the Duke of Wellington fought when he was in India (1800-1805).

* See also Eastern Command (India), page 21.

The Corps was raised in November, 1942, to command the 19th and 25th Indian Divisions, the 251st Indian Tank Brigade, and other formations and units allocated for the defence of Southern India.

A sword and trident, crossed, and superimposed on geometrical wings, the design in white on a black or dark blue background, was subsequently adopted on the change in the role of the Corps. The design was also worn on a background of Corps colours of red, white and red.

Intended as an amphibious expeditionary force, the badge was made up of the trident to represent the Royal Navy; the sword for the Army, and the wings for the R.A.F.—a similar motif to the Combined Operations badge.

From 3rd April, 1944, to 27th May, 1945, 33 Corps travelled a distance of 1,127 miles, from Jorhat to Rangoon, liberating some 55,500 square miles of enemy-occupied territory. The Corps had the task of halting the northernmost Japs' drive at Kohima, following the reopening of the land route to Imphal. By continuous action through the 1944-45 monsoon the Jap 15th Army was driven back across the Chindwin from where the drive to the Irrawaddy was launched, culminating in the capture of Mandalay on 19th March, 1945. Operating south on the line of the Irrawaddy the Corps cleared the oilfields area around Yenangyaung to link with troops pushing north from Rangoon on 15th May, 1945. The Corps, under the command of Lieut.-General Sir Montagu Stopford, was converted into Twelfth Army at the end of May, 1945.

34 INDIAN CORPS.

A leaping panther in black on a circular background divided into Corps colours of two red and a central white band, was the badge adopted by the 34 Indian Corps, which was raised for the invasion of Malaya in 1945. Although this was the badge officially approved for the Corps, the badge actually worn was a leaping black panther on a red circle with a black border.

The Corps was being embarked for Malaya at the time of the Jap surrender. Two of its divisions, however, actually carried out landings in Malaya as had been planned.

THE INDIAN DIVISIONS

2nd INDIAN DIVISION.

A yellow hornet on a black rectangular background was the badge adopted by this formation, which was raised in Iraq in March, 1942. It was said that the formation badge was adopted owing to the prevalence of the hornets in the area at the time of its formation. The Division was formed from No. 2 L. of C. Area (Southern Iraq and South-West Persia). It remained in Iraq as an L. of C. formation.

3rd INDIAN DIVISION (The Chindits).

A golden Burmese Dragon on a blue circular background was the badge of the 3rd Indian Division—Wingate's Chindits—who made history with their airborne invasions of Burma. The Chindits were first in action in Japanese-occupied Burma as long-range penetration troops in the expedition led by the late Major-General Orde C. Wingate, D.S.O. As part of the Fourteenth Army, the Division was subsequently engaged in the Chindwin area harassing and disorganizing the Japanese lines of communication.

4th INDIAN DIVISION.

The 4th Indian Division was the first formation to leave India. It embarked for Egypt, where it concentrated in the autumn of 1939 and formed part of the original desert force under command of General (later Field-Marshal) Lord Wavell. At Sidi Barrani, the Division shared with the 7th Armoured Division the honours of that complete victory over the Italians. The formation was then withdrawn from the Western Desert to participate in the campaign in East Africa. It joined General Platt's forces in Eritrea, where it took part in the operations leading to the defeat of the Italians at Keren, where the Division fought with the 5th (Indian) Division in securing a complete victory. The 4th (Indian) Division then hurriedly returned to Egypt to meet the threat of the Afrika Korps. One Brigade (the 5th) was withdrawn to Syria, where it took part in the operations against the Vichy French Forces. The rest of the Division remained in the Western Desert, where one brigade (the 11th) participated in the action at Halfaya Pass in June, 1941. The whole Division took part in the Allied offensive of November, 1941, advanced to Benghazi and then withdrew to the Gazala line. In April, 1942, the Division was withdrawn from the Desert, one brigade going to Cyprus, another to Palestine, and the third to the Canal Zone. These last two brigades returned to the Desert when Rommel attacked in May, 1942, one (the 11th) was lost in Tobruk, but the second withdrew to El Alamein. The Division re-formed at Alamein in September, 1942, and took part in the Eighth Army's attack in October. It was composed then of the 5th, 7th and 161st Indian Infantry Brigades. the British element of which was the 1st/4th Bn. Essex Regiment, 1st Bn. Royal Sussex Regiment, and 1st Bn. Argyll and Sutherland Highlanders. After Alamein the Division was not engaged until Tunisia was reached. There, with only the 5th and 7th Brigades, they took part in the attacks which outflanked the Mareth Line, burst through the enemy's defences at the Wadi Akarit, and were checked in the hard fighting around Enfidaville. Together with the 7th Armoured Division and the 201st Guards Brigade, the Division joined First

Army for the last attacks which ended in the complete defeat of the Axis forces in North Africa. The Division next joined the Allied armies in Italy on the Orsogna front in December, 1943, took part in the fighting at Cassino in February and March, 1944, advanced through Central Italy and was first to break into the Gothic Line at the end of August, 1944. Withdrawn from Italy in the autumn of 1945, the Division formed part of our forces in Greece until it returned to India in January, 1946.

The Division's badge was a red eagle in flight on a dark blue background. The badges worn in the Western Desert were the gift of the women of the Punjab at the instance of the late Sir Sikander Hyat Khan, Prime Minister of the Punjab, who visited the Division in the Middle East.

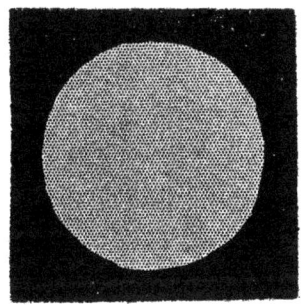

5th INDIAN DIVISION.

The 5th Indian Division, composed of the 9th, 10th and 29th Indian Infantry Brigades, left India in September, 1940, and embarked for the Sudan. The Division formed part of General Platt's forces in Eritrea and played a leading part in the capture of Kassala and at Keren. The 5th followed up the broken Italians to the capture of Asmara and Massawa and received the surrender of the Duke of Aosta at Amba Alagi. After this surrender, in July, 1941, the Division moved to Egypt, then to Iraq and, by the end of the year, to Cyprus. It relieved the 4th Indian Division with the Eighth Army in the Western Desert, and during April, 1942, took part in the costly fighting around Tobruk and in the withdrawal to Alamein, where it helped in stabilizing the line. In September, after Rommel's final attacks had been defeated, the Division was relieved at El Alamein by the 4th Indian Division and moved to "Paiforce," and in May and June, 1942, returned to India with only 9th and 161st Brigades, moving into the Arakan, being one of the two forward divisions in the advance of 15 Indian Corps. The 5th took part in the defence of Imphal and the reoccupation of Tiddim. It formed part of the Fourteenth Army in the final operations in Burma. In April, 1945, the Division was withdrawn from north of Rangoon to take part in "mopping-up" operations until it embarked for Malaya. The Division was first ashore at Singapore, reoccupying the city on the 5th September, 1945. Two months later the formation moved to Java where it was engaged in restoring peace among the Indonesians. The badge of the 5th Indian Division was a red circle on a black background.

6th INDIAN DIVISION.

This Division was formed in India in March, 1941. By October, 1941, the Division had moved to Iraq with the 24th, 26th and 27th Indian Infantry Brigades, where it was engaged largely on protection of the supply routes to Russia, and where it remained until returning to India in November, 1944. On its return to India the Division was disbanded. One brigade, the 26th, was sent to Egypt when the Eighth Army withdrew to El Alamein, and served for a while with the 50th Division. This same brigade returned to India in July, 1944, ahead of the Division, and by the end of the year was serving in Burma.

This formation's badge was the head of a Deccan tiger in black and yellow on a square black background.

7th INDIAN DIVISION.

Known as the "Golden Arrow" Division. A yellow arrow on a black square or circle was the badge of the 7th Indian Division. The badge was chosen to indicate the direction of the line of advance to the protection of the North-West Frontier of India, which the Division was raised to protect, but all its fighting took place in the north-east. This formation saw much hard fighting in the Arakan, and was cut off for sixteen days in the Ngakyedauk pass, where it formed the famous "box" at Sinzweya and held off all the Japanese attacks, stopping the enemy advance towards India.

This formation later formed part of the Fourteenth Army in the advance into Burma. Crossing the Irrawaddy on 14th February, 1945, it established at Nyanugu a bridgehead which enabled the 17th Indian Division to make their dash to Meiktila, the capture of which by the latter formation and 255th Indian Armoured Brigade caused the Japanese resistance in North Burma to crumble. The 7th Division later took part in the hard fighting which drove the Japanese from Myingyan and Yenangyaung. In September, 1945, it was flown to Siam where it concentrated and disarmed over 113,000 Japanese troops. In April, 1946, the Division arrived in Malaya where it remained till the end of the year, when it returned to India.

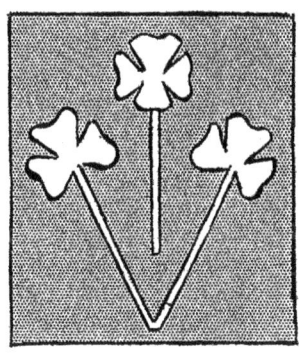

8th INDIAN DIVISION.

Formed in October, 1940, this Division moved to Iraq in June and July, 1941. It took part in the operations in Persia in 1941, advancing through Khoramshah to Ahwaz. Thereafter, the Division served in "Paiforce" until June, 1942, when one brigade moved to Syria and one to Egypt. This latter brigade suffered heavy losses at El Alamein and was disbanded in September, 1942. The remainder of the Division again concentrated in Paiforce. After a short spell of training in Syria during mid-1943, the Division embarked for Italy, landed at Taranto in September, 1943, and formed part of Eighth Army in the advance up the Adriatic Coast. It crashed through the German defences on the Trigno and Sangro Rivers, and spent the winter in the line between Ostona and Orsogna. The Division played a big part in the final breaking of the enemy's defences at Cassino in May, 1944, and in the pursuit northwards to the Gothic Line, where again it was heavily engaged in the high Apennines. In December, 1944, the Division checked the German counter-offensive in the Serchio Valley, and was later in the van of Eighth Army's attack across the Senior River when the final and decisive Allied offensive was launched in the Po valley.

The Division returned to India in July, 1945, with the intention of participating in the operations against the Japanese.

Three yellow clover-shaped leaves on long stems on a dull red background was the badge of the 8th Indian Division.

The Divisional badge was originally the crest of the G.O.C., Major-General C. O. Harvey, C.B., C.B.E., C.V.O., M.C., who commanded the formation in Paiforce. This crest was a bunch of wheat and clover above the motto " Carpe diem," set on a black background, but this was later changed to the three yellow clover-shaped leaves on long stems on a dull red background. The stems were set to form a " V " for Victory, with an " I " for India in the apex. The central clover leaf was of the four leafed variety—for luck.

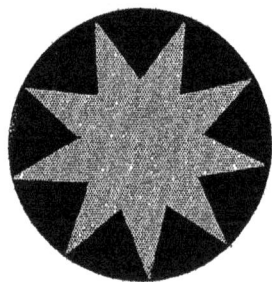

9th INDIAN DIVISION.

The 9th Indian Division embarked for Singapore in 1940 and rormed part of our forces in Malaya at the time of the Japanese invasion.

The division was located in the Eastern Coastal Area of the Peninsula when the Japanese attacked.

It took part in the hard fighting, and suffered heavy casualties in the withdrawal down the mainland to Singapore Island, where it linked up with the 11th Indian Division, and was lost when the Command was forced to capitulate at Singapore in February, 1942.

The divisional badge was a nine-pointed star, in royal blue, set on a black circle.

10th INDIAN DIVISION.

This formation was raised in January, 1941, at Ahmednagar. It arrived in the Persian Gulf in the late spring of that year and took part in the defence of Habbaniyah and later in the capture of Baghdad. The Division also saw action in Persia, one column occupying Teheran. It joined the Eighth Army in Libya in 1942, moving from Iraq to Cyrenaica in fourteen days, and took part in the hard fighting when Rommel attempted to break through into Egypt. The formation was then withdrawn to Cyprus. The Division next saw action in Italy, where it arrived in March, 1944. It went first to Ortona, then to the Tiber basin and the Central Apennines, and back to the Adriatic coast in October to form part of the Eighth Army in the final operations in the Po Valley in April and May, 1945.

The badge of the 10th Indian Division was a black square, on it two diagonal bands of pink or red and blue, forming a cross.

11th INDIAN DIVISION.

The 11th Indian Division formed part of our forces in Malaya at the time of the Japanese invasion. The Division was, at the outset of the brief ten weeks campaign, located in the north of the Malay Peninsula on the Thailand border, and was the first formation in action in North Kedah against the Japanese when they launched their attack on 8th December, 1941. The formation saw much hard fighting and sustained heavy casualties in the withdrawal through Malaya, the two British battalions of the Division, the 1st Leicesters and the 2nd East Surreys being amalgamated and designated "The British Battalion." The Division was finally compelled to withdraw to Singapore Island where following the increasing intensity of the Japanese assaults, the Command capitulated.

The badge of the 11th Indian Division was an eleven-spoked wheel on a yellow or gold background. The badge was retained whilst the Division was in captivity, and at Changi the entrance to the P.o.W. camp was decorated with the badge to which was added in "dog Latin" the motto, *"Qui Ultime Melior Ridet"* ("He who laughs last, laughs best"). This for a considerable time was accepted by the Japanese with all solemnity as the divisional motto without realizing the purport, and the fact that it had been added for their discomfort.

12th INDIAN DIVISION.

This Division also served in Persia and Iraq. Its badge was a Persian lion outlined in blue set on a yellow background.

14th INDIAN DIVISION.

The Division was formed in India, and in May, 1942, served in the Eastern Army, taking part in the hard-fought campaign in the Arakan, before the formation of the Fourteenth Army, taking part in the operations in the Mayu Peninsula before being forced to withdraw when Maundu and Buthidaung were evacuated. In May, 1943, the Division was moved back from the Arakan to Central Command, India, assuming the role of a training formation. The Divisional badge depicted a mountain range in black—the centre peak being Pakatu—set in a white frame on a dark background, the white frame taking the form of a "Q" to link the formation with Quetta, where it was raised in May, 1942, by Major-General H. H. Rich.

17th INDIAN DIVISION.

Raised in Ahmednagar in the spring of 1941, this Division, under the command of Major-General J. G. Smythe, V.C., less one brigade, moved to Burma in November, 1941. The Division was in action against the Japanese in Burma and Assam, with a few short breaks for reorganization and training, from January, 1942, until the Japanese surrender in August, 1945, and fought against the Japanese for a longer period than any other British or Indian formation.

The 17th saw much hard fighting in the Chin Hills and in the Tiddim and Imphal areas. It crossed the Irrawaddy in February, 1945, and, after bitter fighting, captured Meiktila in March—a victory which led to the destruction of the Japanese forces in Burma. The Division was twice reported by the Japanese to have been annihilated but, in spite of this, played a major part in the Fourteenth Army's victorious campaign in Burma.

The divisional badge was a black cat on a khaki square background. This badge was adopted in 1943, and replaced a dark blue square which had been introduced in 1942.

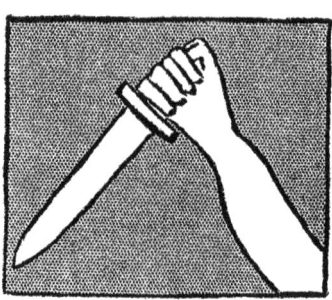

19th INDIAN DIVISION.

Known from its formation badge—a yellow dagger held in a clenched hand on a red background—as the "Dagger Division," this formation served with the Fourteenth Army in Burma under the command of Major-General T. Wynford Rees, C.B., C.I.E., D.S.O., M.C., and in the fighting which led to its liberation. It was the 19th Indian Division which, after severe fighting, eventually established the Irrawaddy bridgehead at Kyaukmyaung which enabled them to drive through and capture Mandalay, where they raised the Union Jack over Fort Dufferin on 20th March, 1945.

20th INDIAN DIVISION.

An Indian sword, a tulwar, in silver, raised aloft by a clenched hand set on a black circle, was the badge of the 20th Indian Division. The sign was chosen to symbolize the "swift and deadly execution" of the Japanese armies. The Division was raised in Bangalore on the 1st of April, 1942, by General Sir Douglas Gracey, K.C.I.E., C.B., C.B.E., M.C., who commanded the formation through its training in Ceylon and its active service in Assam, Burma and Indo-China, until it was disbanded in April-May, 1946.

The Division distinguished itself in the Burma campaign, particularly during the defence of the Imphal plain in the spring and early summer of 1944, and in the breaching of the Irrawaddy line a year later. In September, 1946, the Division moved to French Indo-China where it concentrated and disarmed 70,000 Japanese.

21st INDIAN DIVISION.

This designation was temporarily given to the H.Q. of the 44th Indian Armoured Division when the formation ceased to operate in an armoured role on moving into Assam in May, 1944.

The badge of the 44th Indian Armoured Division was a charging buffalo* and the badge chosen for the 21st Indian Division to link with this was a buffalo's head in white, with red horns, set on a blue background. This badge was subsequently retained, on the splitting up of the formation, by the 268th Lorried Infantry Brigade.†

23rd INDIAN DIVISION.

A red fighting cock on a light yellow circle was the badge of the Division, which was designed by Major-General Savoy, the G.O.C. It was intended as being symbolic to both British and Indian troops and, in the case of the latter, without giving offence to either Muslim or Hindu. In 1942 the Division covered the withdrawal of General Alexander's army through Imphal and later fought with distinction round Shenam, Palel and Tamu during the Japanese offensive against Imphal in 1944.

In 1945 the Division took part in Operation "Zipper," landing in Malaya in September. In the same month it moved to Java where its main task was the evacuation of internees and the restoration of law and order during the Indonesian disturbances.

---
* See 44th Indian Armoured Division, page 127.
† See also 268th Indian Infantry Brigade, page 135.

25th INDIAN DIVISION.

The 25th Indian Division's badge was a black ace of spades set on a green background. The Division was formed in Southern India in August, 1942, under the command of Major-General H. L. Davies, C.B.E., D.S.O., M.C. Under the command of the 15th Indian Corps the Division first saw action in the Arakan in March, 1944, where it fought with distinction in 1944 and 1945, notably at Kangaw, which was one of the fiercest fought battles of the entire Arakan and Burma campaigns. The Division formed part of the Fourteenth Army in the hard jungle fighting which led to the liberation of Burma. In January, 1945, the Division took part in the first large-scale amphibious operation in South-East Asia, which ended in the liberation of Akyab when the formation was ferried across the four-mile-wide Mayu estuary to land on the northern beaches of Akyab Island. In the course of combined operations during the weeks that followed, the Division occupied Myebon and Ru-Ywa.

26th INDIAN DIVISION.

This Division was raised in April, 1942, and moved into the Arakan in the winter of 1942. It first saw action in January, 1943, in the Kalapinzin valley and south of the Maungdaw–Buthidaung road. The Division fought its way to the relief of the 7th Indian Division in their "box" at Sinzweya. The formation took part in the amphibious operations down the Burma coast in support of the main Fourteenth Army offensive through Mandalay, Meiktila and down the Irrawaddy. The Division was allotted the task of the capture of Rangoon by sea. Troops landed ten miles south of the city on 2nd May, 1945, and captured Rangoon before the arrival of the main body of the Fourteenth Army advancing southwards from Pegu. After the capture of Rangoon the Division returned to India as part of 34 Corps, but subsequently served in the Netherlands East Indies.

The formation badge was a yellow and black Royal Bengal tiger stepping out of a blue triangle set on a black triangular background, and from this badge the formation became known as the "Tiger Head" Division. The triangle was taken from the Greek letter Delta, for it was in the Hoogli Delta that the Division was raised from the H.Q. Presidency and Assam District.

39th INDIAN DIVISION.

An Indian sword in white, held aloft in a clenched brown hand on a dark green circle, was the 39th Indian Division's badge. Originally designated 1st Burma Infantry Division, composed of the 1st and 2nd Burma Brigades and an Indian brigade, this formation was known as "Burdiv" and took part in the withdrawal from Burma in 1942. Whilst in India it was redesignated 39th Indian Division, and in 1943 became a training formation.

31st INDIAN ARMOURED DIVISION.

A black elephant on a green background was the badge of the 31st Indian Armoured Division, which was raised in India in 1941 and later saw service in Iraq, Iran, Syria and Egypt. It was redesignated 1st Indian Armoured Division in the latter part of 1945, and returned to India early in 1946.

42nd INDIAN ARMOURED DIVISION.

This Division was raised in 1941. Its badge was a rhinoceros head in grey, picked out in black on a red circle; below the head the motto, "Laro Aur Larte Raho" ("Strike, and keep on striking"). The Division was amalgamated in May, 1943, with the 43rd Indian Armoured Division to form the 44th Indian Armoured Division.

44th INDIAN ARMOURED DIVISION.

This Division was raised in Secunderabad in January, 1943, by the amalgamation of the 42nd and 43rd Armoured Divisions.

In April, 1944, it was announced that the formation was to be converted into an Airborne Division, and the Armoured and Lorried Infantry Brigades to become independent brigades.

Before the change was made the Divisional H.Q. was hurriedly moved to Assam to command certain detached brigades of the L. of C. The H.Q., then redesignated 21st Indian Division,* concentrated at Jorhat in May, 1944, with the task of controlling operations in the Silchar area and L. of C. in rear of 33 Indian Corps. As the advance progressed along the Imphal road the Division moved to Kohima and became responsible for the security of the communications between Dinapur and 33 Corps.

The Division was then split up to become 255th Indian Tank Brigade; 268th Lorried Infantry Brigade and the nucleus of 44th Indian Airborne Division.

The Divisional badge was a charging buffalo, in black, with red horns, hooves and eyes, below an inscription in Urdu—" Laro Aur Larte Raho " (" Strike, and Keep on Striking "). The design was on a white background within a black circular border.

This badge was subsequently retained by 255th Indian Tank Brigade.†

---

* See 21st Indian Division, page 124.
† See 255th Indian Tank Brigade, page 131.

44th INDIAN AIRBORNE DIVISION.

Raised in May, 1944, from elements of the 44th Indian Armoured Division. The 50th Parachute Brigade of the Division was in action at Imphal in 1944 and again in May, 1945, when it made an airborne landing south of Rangoon in support of the 26th Indian Division.

The badge of this Division was the same as that worn by the British airborne divisions, the well-known Pegasus, with the addition of the word "India" in pale blue below the hooves.

* * * * *

INDIAN ARMOURED AND TANK BRIGADES

2nd INDIAN ARMOURED BRIGADE

A white Fleur-de-lis on a scarlet square background.

3rd INDIAN ARMOURED BRIGADE.

A small replica of the badge of the Fourteenth Army, set on a square yellow background.

3rd INDIAN MOTOR BRIGADE.

This Brigade was formed from the pre-war 2nd (Sialkot) Cavalry Brigade of three Indian cavalry regiments, and wore as its badge a red horseshoe on a black circle. The Brigade moved overseas to Egypt in January, 1941, and in April suffered heavy casualties at Mechile, when it sacrificed itself, thereby gaining time for Tobruk to be occupied. One regiment went into Tobruk with the Australians, where it remained for almost the whole period of the siege. The remainder of the Brigade was stationed in Egypt and Syria for a year before returning to the Desert in time to meet Rommel's attack in May, 1942. Near Bir Hacheim the Brigade took the first blow from the enemy and again suffered heavy losses. The Brigade was then withdrawn to Egypt and, ultimately to Iraq, where it joined the 31st Indian Armoured Division. In January, 1943, the cavalry regiments returned to India and infantry battalions took their place. In February, 1943, the Brigade was renumbered and redesignated the 43rd Lorried Infantry Brigade.*

50th INDIAN TANK BRIGADE.

A clenched fist in white on a black circle was the badge of this Indian Tank Brigade. This Brigade originally formed part of the Indian Expeditionary Force. and later 33 Indian Corps. In November, 1944, the Brigade was moved to the Arakan and took part in the hard fighting following the seaborne landings carried out under 15 Indian Corps. In March, 1945, the Brigade was withdrawn to India to prepare for the assault on Malaya under 34 Indian Corps.

---

* See page 132.

251st INDIAN TANK BRIGADE.

This Brigade was formed in 1942 and initially employed in the defence of Southern India under command of 33 Indian Corps. The formation was broken up in the latter part of 1943, personnel going to provide reinforcements for the Chindits. The Brigade badge was officially described as "the forequarters of a tiger rampant with white eyes, teeth and claws, on a red background."

254th INDIAN TANK BRIGADE.

This Brigade was raised at Risalpur in April, 1941, by Brigadier W. T. Gill, M.C., as the armoured brigade of the 32nd Indian Armoured Division. Its original designation was the 4th Indian Armoured Brigade. This was changed to 254th Indian Armoured Brigade at the end of the year.

In May, 1943, the Brigade moved to Ranchi and in October part of the formation moved into the Arakan, going ashore on the beaches from landing craft. The Brigade distinguished itself in the subsequent operations. In October, 1944, the formation moved into the Imphal area and, under command of the 7th Indian Division, advanced down the Kabaw valley on the Tamu-Kalewa-Gangaw-Pauk axis, crossing the Irrawaddy in mid-February, 1945, when it made its first contact with the Japanese. Eleven days after the establishment of the bridgehead, it assisted the 17th Indian Division in annihilating the Meiktila garrison after some of the severest fighting of the Burma campaign, and later advanced 300 miles in thirty days from Meiktali to Hiegu, thirty miles north of Rangoon, capturing Toungoo and Pegu *en route*.

The Brigade's badge was a geometrical design in black set on a red inverted triangle, the design representing tank tracks and three drops of blood, significant of the Brigade motto, "Blood on the Tracks."

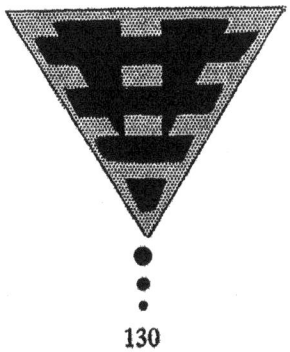

255th INDIAN TANK BRIGADE.

A charging buffalo, black body with red eyes, hooves and horns, set on a blue triangular background, was the badge of this formation, which originally formed part of the 44th Indian Armoured Division. The Brigade's badge was a modified version of the Divisional sign, which was retained when the Armoured Division ceased to exist.* Shortly after the disbandment of the Division, this Brigade was dispatched to Burma where it took part in the final operations of the Fourteenth Army. After the capture of Rangoon the Brigade was allotted to 15 Indian Corps for operations in Malaya.

★ ★ ★ ★ ★

INDIAN INFANTRY BRIGADES

38th INDIAN INFANTRY BRIGADE.

A crane bird, with red head, neck and legs, and a blue body.

---

* See 44th Indian Armoured Division, page 127.

43rd INDIAN LORRIED INFANTRY BRIGADE*

This Brigade was formed in Iraq in January, 1943, as the Lorried Infantry Brigade of the 31st Indian Armoured Division. The Brigade was detached from its parent formation and dispatched to Italy, where it joined the 1st British Armoured Division prior to the Eighth Army's attack on the Gothic Line in August, 1944. Later the Brigade became a Corps and Army Troops formation, serving with the 10th Indian Division, the 2nd New Zealand Division, the 56th Division, and the Polish Corps in the Po Valley. It adopted the badge of two crossed kukris in white on a dark green background, denoting the unusual brigade formation of three Gurkha battalions.

52nd INDIAN INFANTRY BRIGADE.

A black design of a castle, mural crown and leaves flanked by two fish in green on a white background. This badge was adopted from the old Moghul crest of Bhopal State, where the Brigade was located at the time of its adoption. This Brigade was made up of British units, and its role was that of a training formation for training reinforcements for British units in Burma in jungle warfare.

---

* Sometimes known as the 43rd Gurkha Lorried Infantry Brigade.

60th INDIAN INFANTRY BRIGADE.

Two crossed lances with red and white pennants, surmounted by a bugle horn in white, the whole on a black square, was this Brigade's badge, which was chosen when the formation was in Iraq as a motorized brigade and composed of two former Indian cavalry regiments (represented by the lances), and one rifle regiment (the 5th Frontier Force Rifles), represented by the stringed bugle.

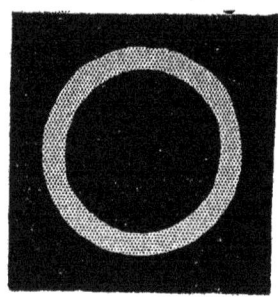

72nd INDIAN INFANTRY BRIGADE.

A red circle on a square black background was the badge of this Brigade, which was composed of the 10th Bn. The Gloucestershire Regiment, the 9th Bn. The Royal Sussex Regiment and the 6th Bn. The South Wales Borderers. The Brigade was formed from the 267th Armoured Brigade in March, 1943, when the 43rd Indian Armoured Division was broken up. It had been composed of three British battalions which had arrived in India in July, 1942, and had been converted to armoured regiments to form the 267th Brigade. In March, 1943, when the 32nd and 43rd Armoured Divisions were amalgamated, the Brigade was reconverted to infantry. The Brigade subsequently formed part of the 36th Division with the 29th Infantry Brigade. The badge of the 29th was a white circle on a black background and this, linked with the red circle of the 72nd, became the Divisional badge.*

---

* See 36th Division, page 55.

109th INDIAN INFANTRY BRIGADE.

This was an Independent Brigade which formed part of the Fourteenth Army in Burma. For some time it was located at Aigal, in the hills south of Silchar, with the object of providing some degree of protection to the right flank of 4 Corps. It took nearly three weeks to reach the brigade from Corps Headquarters through jungle tracks. The Brigade adopted its own badge, which was a representation of the goad used by a mahout to urge on his elephant. This was a good-natured "dig" at 4th Corps Headquarters, whose badge was a charging elephant, and whom owing to the difficulties of communications they had, it was said, to press for their requirements.

116th INDIAN INFANTRY BRIGADE.

A yellow Indian battle-axe on a royal blue rectangular background within a narrow yellow border. This Brigade reoccupied the Andaman Isles when the Japanese occupation troops surrendered.

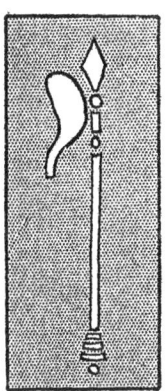

150th INDIAN INFANTRY BRIGADE.

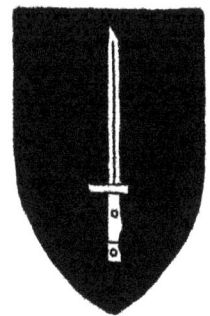

A vertical bayonet, point uppermost, in yellow set on a black shield was the badge of this Brigade, which was raised in May, 1944, to train Indian units in jungle warfare. In December, 1945, the Brigade was moved to Hong Kong.

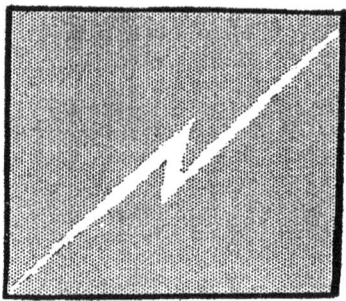

155th INDIAN INFANTRY BRIGADE.

A yellow lightning flash set on a royal blue oblong background.

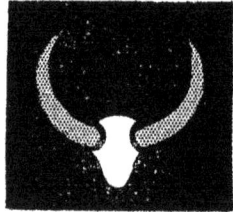

268th INDIAN INFANTRY BRIGADE.

Originally forming part of the 44th Indian Armoured Division, this was an independent all-Indian infantry brigade and formed part of 33 Indian Corps with the Fourteenth Army in Assam and Burma, serving under the command of 21st Indian Division in the maintenance of communications between Dinapur and 33 Corps. After the battle of Kohima this Brigade, under the command of Brigadier M. G. Dyer, D.S.O., was employed, until the end of operations in Burma, in an independent role under 33 Corps. The composition of the Brigade changed continually. At the end of 1945 this Brigade was selected as the Indian element of B.C.O.F. and was moved to Japan early in 1946.

Its badge was a buffalo's head in white with red horns set on a square blue background.*

---

* See also 21st Indian Division, page 124, and 254 L. of C. Sub-Area page 185.

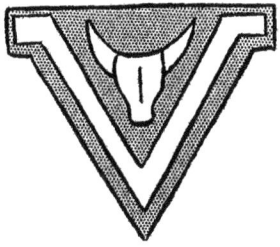

LUSHAI BRIGADE.

A buffalo's head in white, set in the apex of a "V"—for Victory—on a red background, was the badge of this formation which served in Burma with the Fourteenth Army, and saw much hard fighting in the jungle-covered hill country between Manipur State and the Arakan, through which the Brigade advanced to capture Gangaw.

The Brigade was formed in March, 1944, and was in continuous action against the Japanese until January, 1945. In clearing the west side of the Chindwin the Brigade materially assisted the 33 Corps advance on Tiddim and Kalemyo.

INDIAN CONTINGENT IN U.K.

This Indian unit's badge was made up of a five-pointed star, the star of the Order of the Star of India set on a circular band bearing the legend "Heaven's light our guide" in light and dark blue. Surrounding the badge was a circle of golden flames. The whole design was set on a light blue square background.

This contingent was originally "Force K.6," four mule companies and administrative units, which sailed from India and landed in France during December, 1939. These companies served on the Belgian frontier with 1 and 2 Corps, and in the Maginot Line with 51st Highland Division. When France fell one company was captured but the others were transferred to England, where the title was changed to "The Indian Contingent." Until returning to India in January, 1944, the contingent was engaged largely in training with British formations for mountain and arctic warfare.

INDIAN UNITS—BRITISH COMMONWEALTH OCCUPATION FORCE (JAPAN).

On joining the British and Indian Division ("Brindiv") in Japan in September, 1945, the 268th Indian Infantry Brigade* ceased to wear their war-time badge and adopted the Star of India in gold on a blue background. This badge was worn below the "Brindiv" Union Jack on the left arm, with the B.C.O.F. badge on the right.† The wearing of this Star of India badge was confined to the Brigade H.Q. and the three infantry battalions—the 5th/1st Punjab Regiment, the 1st/5th Mahratta Light Infantry and the 2nd/5th Royal Gurkha Rifles.

MILITARY ADVISER-IN-CHIEF— INDIAN STATE FORCES.

A white five-pointed star set on a background evenly divided top half light blue-grey, lower half dark blue.

---

* See 268th Indian Infantry Brigade, page 135.
† See also B.C.O.F., page 192.

INDIAN STATE FORCES

The Indian State forces played their part in the active defence of India, and most of the units adopted a distinctive formation sign in addition to their recognized badges.

COOCH BEHAR STATE FORCES.

A shield, divided into three verticle bars, red, yellow and green, the edges in black. On the red bar is a white ring, on the central yellow bar a white trident, and on the green bar a white five-pointed star.

JAIPUR STATE FORCES.

A full sun—yellow in colour—on a circular red background, was the badge of the Jaipur State Forces. The sun denotes the lineage of the ruling house of Jaipur, which claims descent from Surya Vansh, the Solar Dynasty.

BAHAWALPUR STATE FORCES.

A white pelican on a black shield, was the formation badge of the Bahawalpur State Forces, pelicans being the supporters in the coat of arms of Bahawalpur State, which is also the cap-badge of the State Forces.

THE EAST AND WEST AFRICAN FORMATIONS

EAST AFRICAN EXPEDITIONARY FORCE (E.A.E.F.).

A rhinoceros in black on a white circular background within a black circle was the badge of the H.Q. of the East African Expeditionary Force which served under South-East Asia Command in Burma with the Fourteenth Army.

WEST AFRICAN EXPEDITIONARY FORCE.

The badge of the R.W.A.F.F. (Royal West African Frontier Force) in yellow, outlined in black, set on a green circle was the distinguishing badge of the West African Expeditionary Force.

11th (AFRICAN) DIVISION.

This Division was formed in 1940 in East Africa and was composed of the 22nd (East African) and the 23rd (Nigerian) Brigades. It formed part of the force responsible for the defence of Kenya and later formed part of Lieut.-General Sir Alan Cunningham's force which advanced into Italian Somaliland and Abyssinia, in the campaign which broke the Italian armies under the Duke of Aosta. The Division took part in the operations which led to the capture of Harar and Addis Ababa and in the final rounding up of the broken Italian forces at the conclusion of the campaign. A black ace of clubs on a white square was the formation badge.

12th (AFRICAN) DIVISION.

Raised in East Africa in 1940, the Division comprised the 21st (East African); 24th (Gold Coast); and 25th (East African) Brigades. The 1st South African Brigade joined the Division for the first advance into Italian territory to El Wak in December, 1940. The formation formed part of Lieut.-General Sir Alan Cunningham's force which drove the Italians from Somaliland and advanced into Abyssinia, routing the Italians at Jelib and Wadara, breaking through the Juba line on to Hara and Addis Ababa, and taking part in the final rounding up of the scattered Italian army. A kudu in white on a square black background was the Divisional badge.

11th (EAST AFRICAN) DIVISION.

The head of a rhinoceros was the badge adopted by the 11th (East African) Division. This formation served with the Fourteenth Army in Burma, taking part in the hard jungle fighting which led to the liberation of Burma. Originally the rhino's head in brown was set on a buff oval background, but this was later changed to a black head on a red oval.

22nd (EAST AFRICAN) BRIGADE.

An elephant in white on a black circular background was the badge adopted by this brigade. It formed part of the 12th (African) Division in the conquest of Italian East Africa and Abyssinia and later served in S.E.A.C. with the Fourteenth Army.

28th (EAST AFRICAN) BRIGADE.

The panga is to the African askari what the kukri is to the Gurkha, and was carried by every man of the King's African Rifles in the 28th (East African) Brigade, so the formation adopted as their badge an upright panga, white blade and black hilt set on a red shield within a black border. The formation formed part of the Fourteenth Army in S.E.A.C., as an Independent Brigade, and the red shield was chosen to conform in colour, shape and size to that of the Fourteenth Army, so matching the Army badge which was worn on the right arm whilst the Brigade badge was worn on the left.

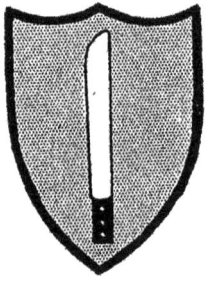

81st (WEST AFRICAN) DIVISION.

The 81st (West African) Division chose as their badge a black tarantula spider on a yellow circle. In the folklore of the West African tribes (equivalent to Aesop's Fables) it is the spider who comes out on top at the end of many of the tales. This Division, under the command of Major-General C. G. Woolner, C.B., M.C., formed part of the Fourteenth Army in the hard-fought campaign which liberated Burma. It was made up of native troops of each of the four West African colonies, was assembled in Nigeria in March, 1943, and was dispatched to India in August, 1943. One brigade was taken to form part of General Orde Wingate's Special Force and was trained in long-range penetration. In December, 1943, the Division crossed the hills into the Kaladan valley and operated on the left flank of the main advance in the Arakan, being the first large formation to be supplied wholly by air. In the following year it again advanced down the Kaladan and took part in the successful assault on Myohaung.

82nd (WEST AFRICAN) DIVISION.

Two spears, crossed on a native carrier's head band, set on a yellow shield was the distinguishing badge of the 82nd (West African) Division. It was dispatched to India in July, 1944, and served in S.E.A.C. as part of the Fourteenth Army, joining the 81st (West African) Division in the assault on Myohaung and in the victorious advance through Burma to the liberation of Mandalay and Rangoon.

COMBINED OPERATIONS
COMMANDO AND BEACH FORMATIONS

COMBINED OPERATIONS HEADQUARTERS.

This familiar badge incorporated emblems of the three Services: in red, on a dark blue circle, a naval anchor,* the tommy-gun and the R.A.F. albatross were linked in the sign symbolic of close co-operation which welded the combined forces of the three Services into the efficient organization which controlled and organized all combined operations. It was in 1940 that the need for such specially trained units became necessary, and selected independent companies were formed to carry out raids into enemy-occupied territory. These were the Special Service Troops, made up of Independent Companies, which were later designated Commandos—the name becoming a household word in consequence of their daring and spectacular exploits at the time when Britain stood alone in Europe. Raids commenced on a small scale, but under the direction of the late Admiral of the Fleet Lord Keyes, who became the first Director of Combined Operations at the newly formed Combined Operations Headquarters (C.O.H.Q.), the size, nature and scope of the Commandos' tasks were increased. Lord Keyes was succeeded in 1941 by Captain (later Admiral) Lord Louis Mountbatten, G.C.V.O., C.B., D.S.O., and the work went on. From the French coast the Commandos' activities moved to Scandinavia, and thence all over the world wherever the enemy presented a vital target in a coastal area. The Lofoten Islands, Spitzbergen, Vaagso, Maaloy, Bruneval, St. Nazaire, Crete, the Libyan coast, the Channel Islands, Diego Suarez, Arakan, Rangoon, Singapore, all saw the Commandos on their beaches coming ashore from their landing-craft under the protection of the Navy and with R.A.F. air cover. Then Dieppe, and finally the invasions of Sicily, Italy and the greatest combined operation of all time, the landings in Normandy on 6th June, 1944.

---

* The anchor is the stockless pattern actually in use instead of the conventional old style stocked anchor.

BEACH GROUPS.

The fouled anchor in red on a pale blue background within a red circle was the badge of the Beach Groups. These groups were composed of specialist units of the Army, Navy, and R.A.F. formed in a complete amphibious formation. The naval element was made up of R.N. Signals and R.N. Commandos; the R.A.F. provided a balloon barrage section for the defence of the beaches and specialists who prepared the way for the R.A.F.'s airstrips; the Army provided an infantry battalion for the seizing of the beach and the defence of the beachhead perimeter, Royal Engineer Field Companies, Mechanical Equipment Platoons, a Stores Section and Transportation units, R.A.S.C. general transport companies with DUKWs, a D.I.D. and Petrol supply unit, an R.A.M.C. unit, C.M.P. traffic control, and an R.E.M.E. Recovery Section and Pioneer Companies.

Beach groups first operated in the landings in Sicily. On 6th June, 1944, D Day, on the Normandy beaches beach-group troops landed with the assault troops and distinguished themselves in the establishment and maintenance of the beachhead.

INDIAN BEACH GROUPS.

Beach Groups which operated under South-East Asia Command wore a different badge. This took the form of a red sword and wings, and dark blue sea on a pale blue background within a red circle. These groups were also employed, in Burma, in an air supply role.

22nd BEACH BRIGADE.

This Brigade, commanded by Brigadier R. Chandler, adopted a black and white penguin on a khaki background as its formation badge. The penguin was chosen when it was decided that a flight of communication aircraft would not be included in the Brigade's order of battle—for the penguin, although amphibious, does not fly.

COMMANDO BRIGADES.

A red, unsheathed dagger, blade pointing upwards, set on a black background was the badge of the Commando Brigades.

No. 1 COMMANDO.

A green and black salamander passing through red and yellow flames, the design on an oval patch, was No. 1 Commando's badge.

No. 2 COMMANDO.

A Commando dagger in silver, hilt uppermost flanked by a silver letter "S" on each side of the hilt, on a black background.

H.Q. SPECIAL SERVICE BRIGADE.

Two silver Commando daggers set horizontally, with the hilt of each dagger in the shape of a letter "S" in red, against a black rectangular background was the S.S. Brigade's badge.

* * * * *

ROYAL MARINE FORMATIONS AND UNITS

MOBILE NAVAL BASE DEFENCE ORGANIZATION.

This Royal Marine formation's badge was circular; on it were five diagonal stripes, blue, yellow, green, red and blue, and on these a polar bear superimposed. The function of the M.N.B.D.O. was to provide the Fleet with a base in any theatre of operations, on an island or on the mainland coast, and defend it after its establishment. The M.N.B.D.O. was about 8,000 strong and composed of a H.Q. and Landing and Maintenance Group and a Land Defence Force, including Anti-Aircraft and Coast Defence Gunners. The Landing and Maintenance Group was made up of skilled technicians and was responsible for the collection and landing of stores and the construction of wharves, jetties, roadways and accommodation. Workshop and signal units were included in the organization, together with all types of administrative personnel.

The 1st M.N.B.D.O. was raised early in 1940. During the Battle of Britain its Anti-Aircraft and Searchlight Batteries were in action in A.D.G.B., whilst other units assisted in mounting and manning Coast Defence Batteries on the East and South-East Coasts.

The 1st M.N.B.D.O. embarked for the Mediterranean early in 1941 to be employed with the Fleet, and after the evacuation from Greece it was employed in providing a naval base in Crete. Only part of the force was landed and this element took part in the stubborn defence of Canea and Suda Bay against the German airborne invasion. The M.N.B.D.O. lost over 1,000 all ranks in the hard fighting and the subsequent evacuation from Crete, the Marines being among the last to leave the island; the survivors returned to Egypt, where the organization was re-formed for service in the Middle East, taking part in the defence of the Canal Zone. It later served in Syria and took part in the seaborne landings at Tobruk. In June, 1943, the formation moved to Ceylon, where it was re-formed into two brigade groups. One served in India, the other remaining in Ceylon, detachments from which served in the Maldive Islands. The anti-aircraft element of the Brigade in India later served with 33rd Corps.

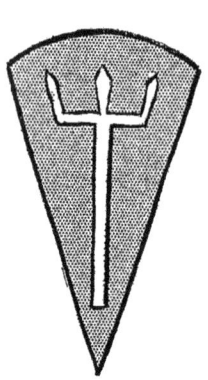

ROYAL MARINE DIVISION.

Neptune's trident in yellow, set on a scarlet background of an inverted isosceles triangle with a circular base, was the badge of the Royal Marine Division. When this formation was disbanded the badge continued to be worn by the 116th (Royal Marine) Independent Infantry Brigade.

116th (ROYAL MARINE) INFANTRY BRIGADE.

This Brigade was raised in 1945 and was composed of the 27th, 28th and 30th Battalions Royal Marines. Under the command of Brigadier C. F. Phillips, the Brigade served with 21st Army Group in North-Western Europe, going into action on the Lower Maas and later taking part in the advance into Germany to Oldenburg. The Brigade wore the badge of the former **Royal Marine Division** (*see above*).

117th (ROYAL MARINE) INFANTRY BRIGADE.

This Brigade was also formed in 1945 from Royal Marine boat crews, retrained for land service to meet the shortage of infantry. The badge adopted by the Brigade was a Naval fouled anchor in yellow on a red circle set in the centre of a yellow eight-pointed star; the design set on a khaki background. The badge was based on the Royal Marine cap-badge, *circa* 1770-75. The yellow represented the brass and the red the traditional colour of the Infantry.

AMPHIBIAN SUPPORT REGIMENT, ROYAL MARINES.

A yellow anchor, set on an inverted red equilateral triangle (with a narrow yellow edge on the two sides meeting at the apex), superimposed on a dark blue shield, was the badge borne by this Royal Marine unit, which was one of the lesser-known units which came about in the development of the technique in combined operations. The Regiment mobilized at Aldershot in February, 1945. It had been formed as a result of investigations into the Dieppe operation. The Regiment went into action on D Day in Normandy. It was moved to India later in 1945, and it would have taken part in the operations planned to take place in Malaya. The unit, however, did not see action, although it took part in a few minor operations in Java in an infantry role. In April, 1946, it returned to the United Kingdom and was attached to the School of Combined Operations in North Devon.

ROYAL MARINE SIEGE REGIMENT

A bursting grenade with red flames set on a khaki background.

ROYAL MARINE ENGINEERS.

A yellow seven-flamed grenade, set on a red fouled anchor, set on a dark blue shield.

ROYAL MARINES TRAINING CENTRE.

This R.M. Training Centre wore a distinctive badge of a yellow sea-horse set in a royal blue circle against the background of an inverted red triangle, the base of which was curved.

SPECIAL FORCES

"V" FORCE.

This force came into being during the withdrawal from Burma, and was made up of local dispersed troops—in the early days, mainly Kachins. In 1943-44 it operated in the no-man's-land on the right flank of the Tiddim Road in the almost impenetrable hills around Haka and Falam. Its primary task was intelligence and the upkeep of local morale.

When operations recommenced in 1944, after the monsoon season, "V" force operated in advance of the Lushai Brigade in the hill country between Manipur State and the Arakan. In much the same way as it grew up so did the force " fade out " as the Fourteenth Army advanced leaving behind the dense jungle-covered hills which lie between the Chindwin river and the Arakan coast.

The "V" force badge was two crossed daggers—the blades forming a "V"—a letter "V" superimposed on the hilts which rested on a scroll on which was inscribed the word "Force." The design was in white, picked out in black, set on a circular light green background.

"R" FORCE.

This was a force of mixed arms which formed part of 21st Army Group and was allotted a special operational role under the direct command of Field-Marshal Montgomery's H.Q. The badge of the force was a white capital "R" on a black shield.

FORCE 135 (Channel Islands Liberation Force).

This force, which was assembled for the liberation of the Channel Islands, wore as its badge the Arms of Jersey and Guernsey, three yellow lions set on a red shield. The three lions on a red field were part of the coat of arms of Richard I, who was also Duke of Normandy, the Channel Islands being originally incorporated in that Dukedom.

FIRST SPECIAL SERVICE FORCE.

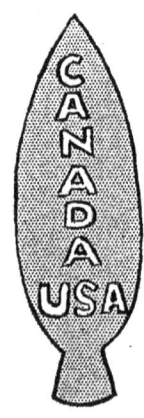

Comprised two U.S. battalions, one Canadian battalion (1st Canadian Special Service Battalion) and an S. and T. company. This force was trained in parachute, ski, beach assault, and other infantry roles, including the use of all forms of Allied and enemy small arms and M.T. All equipment, including uniforms, was American. The force, after training in U.S. and Canada, proceeded to Italy and came under command of Fifth Army in December, 1943. It served with great distinction at the first Anzio landing and subsequent fighting; and also served in the invasion of Southern France; and was then disbanded. The force never wore any badge but its own—a red arrow (or spear) head; on it, in white, the words "Canada—U.S.A."

G.R.E.F. (GENERAL RESERVE ENGINEERING FORCE).

When the withdrawal from Burma commenced in the spring of 1942, there was practically no military engineering organization or resources in Assam. Engineer units ; Military engineering services ; Public Works department staffs and Civil engineering firms' resources were rapidly collected together and played a major part in the operations. With the turn of the tide it was necessary to reorganize this Engineer Force which had been hurriedly raised in emergency, and it was decided to form an Engineer Task Force to support our forces on the north-eastern frontier of India. A headquarters was formed at Shillong in May, 1943, and the organization was designated General Reserve Engineering Force (G.R.E.F.) under the command of G.H.Q. India. In October, 1943, the force was placed under command of Fourteenth Army and moved forward into Burma.

The distinguishing badge of G.R.E.F. was a five-pointed yellow star, the letters " G.F. " in dark green, in the centre, the star set on a dark green circle.

★ ★ ★ ★ ★

THE DISTRICTS

(The Districts of the Home Commands were reorganized on several occasions and the detail of some of the badges as follows does not refer to those worn at the final reorganization.)

LONDON DISTRICT.

A mural crown in gold, with a sword in red pointing upwards through the centre, the whole set against a dark blue background, was the badge adopted by London District. The sword was taken from the Arms of the City of London and the mural crown from the crest of the London County Council.

NORTHUMBRIAN DISTRICT (Northern Command).

Formerly 9th Corps District, Northumbrian District came into existence in 1942. Its badge was the St. Oswald's shield of Northumbria, six yellow and red vertical bars set in a shield on a blue background. The shield was a copy of the badge used by the Northumberland County Council. The badge was also worn by the Northumberland Battalions of the Home Guard. The District covered at one period the counties of Northumberland and Durham and the North Riding of Yorkshire, but the latter subsequently became a separate District.

WEST RIDING DISTRICT (Northern Command).

A Golden Fleece set on a green diamond was the badge of this District of Northern Command. The fleece indicative of the wool industry associated with the area of the West and East Ridings of Yorkshire.

NORTH RIDING DISTRICT (Northern Command).

This District's area included the important training area of the Yorkshire wolds, and of Catterick. Its badge was a red cross on a white shield, above it a dark blue bar on which were superimposed three white Yorkshire roses.

NORTH MIDLAND DISTRICT (Northern Command).

The figure of Robin Hood, in Lincoln green, with brown cap feather, gloves, belt, pouch and boots, with his longbow in black, set against a light green background was the appropriate badge of North Midland District, which included Sherwood Forest within its boundaries.

EAST RIDING AND LINCS DISTRICT (Northern Command).

A golden eagle on a square black background was this District's badge, and vehicle marking. The badge was adopted from the device used by the East Riding County Council—a blue eagle on gold—before the grant of arms in 1945. The eagle was taken from the arms of the ancient kingdom of Mercia.

NORTH WALES DISTRICT*⎫
MIDLAND WEST DISTRICT⎭ (Western Command).

The Prince of Wales's feathers, in red, on a dark green circle, was the badge of North Wales District. The district was redesignated Midland West District in 1944 when part of the former West Lancashire District was absorbed into its boundaries.

SOUTH WALES DISTRICT* (Western Command).

The heraldic red dragon of Wales set on a bright green background was the national badge adopted by South Wales District.

---

* It is interesting to note that the two Welsh Districts of Western Command adopted as their badges the Divisional signs carried during the 1914-18 War by the two Welsh Divisions. During World War I, the 38th (Welsh) Division which served on the Western front adopted the Red Dragon of Wales, and the 53rd (Welsh) Division which formed part of our forces in Palestine the Prince of Wales's Feathers.

WEST LANCASHIRE DISTRICT (Western Command).

The red rose of Lancaster formed the basis and background of this District's badge. In the centre of the large rose were the emblems of the Cheshire Regiment (the acorn and oak leaf), Lancashire (the Tudor rose), and Staffordshire (the knot), these counties being within the District's boundaries. The District was disbanded in 1944 and absorbed into the adjacent Districts of Western Command.

LANCS AND BORDER DISTRICT } (Western Command).
NORTH-WESTERN DISTRICT

This District's badge also featured the red rose of Lancaster set on a dark green background within a yellow entwined circular border. The District covered the counties of Westmorland and Cumberland and part of Lancashire. In 1944 it was redesignated North-Western District and absorbed part of West Lancs District on its disbandment.

HANTS AND DORSET DISTRICT } (Southern
ALDERSHOT AND HANTS DISTRICT }   Command).

The District badge, which came into use in 1943, depicted a white winged figure of Victory, set on a saxe blue background representing sea and sky, before her the white points of the Needles. It was in this District's area that a high proportion of the D Day concentrations were assembled, and it was from the District's South Coast ports that the invasion fleet set sail in June, 1944. On the reorganization of Southern Command consequent upon the disbandment of South-Eastern Command in 1944, the area was redesignated Aldershot and Hants District and its boundaries were altered to include the former Aldershot Command, but lost the territory within the county of Dorset.

SALISBURY PLAIN DISTRICT (Southern Command).

The Great Cromlech of Stonehenge, in red, set against a yellow background and green grass base, within a black and red circle was appropriately chosen as the badge of Salisbury Plain District. The District's area originally covered the county of Wiltshire, but on the reorganization of Southern Command in 1944 took in the county of Dorset and was redesignated Wilts and Dorset District.

SOUTH-WESTERN DISTRICT (Southern Command).

This area was, until 1943, known as 8 Corps District, but was redesignated South-Western District on the withdrawal of H.Q. 8 Corps* to train for its operational role with 21st Army Group. South-Western District retained the original 8 Corps District badge—a black Francolin partridge, in flight, set upon a white oval. The District comprised the counties of Devon, Cornwall and Somerset and part of Gloucestershire.

SOUTH MIDLAND DISTRICT (Southern Command).

A yellow bell set on a dark blue background was this District's badge. The sign was chosen to associate the District H.Q. with Oxford, where it was located, the bell depicted in the badge representing "Great Tom" of Christ Church, Oxford. South Midland District's area covered the counties of Oxfordshire and Berkshire and part of Gloucestershire.

EAST KENT DISTRICT (South-Eastern Command).
HOME COUNTIES DISTRICT (Eastern Command).

A shield, on which was depicted Dover Castle above the white cliffs, was the appropriate and distinctive badge of East Kent District. The colouring of the sign was white, black, grey, and light and dark blue. The District was redesignated, in 1946, Home Counties District and formed part of Eastern Command.

---

* See also 8 Corps, page 33.

NORTH KENT AND SURREY DISTRICT (South-Eastern Command).

First style badge.

Second style badge.

The White Horse of Kent, as it appears in the cap badge of the Royal West Kent Regiment, was the badge adopted by North Kent and Surrey District. The horse was set on a green oval-shaped background within a narrow white border. This badge was adopted in 1941; previously the District's badge was a white horse's head on a green circular background within a narrow white border.

SUSSEX DISTRICT (South-Eastern Command).

The head of a black wolf, or Alsatian dog, with open mouth showing a bright red tongue, set in a pale green/blue oval within a black border, was the badge of this District, which was formed to administer the area of South-Eastern Command vacated by Canadian Corps District on its assumption of a field force role.

CANADIAN CORPS DISTRICT (South-Eastern Command).

This District, which subsequently became Sussex District, was the static District of South Eastern Command allotted to the Canadian Corps. Its badge was a Sussex martlet set on a green circle, the martlet being taken from the shield of the Arms of Sussex, which also formed the centre of the badge of the Sussex Yeomanry.

Badge taken from a vehicle marking.

2 CORPS DISTRICT
(Eastern Command).

Two seaxes, from the arms of the County of Essex, in blue, with yellow hilts set on a black shield within a yellow border was the badge of this Corps District which was located in Essex prior to the formation of Essex and Suffolk District of Eastern Command.

ESSEX AND SUFFOLK DISTRICT
EAST ANGLIAN DISTRICT } (Eastern Command).

The badge of Essex and Suffolk District was a shield divided horizontally; in the upper half a Suffolk castle on a light blue background; in the lower against a red background, the three seaxes of the arms of Essex.

On the reorganization of Eastern Command in 1944, this District ceased to exist and a newly created District designated East Anglian assumed this badge, the colours being changed to a black design on a yellow shield.

NORFOLK AND CAMBRIDGE DISTRICT
(Eastern Command).

Members of the coats of arms of East Anglian cities, set in quarters on a shield in black and white, was the badge adopted by Norfolk and Cambridge District.

CENTRAL MIDLAND DISTRICT ⎫
EAST CENTRAL DISTRICT ⎬ (Eastern Command).

The distinctive badge of Central Midland District subsequently re-designated East Central District, depicted a helmet, as worn by Cromwell's "Ironsides," superimposed on crossed cavalry swords and an upright pike, set on a red rectangular background. This design was chosen as the District boundaries included the battlefields of some of the major engagements of the Civil War.

EAST SCOTLAND DISTRICT ⎫
WEST SCOTLAND DISTRICT ⎬ (Scottish Command).

Both these Districts had similar signs, and both incorporated the same basic pattern as set by H.Q. Scottish Command—the lion rampant of Scotland in gold. In the West Scotland District badge the lion was superimposed on a white St. Andrew's cross on a red background, and in the case of East Scotland District the badge was identical but for the colour of the background, which was dark green.

NORTH HIGHLAND DISTRICT (Scottish Command).

The heraldic lion rampant of Scotland, in gold, as it appeared on the H.Q. Scottish Command badge was also the sign of North Highland District, which had its H.Q. at Inverness. The lion was superimposed on a diagonally divided background of purple and green.

NORTHERN IRELAND DISTRICT.

The initial letters of Northern Ireland District, being N.I.D., formed the word "nid," French for nest, hence the white bird in a nest lodged on two black boughs on a dark green background being adopted as the District's sign. The badge was later changed to the sign of the Irish gate, similar in design to that used by B.T.N.I.; in the case of the District badge, the gate was white and the background emerald green.

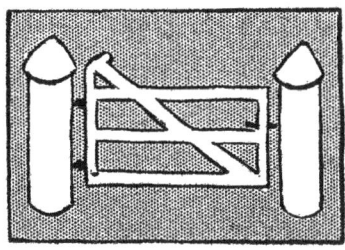

BRITISH TROOPS IN NORTHERN IRELAND (B.T.N.I.).

A typical North Irish three-barred gate between two stone posts, so familiar to the troops in Northern Ireland, was adopted as the badge of B.T.N.I. The gate was red set on a black oblong background.

ORKNEY AND SHETLAND DEFENCES.

The military garrison of the Orkneys and Shetlands, known as "Osdef," was composed mainly of Anti-Aircraft and Coast Defence Gunners and Infantry and adopted as its badge the naval fouled anchor in red on a dark blue background denoting its close association with the naval base at Scapa Flow.

OVERSEAS FORCE AND GARRISON HEADQUARTERS

MALTA FORCE.

All formations in Malta incorporated the Maltese Cross in their distinguishing badge. Command Headquarters adopted the cross in white set on an evenly divided background of Command colours, red, black, red, whilst the Malta Infantry Brigade (later the 231st Infantry Brigade) wore a white Maltese Cross on a red shield.*

FIELD DEFENCES—MALTA.

A Maltese cross, the arms each divided evenly into silver and red, the badge on a square black background was the distinguishing sign of the troops of Malta's field defences.

GIBRALTAR GARRISON.

The appropriate badge of the Fortress Headquarters was the Gibraltar "Key to the Mediterranean" which figures in the Rock's coat of arms. The badge was a yellow key, upright, on a scarlet rectangle. The R.A. units of the garrison wore this badge on a diagonally-divided background of red and blue.†

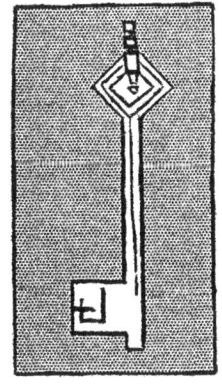

---

* See Malta Command, page 22; R.A. Units, Malta, page 217; and 231st Infantry Brigade, page 208.
† See R.A. Units, Gibraltar, page 217.

FAEROE ISLANDS FORCE.

These North Atlantic Islands were occupied by British forces in 1940 as a preventive measure against German aggression and the possible establishment of a hostile base which would threaten our sea communications. The Force H.Q. was at Thorshaven, and the original garrison was made up of the Lovat Scouts, Royal Artillery, Coast Defence and Heavy and Light A.A. Batteries, and R.E. L. of C. and Works Units.

The badge of the Faeroe Islands Force depicted a "Tjaldur" (an oyster catcher)—the national emblem of the Faeroes. The bird, in natural colours of black and white, stood on a black rock against a background of sea and sky in dark and light blue.

ICELAND FORCE.

The well-known polar bear badge of Iceland Force was originally chosen as their badge by the first brigade of the 49th (West Riding) Division to land in Iceland in May, 1940. Previous to this the 49th Division had worn the white rose of Yorkshire as their sign.* The white polar bear on the black background was subsequently adopted by the rest of the 49th Division when they disembarked in Iceland, and also by the Force H.Q. at Reykjavik and all the non-divisional British troops under command.

* See also 49th (West Riding) Division, page 62.

NEW GUINEA FORCE.

This force was formed from 2 Australian Corps* and its staff formed the operational and administrative Headquarters for all Australian troops in New Guinea. The formation was disbanded in 1944 and reformed as a Corps. Its badge was a parakeet's head above a boomerang.

DODECANESE FORCE.

A red leaping goat above three wavy blue lines set on a square white or khaki background was the badge of the Dodecanese Force which was originally designated Force 281.

H.Q. PALESTINE and TRANSJORDAN.

An Arab dagger, white blade, black hilt, on a red square background was the distinguishing badge of H.Q. Palestine and Transjordan.

---

* See also 2 Australian Corps, page 97.

H.Q. SUDAN and ERITREA.

In black silhouette on a white square background, a camel and rider, the badge of Sudan Defence Force, was adopted by H.Q. Sudan and Eritrea. This badge has been the emblem of the S.D.F. since 1924 and was taken from the design on the postage stamps of the Sudan.

H.Q. BRITISH TROOPS ADEN.

A white Arab dhow in full sail on a black square background was the badge of Aden District.

H.Q. BRITISH TROOPS IN IRAQ.

The same badge as was formerly used by "Paiforce"*—a red elephant's head with white tusks on a blue background—is worn by H.Q. British Troops in Iraq.

---

* See Persia and Iraq Command, page 22.

H.Q. LAND FORCES HONG KONG.

Established on the liberation of Hong Kong, this H.Q. has adopted as its badge a China dragon in gold set on a rectangular background of Command colours, red, black and red.

H.Q. BRITISH TROOPS IN THE LOW COUNTRIES.

Formerly H.Q. L. of C. 21st Army Group,* this Headquarters continued to wear its former badge; a dark blue cross on a yellow shield. With its Headquarters in Brussels it was the Administrative H.Q. for all British troops located in Belgium and Holland after the cessation of hostilities in North-Western Europe.

H.Q. BRITISH FORCES IN GREECE (B.F.I.G.).
H.Q. LAND FORCES, GREECE.

H.Q. 3 Corps on arrival in Greece assumed command of all British land forces in that country, the Headquarters being redesignated accordingly. The formation Headquarters continued to wear the badge of the green fig leaf on a white background, and this badge was retained when the Headquarters was later renamed British Forces in Greece.†

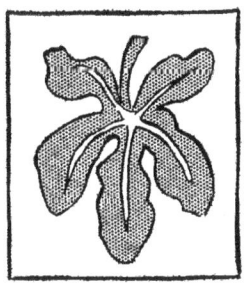

---

* See H.Q. L. of C., 21st Army Group, page 172.
† See 3 Corps, page 31.

BRITISH TROOPS IN NORWAY.

A Viking's galley with three wavy lines below to denote the sea, and on the horizon, the midnight sun, the whole design in white on a pale blue background, was the badge of British Troops in Norway. This force, which formed part of the Allied Liberation Force (American, Norwegian and British) under the direction of S.H.A.E.F., was composed of the 1st Airborne Division, commanded by Major-General R. E. Urquhart, C.B., D.S.O., the Headquarters of the 50th (Northumbrian) Division (which later became H.Q. British Land Forces, Norway), the 1st S.A.S. Brigade, commanded by Brigadier J. M. Calvert, D.S.O., the 303rd and 304th Infantry Brigades and 88 Group, R.A.F., together with L. of C. units withdrawn from 21st Army Group. The Allied force landed in Norway on the 9th May, the 1st Airborne Division going ashore at Oslo and Stavanger. The task of this force was to control, disarm and evacuate the German occupation forces, to assist Allied prisoners of war and displaced persons, and to help the Norwegian authorities in the re-establishment of their power. A composite battalion of the Guards later joined the force and replaced the Airborne units.

BRITISH TROOPS IN EGYPT.

A scarlet pyramid and two palm trees on a white background was the badge of B.T.E. (British Troops in Egypt) and was worn by H.Q. B.T.E. and troops under command stationed in the Delta, the Canal Zone, Western Desert and in Cairo and not belonging to any formation having its own distinguishing badge.

BRITISH TROOPS IN SIAM.

A native ceremonial dancer in black silhouette on a yellow background within a narrow black border was the badge adopted by our forces which occupied Siam after the defeat of the Japanese.

LAND FORCES ADRIATIC (L.F.A.).

This force, which operated in Yugoslavia and in Albania, had its base at Bari in Italy. Its primary task was to aid the partisans of Marshal Tito's forces in Bosnia and Montenegro. After a year's successful activities the force was disbanded in June, 1945. Its badge, which linked with the amphibious activities of the force, was a white winged horse—Pegasus—swimming, set on a dark blue oval background. The badge was symbolic of the airborne and amphibious activities of the force.

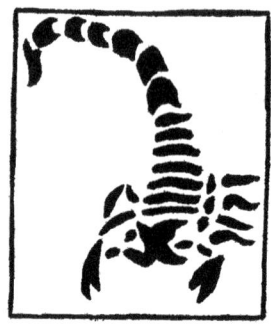

TRANSJORDAN FRONTIER FORCE.

This force wore one distinguishing badge of a black scorpion on a white background. The Transjordan Frontier Force was raised in Palestine in 1926 under the auspices of the Colonial Office. N.C.Os. and men of the Palestine Gendarmerie formed the cadre on which the force was built. The officers were British, and the men were of various nationalities—Arabs, Sudanese, Circassians and Jews.

The force was originally horsed, but was subsequently partly mechanized. With its headquarters in Zarga, the force had two main tasks—internal security and guarding the frontiers of Transjordania.

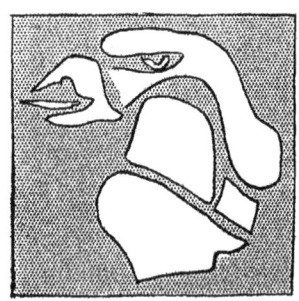

THE ARAB LEGION.

This was a Middle East force. Its badge a falcon's head in white on a red square. The badge, it was said, was chosen as falconry is a favourite Arab sport in the Desert.

The famous Arab Legion was established in Transjordan after the 1914-18 War by Major Peake Pasha, who built up this force in order to check the raiding Bedouins and to maintain Transjordan's frontiers.

Under the command of Brigadier Glubb Pasha the Arab Legion served the Allied cause during the 1939-45 War.

Among its most essential roles is that of guarding the pipeline which lies across the country by means of men operating from small forts.

OVERSEAS DISTRICTS AND L. of C. AREAS

21st ARMY GROUP (G.H.Q. and L. of C. TROOPS).

The H.Q. 21st Army Group sign, minus the crusaders' swords—*i.e.*, a blue cross on a red shield—was worn by all ranks of the 21st Army Group G.H.Q. troops and L. of C. formations and units not allotted to any lower formation which had its own distinguishing badge.

HEADQUARTERS L. of C. 21st ARMY GROUP.*

Of similar design to the 21st Army Group G.H.Q. troops badge was that of the H.Q. Lines of Communication 21st Army Group and the L. of C. and Base Sub-Area H.Qs. This was a dark blue crusader's cross on a yellow shield and was worn by all ranks, and stencilled on the vehicles of the H.Qs. of the L. of C. and certain formations and units under direct command of those Headquarters—*i.e.*, Chief Engineers (Works) and Cs.R.E. (Works), etc.

---

* See also British Troops in the Low Countries, page 168.

NETHERLANDS DISTRICT.

Originally designated West Holland District, this formation came into existence early in 1945 for service in B.L.A. as one of the Districts of 21st Army Group's L. of C. The District was formed to cover, initially, the liberated area of Holland from Walcheren and the Scheldt estuary and south of the Waal, but later assumed responsibility for the military administration and rehabilitation of the Netherlands following the German surrender in May, 1945. It was then that the District was redesignated "Netherlands" and its H.Q. was established at The Hague. The District's badge was a typical Dutch scene, a windmill, cottage, and a dyke by the banks of a canal, the design being in light blue on a white background within a blue circular border.

H.Q. L. of C. BRITISH TROOPS IN NORTH AFRICA.

Badge taken from a vehicle marking.

Originally H.Q. L. of C. First Army, this formation adopted as its sign a gazelle which appeared in the design as "Bambi" of the Walt Disney film. The gazelle was in black and white and was set on a green background. The formation was, whilst in North Africa, presented with a gazelle, which was adopted as its mascot.

TRIPOLITANIA DISTRICT.

A Barbary pirate's galley in black, set on a square background of a white sky and blue sea, was the Tripolitania District's badge. The design was taken from the emblem of the city of Tripoli, as used by the Italian Colonial authorities during their regime. This was another administrative H.Q. set up when this area was occupied after the conquest of the Italian North African colonies.

CYRENAICA DISTRICT.

Two black pillars on black pavings, representative of the ruins of ancient Carthage, set on a square white background, was Cyrenaica District's badge after its establishment as an administrative H.Q. of this conquered and occupied former Italian colony. The badge was significant of "the *parts* of Libya about Cyrene" (*Acts, ch.* 2, *verse* 10). The badge was subsequently changed, the design being in white on a black background. It was only used as a vehicle marking sign.

No. 15 AREA, M.E.F. NORTH PALESTINE DISTRICT

This Middle East administrative area had as its badge a blue dolphin on a square black background. At one period this area was designated "Northern Area" and after the war became North Palestine District.

No. 16 AREA M.E.F.

Located in the Alexandria Area, this District adopted as its badge a typical caique as used by the Egyptians. The craft was in white, on a black sea, against a dark blue sky.

No. 17 AREA M.E.F.

This Area H.Q. was located in Cairo and had as its badge a black mosque flanked by two minarets set on a white background representing the Mohammed Ali Mosque within the citadel of Cairo, which as a fortress on the Muquattan Hills dominating the city has been long associated with its military history.

No. 18 (SUEZ CANAL) AREA M.E.F.

Originally designated Canal Zone, and later Suez Canal Base Sub-Area, 18th Area, M.E.F. H.Q. adopted the appropriate badge of a yellow ground, representing the desert, across it a diagonal blue line for the canal, and on it a dhow with one white triangular sail.

CYPRUS DISTRICT.

The badge of Cyprus is two red lions "passant guardant" (taken from the Arms of Richard Cœur de Lion*) on a white background.† The two lions also formed part of the heraldic arms of the Lucignian Kings of Cyprus, *circa* 1192-1489, and the badge of Cyprus District, which forms part of the Middle East Land Forces, has been adopted from the Cyprus badge and consists of a yellow lion on a green background.

NORTH LEVANT DISTRICT.

Originally the badge of the Ninth Army.‡ A charging elephant in red, on its back a small castle carrying a flag, set on a black circular background was the badge of North Levant District.

IRAQ BASE AND L. OF C. AREA

An Arab sheathed knife in black, set on a white jagged-edged background on a dark green square, was the badge of this Base and L. of C. Area.

---

* See also Force 135, page 151.
† This badge, set on a shield, is also the badge of the Cyprus Regiment which was raised in 1940.
‡ See also Ninth Army, page 26.

No. 21 AREA, M.E.F.

This Middle East Forces area badge was made up of a white crusader's sword, point uppermost, on a black shield, superimposed on the flag of St. George—a red cross on a white background. 21 Area was located in the Lydda District, reputed to be the place where St. George was buried, hence the adoption of the St. George's cross and the crusader's sword.

No. 88 AREA M.E.F.

A red sea shell on a yellow square was the badge adopted by this Middle East Administrative Area.

No. 1 DISTRICT C.M.F.

A husky dog, white head and with red ears and tongue set on a pale green circle was the badge of No. 1 District C.M.F. Formerly H.Q. Tunisia District the formation was moved to Sicily. The code name for the move was Operation "Husky" hence the adoption, in Sicily, of the District's badge.

No. 2 DISTRICT C.M.F.

Two white columns, typical of Roman architecture, set on a black background was the vehicle marking of No. 2 District C.M.F. in Italy, whilst the District's badge depicted a horizontal dagger from which, suspended by two links, hung an anchor. The design was in black on a red background. This District at the conclusion of hostilities occupied one north-western area of Italy.

No. 3 DISTRICT C.M.F.

The District Commander, Major-General A. L. Collier, C.B.E., M.C., was formerly G.O.C. Cyrenaica District, which had as its badge two columns representative of the ruins of ancient Cyrene.* When No. 3 District C.M.F. was established, the Commander retained the architectural basis for the new badge and No. 3 District's badge became the three pillars of the Temple of Castor and Pollux in Rome, in white set on a black background, the pillars being identified with the Roman figure III and the District's number.

---

* See also Cyrenaica District, page 174.

No. 56 AREA C.M.F.

A black torch, with a red flame—similar to that in the G.H.Q., C.M.F. badge—held in a white hand, set on a buff or yellow background was the badge of this area which was used as a vehicle sign and not worn by personnel.

NORTH CARIBBEAN AREA.

The H.Q. of this area was located in Jamaica. Its badge was a sea-horse, in black picked out in white, above a red bar, set on a khaki background. This was changed to a black seahorse on a yellow background.

SOUTH CARIBBEAN AREA.

With its H.Q. in Trinidad, this area administered the British troops and auxiliary forces in the South Caribbean. Its badge was composed of two crossed swords, a rapier and a cutlass, in black, set on a yellow background within a black border.

GOLD COAST AREA.

An elephant, and a palm tree, as appear in the badge of the Colony, in white on a black circle.

NIGERIA AREA.

A crown bird in black on a white rectangular background.

GAMBIA AREA.

A native craft in full sail in white set on a black circle within a white square.

SIERRA LEONE AREA.

A lion and a palm tree in yellow on a black circle or rectangle.

★   ★   ★   ★   ★

INDIAN and S.E.A.C. DISTRICTS and L. of C. AREAS

101st (BIHAR AND ORISSA) L. of C. AREA.

A rampant unicorn in red on a yellow circular background, was the badge of this area which had its H.Q. at Jhansi.

105th (MADRAS) L. of C. AREA. MADRAS AREA.

This L. of C. Area wore as its badge a golden phœnix, with outspread wings and a red eye, rising from red flames surmounted by a red seven-pointed corona. The design was set on a square black background. Originally designated Madras District, it was, in November, 1942, renamed, for security reasons, 105 L. of C. Area. On the 1st April, 1946, it assumed the title of Madras Area. The following is an extract from Madras Area Orders dated 30th October, 1946 :—

"The mythological story of the Phœnix varies as told by different authors. The salient points of the story are, however, similar. The bird was always male, and there was never more than one alive at any one time. It died by setting its nest on fire and burning itself alive ; from the ashes another Phœnix was born. India is one of the countries in which the Phœnix is said to have lived. In July, 1942, when the question of the Area sign was being considered, the Phœnix was thought appropriate because it indicated that the Madras District was determined to rise again to renewed heights of martial vigour and achievement for which, in times of stress, the Southern Indian peoples have won fame in the past." The sign was adopted in August, 1942.

This badge was intended to represent the new warlike spirit of Madras rising from the ashes of the old Madras Army which, with the exception of the Madras Sappers and Miners, had been disbanded after the 1914-18 war.

106th L. of C. AREA.

This Area adopted as its badge two battleaxes in red, crossed, and superimposed on a white circle on a black background. The Area covered the whole of Hyderabad State and the northern part of Madras Province, including Vizagapatam.

107th L. of C. AREA.

The badge of this Area, which included the whole of Bombay Province, depicted "The Gateway of India" at Bombay (where all the Viceroys landed on first entering the country) in black and white set on a red square.

108th (BOMBAY) L. of C. AREA.

The first badge of this Area was a white swan set on a blue circular background (jokingly referred to as the "Bombay Duck") which had been the badge of Bombay Fortress Area (later designated "Bombay Defended Port Area"). When 107 L. of C. Area was disbanded, 108 L. of C. Area adopted the Gateway of India badge formerly used by 107 L. of C. Area.

109th (BANGALORE) L. of C. AREA.

A yellow palm tree on a red background.

110th (POONA) L. of C. AREA.

Two Mahratta swords crossed below a circular shield. The design in black on a red square with a black border.

202nd (ASSAM) L. of C. AREA.

A black arrow representing a Naga spear pointing upwards through a blue wavy band, representing the River Bramaputra, on a white circle within a black border and set on a khaki square.

303rd (BENGAL) L. of C. AREA.

A round of .303 ammunition, the case in yellow, the bullet in white set diagonally on a red square.

404th (EAST BENGAL) L. of C. AREA.

A white paddy-bird on a red square.

505 L. of C. DISTRICT.

This district was formed in Chittagong, in March, 1945, under the command of Major-General A. H. J. Snelling, C.B., C.B.E. At the end of the month the H.Q. flew to Shwebo and took over command of No. 551 Sub-Area at Kalewa, and later assumed command of No. 253 Sub-Area, Mandalay, and No. 553 Sub-Area at Myitkyina.

The H.Q. moved in May to Meiktila and assumed control of No. 445 Sub-Area at Magwe, and 552 Sub-Area at Myingyam.

The district's badge was composed of two strong arms holding a circle below the Roman figures " XIV," the design was in black set on a red shield of similar pattern to that of H.Q. Fourteenth Army and was linked with the District's role—the support of the Army. The two arms and the circle together formed " VOV " or " 505."

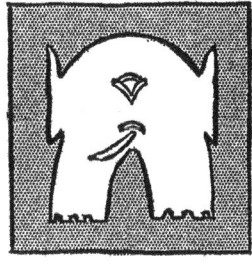

253 L. of C. SUB-AREA.*

The rear view of an elephant in white on a khaki background. 253 L. of C. Sub-Area was the base for 4 Corps. The Corps badge was a charging elephant, hence the selection of the Sub-Area badge—the base of the Corps.

---

* See 4 Corps, page 32.

254 L. of C. SUB-AREA.

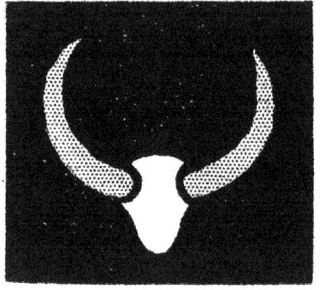

This L. of C. Sub-Area, which operated in the Fourteenth Army in the Kohima area on the Dimapur–Imphal road, bore as its sign the same buffalo's head in white with red horns set on a square blue background as was worn by the 268th Indian Infantry Brigade.

SIND DISTRICT.

A native craft in full sail in white on a maroon background.

PESHAWAR DISTRICT.

A white frontier fort on a red background. The badge represented Jamrud Fort at the entrance to the Khyber Pass.

DELHI DISTRICT.

A leopard, in black and yellow, on a red background.

RAWALPINDI DISTRICT.

A white eaglet on a square red background.

LAHORE DISTRICT.

An old pattern cannon, in black, on a red background, was the badge of Lahore District. The badge was representative of the gun Zam-Zammah which stands outside the Lahore Museum, and is referred to in Rudyard Kipling's "Kim"—"Who hold Zam Zammah, that 'fire-breathing dragon,' hold the Punjab; for the great green bronze piece is always first of the conqueror's loot."

WAZIRISTAN DISTRICT.

Two white crossed daggers on a red background.

NAGPUR DISTRICT.

A black and yellow cobra on a red square edged in black was the badge of this District, which was renamed in 1946 and became Deccan Area, the badge undergoing a slight change, the tail of the cobra being changed to yellow.

KOHAT DISTRICT.

A white dog-fish above three wavy white lines on a red background.

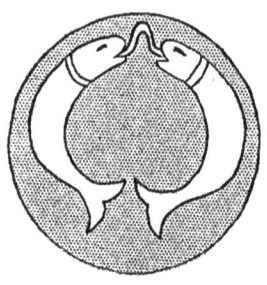

UNITED PROVINCES AREA.

Two blue-grey fish ("The Fishes of Oudh"), set on a red circular background, was the badge of the U.P. Area. Its H.Q. was in Lucknow.

BALUCHISTAN DISTRICT.

A head and horns of a gnu in white set on a red background.

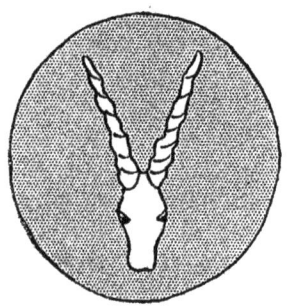

MADRAS DEFENDED PORT AREA.
MADRAS FORTRESS AREA.
(164 L. of C. Sub-Area.)

Originally designated Madras Fortress Area, later as Madras Defended Port Area, this formation wore as its badge a yellow coconut palm tree and square black background.

This badge was similar to that of the 109th (Bangalore) L. of C. Area. The Madras Defended Port Area badge differed in colour and slightly in design.

NORTH CEYLON ADMINISTRATIVE AREA.

A vertical white directional arrow set on a shield divided, upper half red, the lower dark blue, was the North Ceylon Administrative Area's badge.

COLOMBO SUB-AREA.

A square quartered patch. The top quarters red and green, the lower green and red—the L. of C. colours.

TRINCOMALEE FORTRESS AREA.

This Ceylonese Garrison adopted as its badge a head and antlers in black set on a yellow square or circular background.

H.Q. L. of C. S.E.A.C.
SOUTH BURMA DISTRICT.

A white flying stork, with red beak and legs set on a pale green rectangular background with a narrow white border, was the badge of this formation. This badge was originally designed for H.Q. L. of C. Command S.E.A.C., which was formed in October, 1944, under the command of Major-General G. W. Synes, C.B., M.C., to relieve H.Q. Fourteenth Army of the responsibility of the Lines of Communication from India up to the fighting line between Imphal and Maungdaw. One of the main functions of this H.Q. was the flying in of supplies to the Fourteenth Army, hence the adoption of the flying stork badge, although it was jokingly said that the badge was adopted as the staff were always "carrying the baby." In July, 1945, this formation was moved to Rangoon and became South Burma District and, as such, was disbanded on the 31st December, 1945.

No. 2 AREA S.E.A.C. (SINGAPORE)

Headquarters No. 2 Area was formed in S.E.A.C. in April, 1945, as a planning staff for the reoccupation of Singapore and the establishment there of an advanced base. In June, 1945, under the command of Brigadier J. A. E. Ralston, O.B.E., the formation moved from Calcutta to Kurunegala, Ceylon, where it combined with the offices of the Flag Officer (R.N.), Malaya, 77 Base R.A.F. and Civil Affairs. In August the staffs left Ceylon and No. 2 Area was established in Singapore with its headquarters in Fullerton Building in September. The area of responsibility included Singapore Island, the Dutch Riow Archipelago, and a major portion of Johore State. Towards the end of 1945 the designation was changed to Singapore District and the Johore Causeway became the northern boundary. The badge of No. 2 Area was a red figure "2" set on a black anchor on a blue circular background with a black border.

★ ★ ★ ★ ★

OCCUPATION FORCES

H.Q. BRITISH ARMY OF THE RHINE.

When H.Q. 21st Army Group was in August, 1945, redesignated H.Q. British Army of the Rhine, the H.Q. 21st Army Group badge,* two crusaders' swords in gold, set on a dark blue cross on a red shield, was retained by H.Q. B.A.O.R.

BRITISH TROOPS BERLIN (B.T.B.)*

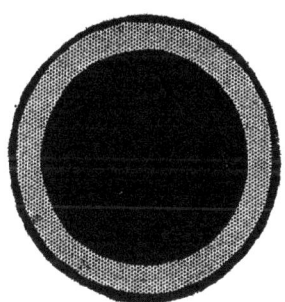

Originally designated Berlin District (and later "Area"), the designation, British Troops, Berlin, was adopted shortly after the occupation of the British Zone by the 7th Armoured Division and attached troops, for the Administrative H.Q. of the British sector. The formation badge was a black circle surrounded by a scarlet ring—symbolic of the encirclement of the black spot of Europe.

H.Q. BRITISH TROOPS IN AUSTRIA.

The Headquarters of our occupational force in Austria adopted the badge of the Eighth Army†; the golden cross set on a white shield on a dark blue background.

---

* See H.Q. 21st Army Group, page 14.
† See Eighth Army, page 25.

CONTROL COMMISSION FOR GERMANY.

The familiar blue cross on a scarlet shield of 21st Army Group was adopted as the badge of the Control Commission for Germany; the letters " C.C.G." linked, in yellow, being superimposed on the cross. This distinguishing badge is worn by all members, military and civil,* of the Control Commission for Germany and Military Government. Field-Marshal Viscount Montgomery, in his capacity as Commander-in-Chief, B.A.O.R., adopted the wearing of the Control Commission for Germany badge on his left sleeve, retaining the former 21st Army Group (now H.Q. British Army of the Rhine) badge on his right.

ALLIED CONTROL COMMISSION FOR AUSTRIA.

This Civil Affairs/Military Government formation set up for the control of Austria adopted as its badge that of the Eighth Army (and H.Q. British troops in Austria). The yellow Crusader's cross in a white shield on a dark blue background with the addition of a white scroll above the shield, upon it the letters " A.C.A." (Allied Control Austria) in blue.

---

* When in uniform. Battledress blouse and trousers were worn by civil members of the Control Commission for Germany. A green epaulette on the blouse bearing, in yellow, the words " Civilian Military Government Officer " or in black " Civilian Military Government."

BRITISH COMMONWEALTH OCCUPATION FORCE (JAPAN).

The British Commonwealth Occupation Force (Japan) was composed of "Brindiv" (British Indian Division), made up of the 5th British Infantry Brigade (ex-2nd-Division), and the 268th Indian Brigade together with the 34th Australian Infantry Brigade and the 9th New Zealand Brigade. The 5th Brigade* was composed of the 2nd Bn. The Dorsetshire Regiment, the 1st Bn. The Queen's Own Cameron Highlanders, and the 2nd Bn. The Royal Welch Fusiliers. The 268th Indian Brigade† was composed of the 5th/1st Punjab Regiment, the 1st/5th Mahratta Light Infantry, and the 2nd/5th Royal Gurkha Regiment. The Division was originally raised in September, 1945, as Force 153, later redesignated "Brindjap." It joined B.C.O.F. in Japan in March, 1946, as "Brindiv," commanded by Major-General D. Tennant Cowan, C.B., C.B.E., D.S.O., M.C., who had commanded the 17th Indian Division from 1942-45.

H.Q. B.C.O.F. Badge

The badge of H.Q. B.C.O.F. was the Imperial Crown in gold and red, set above a dark blue scroll, outlined and backed in red, on which was the legend in white "British Commonwealth Forces." The design was set on a square dark blue background. The wearing of the badge was not confined to the H.Q. staff, it was worn also by all personnel, British, Indian, Australian and New Zealand, including the R.A.F. It was worn on the right sleeve by all troops of "Brindiv" with the Divisional badge on the left.

Union Jack worn by all "Brindiv"

The divisional badge of "Brindiv" was a small Union Jack (1½ in. × 2½ in.) worn on the left sleeve above the brigade badges. All vehicles of "Brindiv" bore both the Divisional and B.C.O.F. badges.

---

* See also 5th Infantry Brigade, page 201.
† See also page 137.

THE ARMOURED AND TANK BRIGADES

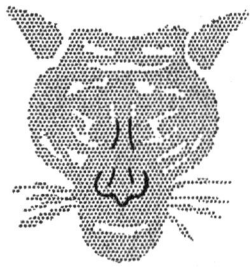

1st ARMOURED BRIGADE GROUP.

A red stencilled tiger's head, on a white background, was the distinguishing badge of this formation, which served in the Middle East.

2nd ARMOURED BRIGADE.

This Brigade continued to wear the white rhinoceros on the black oval of the 1st Armoured Division* when the Division was broken up after the break through the Gothic Line in Italy.

4th ARMOURED BRIGADE.

A jerboa (desert rat) in black on a white square background. The Brigade served in the Middle East with the Eighth Army and in North-West Europe as part of 21st Army Group.

---

* See also 1st Armoured Division, page 40.

6th GUARDS TANK BRIGADE.

The badge of this Tank Brigade was a golden sword, point uppermost, set in the centre of a white shield and superimposed on a diagonal band in Household Brigade colours—equal bars of blue, red, blue. Originally part of the Guards Armoured Division, this Brigade subsequently became an independent tank brigade in North-West Europe with 21st Army Group.

7th ARMOURED BRIGADE.

Another of the armoured formations of the M.E.F. which adopted the jerboa—the desert rat—as its badge. The 7th Armoured Brigade's rat was light green set within a red circle on a circular white background. The Brigade served in the M.E.F. as part of the 7th Armoured Division. It was withdrawn from the Desert and sent to Burma in 1942. It was here that its badge was adopted. The same desert rat as it had worn with the Division in the desert but changed to green and nicknamed the "Jungle Rat." After the withdrawal to the Arakan, the Brigade joined Paiforce. May, 1944, saw the formation in Italy where it fought at Pescara, in the operations which broke the Gothic Line and finally in the Po Valley campaign.

8th ARMOURED BRIGADE.

Of similar design to the badge of the 10th Armoured Division, a fox's mask was the badge of this Armoured Brigade, the 8th Brigade's sign being a reddish-brown fox mask on a yellow circle, with a narrow brown border. The Brigade served in the Western Desert with the Eighth Army and formed part of 21st Army Group, serving in North-West Europe and the occupation forces in Germany.

9th ARMOURED BRIGADE.

The Brigade served in the Middle East and later in Italy. With the Eighth Army at El Alamein the formation was the Armoured Brigade of the 2nd New Zealand Division. The formation badge was appropriate, for the Brigade was composed of one regular cavalry regiment (the 3rd King's Hussars) and two yeomanry cavalry regiments (the Royal Wiltshire and the Warwickshire Yeomanry). A white horse on a square or semi-circular bright green background was the Brigade's badge.

16th ARMOURED BRIGADE.

The two triangles common to most Tank Brigades feature in this badge. They were dark blue, set on a yellow circle, behind the triangles was a red devil. The Brigade served in North Africa and in Italy.

20th ARMOURED BRIGADE.

The armour-clad head of a knight's charger in white on a black square background was this Brigade's badge.

21st ARMY TANK BRIGADE.

Originally this formation wore the usual Tank Brigade "diabolo" in yellow,* but the badge subsequently adopted was a black diabolo superimposed on a vertically divided shield of Royal Armoured Corps colours of yellow and red. This formation served in Italy.

22nd ARMOURED BRIGADE.

A stag's head in red was the badge of this Brigade which served in the Western Desert with the Eighth Army taking part in the sweep into Tunisia. It later served in North-Western Europe.

* See also page 200.

23rd ARMOURED BRIGADE.

A black liver bird, in its beak an olive branch set on a white square or circular background was the badge of this Armoured Brigade, which was composed of the 40th, 46th and 50th Royal Tank Regiments, and the 11th Bn. 60th Rifles (K.R.R.C.). The badge was chosen to link the formation's association with Liverpool, where the Brigade was raised. The Brigade originally wore the badge of the 8th Armoured Division.

The Brigade saw considerable service in the Middle East and in the Mediterranean, taking part in the battle of El Alamein with 51st (Highland) Division and the advance across the Western Desert to Tunisia. The Brigade then moved to Malta and thence to Sicily and Italy, taking part in the Salerno landing—one regiment also took part in the Anzio landing. Withdrawn in 1943, to Egypt, the Brigade rejoined the Eighth Army in Italy later in the year.

The 23rd Armoured was the first formation to move to Greece, where it was engaged in the fighting following the E.L.A.S. rising. The Brigade remained in Greece until it was disbanded in May, 1946.

25th ARMOURED ENGINEER BRIGADE.

Originally designated 25th Assault Brigade R.E., this Brigade was formed, on the disbandment of the 25th Tank Brigade, early in 1945 at Viterbo, the Italian Parachute Depot just north of Rome. It was composed of the 1st Assault Regiment R.A.C./R.E. (originally the "Scorpion Regiment"), which later became 1st Armoured Engineer Regiment R.E.; the Divisional Engineers of the 1st Armoured Division, which became the 2nd Armoured Engineer Regiment;

and the 51st Royal Tank Regiment with a squadron of "Crocodiles" and two of "Flails." The Brigade was equipped on similar lines to the Armoured Engineer Brigade of the 79th Armoured Division in North-Western Europe with A.Vs. R.E. and special assault Engineer equipment.

The Brigade's badge was composed of the familiar diabolo sign of the Tank Brigades, in black, set on a red shield, divided vertically by two royal blue bars (the R.E. Colours).

27th ARMOURED BRIGADE.

A yellow and white sea-horse set on a saxe blue shield was this formation's badge. The Brigade formed part of 21st Army Group with the British Liberation Army in North-West Europe.

32nd ARMY TANK BRIGADE

A white daisy, with a pale green centre, stalk and leaf set on a black square, was the badge adopted by this Brigade, which formed part of our forces in the Middle East.

33rd ARMOURED BRIGADE.

This Brigade's badge varied from the triangular badges of other armoured formations inasmuch as the triangles were equilateral, the top triangle being green and the lower one black. The Brigade formed part of the armoured force of 21st Army Group.

35th ARMOURED BRIGADE.

Similar in design to the badge of the 33rd Armoured Brigade, the colours of the triangles of the 35th Brigade were brown at the top, and green at the bottom.

34th ARMOURED BRIGADE.

A mailed fist clenching a spiked mace in white, picked out in black, superimposed on a red shield divided diagonally by a yellow band, was the 34th Armoured Brigade's badge. The Brigade served in North-West Europe with 21st Army Group.

★ ★ ★ ★ ★

The same pattern of formation badge was adopted by the following Army Tank and Armoured Brigades. In each case the design was a diabolo or two isosceles triangles, one inverted above the other, the apices meeting. The colours of the triangles varied in each case.

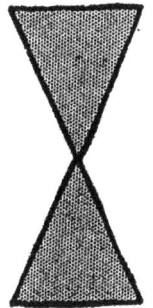

21st ARMY TANK BRIGADE.*

Colour of triangles: Yellow.

23rd ARMY TANK BRIGADE.

Colour of triangles: Green.

24th ARMY TANK BRIGADE.

Colour of triangles: Blue.

25th ARMY TANK BRIGADE.

Colour of triangles: Black. A white maple leaf was added to the centre of the upper triangle to commemorate this Brigade's service with the 1st Canadian Infantry Division in Italy. This Brigade was disbanded early in 1945, part of it being incorporated into the then newly-raised 25th Assault Brigade R.E. (later the 25th Armoured Engineer Brigade). The black diabolo of the Brigade's sign being included in the badge of the new formation.†

31st INDEPENDENT ARMOURED BRIGADE.

Colour of triangles—pale green.

36th TANK BRIGADE.

Colour of triangles: Red (top), black (bottom).

---

* See also page 196.
† See 25th Armoured Engineer Brigade, page 197.

INDEPENDENT INFANTRY BRIGADES AND BRIGADE GROUPS

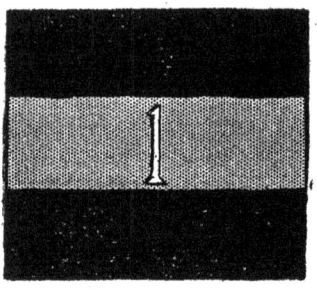

1st INDEPENDENT GUARDS BRIGADE GROUP.

A white figure "1," set in the centre of an oblong divided horizontally into three bands, blue, red and blue.

5th INFANTRY BRIGADE.

Originally forming part of the 2nd Division and composed of the 2nd Dorsets, 1st Camerons and (from 1940-1945), the 7th Worcesters. This Brigade retained the 2nd Division's badge when it joined B.C.O.F. (Japan), with the 2nd Royal Welch Fusiliers, who had replaced the Worcesters in 1945.

When the Dorsets were ordered to take over public duties in Tokio in June, 1946, they were instructed to wear the B.C.O.F. sign as they were the B.C.O.F. Guard Battalion for the time being. This led to the fashion of the two brigades of "Brindiv" wearing three formation badges—the B.C.O.F. badge on the right arm, the Union Jack of "Brindiv" on the left arm, with their brigade badge below the "Brindiv" badge.

24th INDEPENDENT GUARDS BRIGADE GROUP.

An heraldic pinion in red, set on a dark blue background.

29th INDEPENDENT BRIGADE GROUP.

A plain white ring set on a khaki or black background. The white ring was, it was said, intended to be the "O" of General Oliver Leese's name, for he was the first commander of the formation. The Brigade took part in the operations in Madagascar in April, 1942. Moving later to India, it subsequently formed part of the 36th Division with the 72nd Brigade. The 72nd's badge was a red circle in a black background, and this, linked with the white circle of the 29th, became the Divisional badge.*

31st INDEPENDENT BRIGADE GROUP.

An heraldic bull in red rising from a crown, on a dark blue background.

32nd INDEPENDENT GUARDS BRIGADE.

An eight-pointed star, composed of eight diamonds, four red and four blue in alternate colours. This was the badge of the Brigade which subsequently formed part of the Guards Armoured Division.

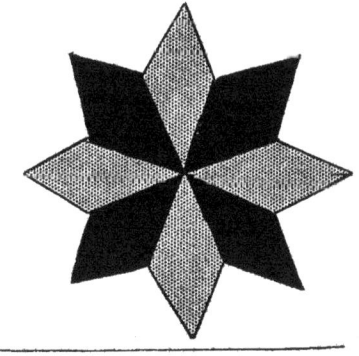

---

* See 36th Division, page 55.

33rd GUARDS BRIGADE.

A sword bayonet point uppermost, set on a rectangle divided horizontally into three bands of the Household Brigade colours, blue, red, and blue.

36th INDEPENDENT INFANTRY BRIGADE.

A Kentish cob nut with green shell and yellow nut on a khaki background. This Brigade formed part of the 12th Division* in the B.E.F., where it saw hard fighting following the German breakthrough to the Channel Ports. Cut off from the Division, the Brigade served for a time with the 23rd and 50th Divisions and with "Petreforce." Coming into contact with a German armoured formation near Albert, it was heavily engaged and but few survivors eventually returned to England. Reorganized in U.K., the Brigade later saw service in North Africa with the First Army.

37th INDEPENDENT BRIGADE GROUP.

A black clock face on a grey background, the hands pointing to seven minutes past three, 0307 hours, a link-up of the Brigade number, " 37." The background of the badge, the grey diamond, was chosen to link the formation with the badge of 12th Division* of which it originally formed part in the B.E.F.

38th INFANTRY BRIGADE.

Composed of Irish Regiments, this formation of the 78th Division wore a Brigade flash of a cut-out green shamrock.

---

* See 12th Division, page 52.

56th INDEPENDENT INFANTRY BRIGADE.

A yellow sphinx set on a black circle within a yellow square. The 56th was one of the independent brigades of 21st Army Group, landing in Normandy on D Day. The Brigade subsequently served with First Canadian Army and the 49th and 59th Divisions and formed part of B.A.O.R.

61st INDEPENDENT INFANTRY BRIGADE.

Composed of the 2nd, 7th and 10th Battalions of the Rifle Brigade, this Brigade, which served in the C.M.F., wore a black and white stringed rifle bugle, surmounted by a crown, and with the figures "95"—the Rifle Brigade's former Regimental Number, superimposed on the bugle cords. The design set on a square divided diagonally into the Rifle Brigade colours of green and black.

70th INDEPENDENT INFANTRY BRIGADE.

A capstan-like design with seven "bars" in red, set on a green circle on a square black background. Green is the Regimental Colour of the Durham Light Infantry—two battalions of which formed part of the Brigade, and red that of the Tyneside Scottish, the Brigade's third Battalion (originally a battalion of the D.L.I.).

71st INDEPENDENT INFANTRY BRIGADE.

The red and white roses of Lancashire and Yorkshire, set on a black oblong background was chosen as the Brigade's badge as it was composed of the 7th Bn. The King's Own Royal Regiment (Lancaster) and the 8th and 9th Bns. The York and Lancaster Regiment.

72nd INDEPENDENT INFANTRY BRIGADE.

A six-pointed white star on a square red background.

73rd INDEPENDENT INFANTRY BRIGADE.

This Independent Infantry Brigade wore the badge of the Devon and Cornwall County Division.* The Arms of Cornwall, fifteen gold bezants on a black shield with a gold border, superimposed on the sword Excalibur, white blade, yellow hilt, set on a dark blue rectangular background.

115th INDEPENDENT INFANTRY BRIGADE.

Two unsheathed crossed swords in black on a scarlet shield. This Brigade formed part of 21st Army Group.

---

* See page 84.

148th INDEPENDENT INFANTRY BRIGADE.

The letters "NM" in black and joined together, set on a khaki background was this brigade's badge. Allotted a training role, the formation subsequently became the pre-O.C.T.U. training establishment, located in South-Eastern Command.

162nd INDEPENDENT INFANTRY BRIGADE.

This Brigade retained the badge of the 54th (East Anglian) Division,* its parent formation, when it became one of the Independent Brigade Groups of 21st Army Group.

204th INDEPENDENT INFANTRY BRIGADE.

A pyramid, composed of three inner triangles incorporating the colours of the regimental facings of the three battalions of the Brigade within a blue border. Grey (7th Bn. Leicestershire Regiment). Salmon buff (7th Bn. South Lancashire Regiment). Green (12th Bn. Sherwood Foresters).

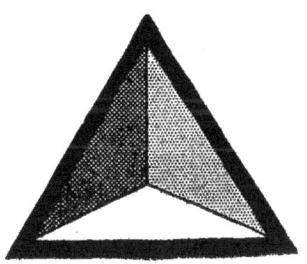

206th INDEPENDENT INFANTRY BRIGADE.

A chessman, the king, in black on a red background.

* See also 54th (East Anglian) Division, page 66.

212th INDEPENDENT INFANTRY BRIGADE.

A red tulip with a green stem and leaf set on a white rectangular background. Originally the badge of the Lincolnshire County Division* this badge was subsequently adopted by the 212th Infantry Brigade.

214th INDEPENDENT INFANTRY BRIGADE.

A Viking's winged helmet in red on a blue background.

218th INDEPENDENT INFANTRY BRIGADE.

A yellow torch, with a red flame, set on a black diamond background.

---

* See Lincolnshire County Division, page 85.

219th INDEPENDENT INFANTRY BRIGADE.

A white phœnix, rising from red flames, in its beak a white torch with red flame, set on a dark blue background within a white circle.

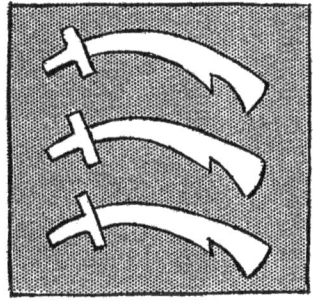

223rd INDEPENDENT INFANTRY BRIGADE.

The three seaxes of the arms of the county of Essex in blue set on a red square background, the same badge as worn by the Essex County Division.*

231st INDEPENDENT INFANTRY BRIGADE.

A white Maltese cross on a scarlet shield was this formation's badge. The Brigade had several titles, and was known at different times as the Malta Infantry Brigade, the Southern Infantry Brigade, 1st (Malta) Infantry Brigade, 231st Infantry Brigade, and finally the 231 (Malta) Independent Brigade Group. It was made up of the three Regular battalions which formed part of the garrison of "George Cross Island" : the 2nd Bn. The Devonshire Regiment, the 1st Bn. The Hampshire Regiment, and the 1st Bn. The Dorsetshire

---

* See page 84.

Regiment. It was pure coincidence that these happened to be three South-West England county regiments from adjoining counties. This Brigade stood ready to oppose any attempts at an Italian invasion during the long months when the island was in a stage of siege, withstanding the combined air attacks of the Italians and the Luftwaffe, during the ordeal of constant bombing and famine. The successes in North Africa of the First and Eighth Armies raised the siege of Malta, and in April, 1943, the Brigade was withdrawn from Malta to Egypt, where it underwent special training and became an Independent Brigade Group. The Brigade took part in the invasion of Sicily and saw much hard fighting from the beaches across the island to the Straits of Messina. The Brigade also took part in the landings on the toe of Italy on the Pizzo beaches and in the left hook attack up the coast of Italy. Joining 50th (Northumbrian) Division, the Brigade returned to U.K. in 1943. In June the following year the formations made their third assault landing, in Normandy, on D Day, and took part in the operations in N.W. Europe until the end of 1944.

301st INFANTRY BRIGADE.

Two crossed cannons, and a cannonball in dark blue on a square red background. The Brigade was made up of converted Coast Artillery Units, hence the choice of the cannon to associate the formation with its R.A. origin, the red background being the traditional infantry colour, and the red and the blue also being the R.A. colours.

303rd INFANTRY BRIGADE.

A white hart's head on a divided background, top half red, the lower blue. The hart's head was taken from the Arms of the Borough of Eastbourne, associating the Brigade's connections with the town. The Brigade, under the command of Brigadier H. G. Smith, C.B., O.B.E., M.C., T.D., formed part of the British force which participated in the liberation of Norway in May, 1945.

304th INDEPENDENT INFANTRY BRIGADE.

This Brigade was composed of three infantry battalions which had been converted from Searchlight Regiments R.A. Its badge was designed to represent three searchlight beams, which were in red on a blue background. This formation, commanded by Brigadier F. W. Saunders, D.S.O., formed part of the Allied Land Forces, Norway, and took part in the liberation of that country in May, 1945.

JEWISH BRIGADE GROUP.

This Brigade Group was formed in Palestine and saw service in Italy and in North-Western Europe. Its badge was the yellow star of David set on a rectangular background divided vertically into three bands, two light blue and a central white band.

★ ★ ★ ★ ★

MISCELLANEOUS BADGES

G.H.Q. LIAISON REGIMENT.

The " P " of this badge stood for " Phantom " the code name of the G.H.Q. Liaison Regiment of 21st Army Group. This unit had a special role in keeping G.H.Q. in touch with every development in operations.

" The Phantoms " operated in the forward areas, patrols moving in armoured vehicles, and radioing information to G.H.Q. about allied troops movements and general battle progress. The Regiment was recognized as the " eyes and ears of the Commanding General." By VE Day the G.H.Q. Liaison Regiment totalled about 150 officers and 2,000 men.

ARMY FILM AND PHOTOGRAPHIC SERVICE.

Army Film and Photographic Units wore the appropriate badge of a camera, in white, flanked by the initial letters " A.F.P.U." in red, set against a black background. This service was established under the control of the Director of Public Relations at the War Office, and sections served in all overseas theatres, whilst an Army Film and Photographic Centre was formed in U.K.

The overseas sections were composed of operational cameramen, developers, camera mechanics and administrative personnel. The sections were responsible for filming the battle sequences from which the Home Centre made the films " Desert Victory," " Tunisian Victory," " True Glory," " Burma Victory," and many other official documentary films.

INDIAN FIELD BROADCASTING UNITS.

Indian Field Broadcasting Units were formed by the "I" Branch of G.H.Q. Fourteenth Army in February, 1943, and before the monsoon of that year the first experimental I.F.B.U. had seen service in the Arakan. The experiment was successful and during the operations in 1943-44 five I.F.B.Us. were employed on the Fourteenth Army front.

I.F.B.Us. were propaganda units and were employed against enemy and inhabitants of Enemy Occupied Territories. During their short existence they met with considerable success, and on three occasions during the Jap attack on the Imphal Plain (April—July, 1944) they were successful in making the Japs show the white flag.

The badge was a deer's head in yellow with black eyes and outlines set on a dark blue circular background.

BRITISH MILITARY HEADQUARTERS IN THE BALKANS.

The head of a phœnix in blue, bearing in its beak the torch of liberty, rising from red flames. The design, on a white oval background, was also used by the staff of the Allied Liaison H.Q. in Greece, Albania and Yugoslavia.

POLITICAL WARFARE EXECUTIVE, M.E.F.

The special badge of this branch of G.H.Q., M.E.F., was a peewit in black and white set on a light blue diamond background with a red border. The peewit being a play on the abbreviation P.W.E. This organization was an offshoot of the Political Intelligence Department of the Foreign Office and was responsible for propaganda in the field by radio, leaflets, etc.

★ ★ ★ ★ ★

Royal Artillery Badges

NEWFOUNDLAND UNITS R.A.

These units wore as their distinguishing badge the head of a caribou, in gold, set on a red oval background.

ANTI-AIRCRAFT AND COAST DEFENCE UNITS R.A (C.M.F.).

During the operations in Italy, it was decided that a special badge should be given to the A.A. and Coast Regiments R.A. of the C.M.F. The badge chosen was two white capital letters "AA," conjoined, set on an evenly divided background of red and blue, the Gunner colours.

COAST ARTILLERY UNITS.

A muzzle-loading gun and a stack of cannon balls in black on a circular background divided in red and blue was the badge of the Coastal Artillery Fire Commands, Regiments and Batteries. This badge was used as a vehicle marking.

First Pattern Badge

MARITIME ANTI-AIRCRAFT ARTILLERY.

The Maritime A.A. Gunners wore a red fouled anchor with a white rope, set on a black square background. Originally the letters " AA " (Anti-Aircraft) in white appeared one either side of the anchor, but these were subsequently changed to " R.A." (Royal Artillery). The Maritime A.A. Artillery came into being in 1941, being formed from the Light A.A. Defence of Coastal Shipping organization which had been set up in 1940, and from volunteers of Anti-Aircraft Command. The Maritime A.A. Artillery consisted of gun crews, each a separate unit, allotted to the Royal Naval D.E.M.S. (Defensively Equipped Merchant Shipping) organization. The gun crews served in troopships, tankers, and Merchant Navy craft of all types, and were armed with 40-mm. Bofors guns or, in the case of smaller coastal craft, with Bren and Lewis light automatics. The crews formed part of Home-based Maritime Anti-Aircraft Regiments and Batteries at Liverpool, London, Glasgow, Leith, Newcastle, Cardiff and other U.K. ports, and also at Cape Town, Alexandria, Halifax (Nova Scotia), Madras, Bombay, Colombo, and other naval stations around the "seven seas." The Maritime A.A. gunners set up a fine record during the Battle of the Atlantic and in the dogged maintenance of our convoy routes around the world.

Second Pattern Badge

1 CORPS ARTILLERY.*

The white spearhead badge of 1 Corps was worn by the Corps Artillery set on a diamond-shaped background of Gunner colours, red and dark blue.

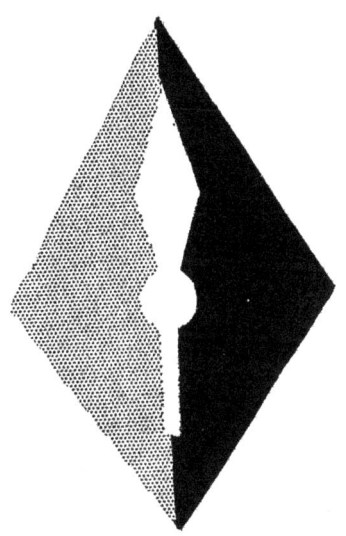

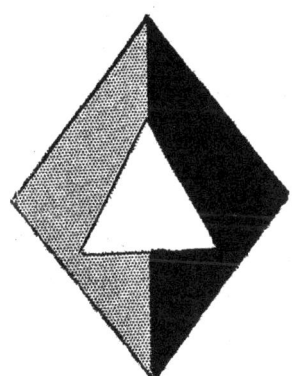

1st DIVISION R.A.†

The white triangle badge of 1st Division was worn by the Divisional Artillery set on a diamond patch vertically divided into Gunner colours of red and royal blue.

6th ARMY GROUP R.A.

This A.G.R.A. was one of the few that adopted a badge of its own—the majority of Army Group formations wore the badge of the higher command. The 6th A.G.R.A., commanded by Brigadier J. St. C. Holbrook, C.B.E., M.C., however, wore the sixth

* See also 1 Corps, page 30.
† See also 1st Division, page 46.

sign of the Zodiac in silver on a black background. White paint, instead of silver, was used for vehicle markings. The badge was worn on the left shoulder, with the Eighth Army badge on the right.

This A.G.R.A. was raised in Egypt in April, 1943. It took part in the Sicily landing and saw much hard fighting in the campaign in Italy.

H.Q. R.A. AND MOBILE ARTILLERY, MALTA.*

A dark blue Maltese cross with red edges—the R.A. colours—set on a square black background was the badge of the Royal Artillery H.Q. in Malta, and was also worn by the mobile artillery units under command.

HEAVY A.A. BRIGADE R.A. MALTA.*

The Heavy A.A. Brigade of Malta's A.A. Defences wore a Maltese cross divided into dark blue and gold set on a black square.

R.A. UNITS, GIBRALTAR GARRISON

The R.A. Units of Gibraltar Garrison wore the yellow key badge of the Garrison H.Q.,† set in a rectangular background divided diagonally into the Gunner colours of red and royal blue. A.A. units wore the plain red background with a yellow letter "A" on either side of the key.

---

* See also Malta, page 164.
† See Gibraltar Garrison, page 164.

Royal Engineer Badges

R.E. DEPOT.

The R.E. Depot was moved in 1941 from Chatham to Halifax, Yorks, where it occupied the pre-war Regimental Depot of the Duke of Wellington's Regiment. The permanent staff of the R.E. Depot wore below the shoulder title the Sapper red and royal blue flash set on a dark blue background, edged with red.

TRANSPORTATION TRAINING CENTRE R.E.

The Royal Engineers' Transportation Training Centre at Longmoor, Hants, adopted as its badge the cross-section of a railway line. This was in royal blue on a red background, with a narrow royal blue border, the R.E. colours.

TUNNELLING COMPANIES R.E.

The Tunnelling Companies of the Royal Engineers wore a distinctive shoulder badge in addition to any formation sign. It was a plain red letter "T." Tunnelling Companies were employed in the B.E.F. in 1939-40, and in U.K. and M.E.F., but their main work was in Gibraltar where they were engaged in the improvement and expansion of the defences of "The Rock."

CHEMICAL WARFARE GROUPS R.E.

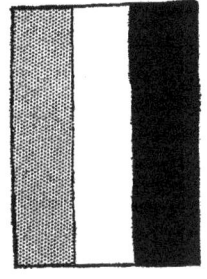

These Groups, each comprising a Headquarters and three C.W. Companies, were raised in 1939 and 1940 and wore a distinguishing flash below the shoulder titles, a rectangle evenly divided into three vertical strips of green, yellow and red.

AIRFIELD CONSTRUCTION GROUPS.

The Airfield Construction Groups were composed of Royal Engineer Road Construction Companies and Pioneer Corps Companies. Their circular badge, divided into three segments, incorporated their colours: the red and blue of the Sappers, and the red and green of the Pioneers. The white or pale blue geometrical design set in the centre of the badge was representative of the airstrips they constructed. Their task was that of rapid airfield construction for fighter strips in the forward areas.

8th G.H.Q. TROOPS ENGINEERS.

Formed in 1940, as 8th Chemical Warfare Group R.E., this formation was converted into G.H.Q. Troops Engineers in 1943 and formed part of the Beach Group which established the Normandy Beachhead on D Day, 6th June, 1944. This formation wore the badge of the Beach Groups, the fouled anchor in red on a pale blue background within a red circle, and continued to wear it when later it assumed a normal G.H.Q. Troops role in 21st Army Group and later in B.A.O.R.

1st CORPS TROOPS ENGINEERS.

The white spearhead badge of 1 Corps* was worn by the Corps Troops Engineers on a background of R.E. colours, red and blue set diagonally on a diamond shaped background.

8th ARMY TROOPS ENGINEERS.

Originally the Edinburgh Fortress Engineers, a First Line T.A. Unit, and converted to Corps Troops Engineers in 1940, the formation became the Eighth Army Troops Engineers whilst in the M.E.F. The Unit had its own badge which was worn in North Africa and in Italy, and finally by the unit's two representatives in the Victory Parade in London.

The central badge was that of the original Submarine Miners, formerly a branch of the R.E. before it became a Royal Naval unit. The Edinburgh Fortress R.E. were formed as a volunteer unit from a former Submarine Miner Company.

The badge was in red, set on a background of R.E. colours, red and blue. When the design was chosen, instructions issued laid down that all Scottish units should have a tartan background. Not having a tartan of its own, the unit selected a portion of the Mackenzie tartan, which although predominantly green, has a dark blue background and stripes of both red and white. The background to the old Submarine Miner badge was therefore chosen and that portion of the tartan which has two red stripes on a blue background. This linked with the R.E. Corps Colours and the tartan of the C.R.E. at the time—Lieut. Colonel W. H. Mackenzie, M.B.E., T.D.

---

* See 1 Corps, page 30.

42nd ARMOURED ENGINEER REGIMENT.

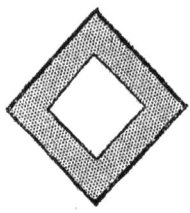

Originally the Divisional Engineers of the 42nd (East Lancashire) Division, and subsequently the 42nd Armoured Division, this Regiment converted into an Assault Regiment, R.E. (later redesignated Armoured Engineers), retaining the 42nd Divisional badge, a small white diamond within a red diamond. The Regiment served in North-West Europe with the Armoured Engineer Brigade of the 79th Armoured Division.

MADRAS SAPPERS AND MINERS.

The head of a Madrassi Sapper in black silhouette on a grey background within a black circle was the badge adopted by the Madras Sapper and Miner groups.

* * * * *

Royal Signals Badges

AIR FORMATION SIGNALS.

White wings set on a dark blue triangle within a white border was the distinguishing sign of the Air Formation Signals. The vehicle marking was, however, a black aeroplane silhouette set on a background of the Royal Signals colours of white and blue. Some units wore their number in the centre of the triangle.

INDIAN AIR FORMATION SIGNALS.

A scarlet five-pointed star and an aeroplane set on a diamond shaped patch which was divided vertically into the Royal Signals colours of blue and white, was the badge adopted by the Indian Air Formation Signals with the Fourteenth Army.

1st DIVISIONAL SIGNALS.

The Royal Signals units of the 1st Division wore a dark blue diamond, with the Divisional badge, a white equilateral triangle in the upper half,* thereby incorporating the Divisional sign with the Royal Signals colours of dark blue and white.

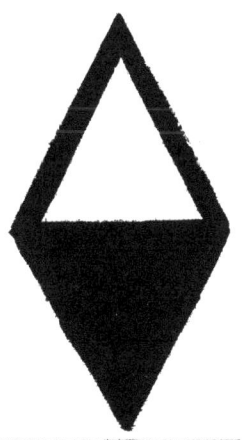

---

* See 1st Division, page 46.

Royal Armoured Corps Badges

R.A.C. TRAINING CENTRE B.A.O.R.

A tank in white, similar to that in the badge of the R.T.R. (Royal Tank Regiment) set in the centre of crossed lances, also in white, emblematic of the cavalry regiments now incorporated in the Royal Armoured Corps, the design superimposed on the blue crusader's cross on the red shield badge of the 21st Army Group G.H.Q. and L. of C. troops was the badge adopted by the Royal Armoured Corps Training Centre of the Rhine Army.

No. 1 ARMOURED REPLACEMENT GROUP C.M.F.

This Group was composed of R.A.C. Forward Delivery Squadrons and supplied A.F.Vs. and personnel to all armoured formations under British Command in Italy. The sign of this group was the head of Mars, in black, a tank blown from his (white) tongue. The design on a divided background of R.A.C. colours—top yellow, and lower half red.

Royal Army Service Corps Badges

AIR DESPATCH GROUP, R.A.S.C.

A yellow aircraft, a Dakota, on a royal blue square was the badge of this R.A.S.C. organization which was first formed in April, 1944, and held in readiness to carry out maintenance by air for any formation that might be cut off during the invasion of the Continent. By July of that year, it had expanded to a strength of over 5,000 and was responsible for air supply and maintenance of all formations including airborne and S.A.S.

The task of the Air Despatch Group, R.A.S.C. was twofold: (*a*) Maintenance by Air and (*b*) Supply by Air. The first task involved a large number of men trained as "Air Despatchers" flying in aircraft of Transport Command, R.A.F., and dropping ammunition, petrol and supplies by parachute, the second task involved the transport of supplies to airfields and loading those which were to land on the Continent.

The Air Despatch Group carried out maintenance by air in the operations in North-Western Europe and dropped supplies to our troops in the Falaise Gap; at Arnhem; and on Walcheren, when troops were cut off owing to weather conditions which made sea communication impossible.

WAR DEPARTMENT FLEET.

The W.D. Fleet is an R.A.S.C. organization composed of Water Transport Companies, Motor Boat Companies, and Boat Stores Depots (for the provision of Marine Stores to the Army). The Motor Boat Companies were divided into Harbour, Ambulance and Fast

Launch Companies and also Oil Barge, Coaster, Floating Workshops, and Fire Boat Companies. The R.A.S.C. Ensign of the W.D. Fleet is a Blue Ensign, on it the crossed swords of the Army badge, and was worn as the shoulder badge of the R.A.S.C. personnel of the Army's own fleet which saw service in Iceland; in the expedition to Spitzbergen; in West and North Africa, the Middle East, the Far East and North-West Europe.

H.Q. PACK TRANSPORT GROUP, C.M.F.

Formed in North Africa as the administrative H.Q. for the Pack Transport Companies raised in Algeria and Tunisia. This unit adopted as their badge, two white horse-shoes on a black background —of similar design to the Divisional sign of the 2nd Cavalry Division of the 1914-18 War.

This Pack Transport Group served in the North African and Sicilian Campaigns and also in Italy.

R.A.S.C. UNIT BADGES

The R.A.S.C. made a feature of unit badges. These, however, were used primarily as vehicle marking signs, and were not worn by the personnel, who wore their Army, Corps, Divisional, Brigade or L. of C. formation badges.

The value of the unit-distinguishing badges on vehicles was proved at times when forward and maintenance routes were packed with convoys; at the same time they fostered an *esprit de corps* among the many varied companies and units of the R.A.S.C.—from the General Transport Columns to the D.I.Ds. The choice of the signs gave ample scope to the ingenuity of designers—unlike the approved formation badge there was a touch of informality, and opportunity for the humorous artist, in the selection of the unit vehicle marking. Some units adhered to formality and heraldic design and association with the formation badge; others made a point of linking their sign with their function, *i.e.*, the predominance of the horse-shoe in the signs of the Pack Transport Companies, and the jerricans of the Petrol Depots and Filling Centres, whilst a third category specialized in the lighter vein, with adoptions of Walt Disney's characters and other animals and figures which became their mascots.

The following are but a few examples of the many R.A.S.C. unit signs which were seen on mudguards and tailboards of the lorries which drove by; in dust; rain or snow; through desert, jungle, mountains, and the rubble of the battlefields, on the forward routes to Victory.

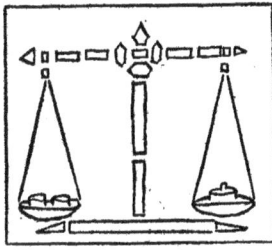

No. 14 C.R.A.S.C.

This unit served in the Middle East and later in Italy at Salerno, under the Command of 10 Corps, and on the Italian L. of C. The unit sign, emblematic of the "Balanced Ration," was a pair of evenly balanced scales.

840 GENERAL TRANSPORT COMPANY.

This unit served with the C.M.F. The unit sign "The Toddler" was selected owing to the youth of personnel on its arrival in Italy.

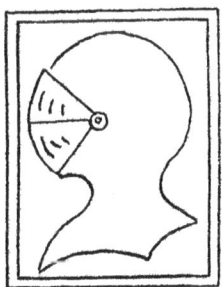

No. 277 ARMOURED DIVISIONAL TRANSPORT COMPANY.

This unit served in Tunisia with the 6th Armoured Division and adopted as its sign the knight's helmet which linked up with the Divisional badge of the mailed fist. The unit subsequently served in Italy.

No. 236 BRIDGE COMPANY.

A representation of Tower Bridge was appropriately chosen as this unit's sign. The company served in Paiforce, the Middle East, and in Italy, where it transported bridging equipment for the assault crossings of the Reno, Senio, Po and Adige rivers.

No. 534 TANK TRANSPORTER COMPANY.

The unit sign was emblematic of its role and depicted the wings of Mercury bearing aloft a tank—signifying speed of delivery of armour into battle. The unit served in North Africa and in Italy.

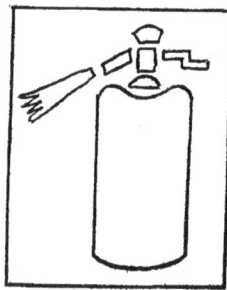

No. 558 WATER TANK COMPANY.

A soda water siphon—quick delivery of water—was the sign chosen by this company which served in the Western Desert and in Italy with the Eighth Army.

No. 234 PETROL DEPOT.

The familiar "jerrican" was the unit sign of this Petrol Depot which took part in the Sicily landing under command of the 1st Canadian Division and later served throughout the campaign in Italy.

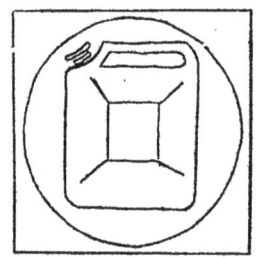

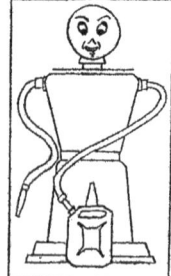

No. 9 MILITARY PETROL FILLING CENTRE.

This unit which served in Tunisia with the First Army and in Italy with the Eighth Army, chose the appropriate sign of a robot-like petrol pump in the act of filling a "jerrican."

No. 36 DETAIL ISSUE DEPOT.

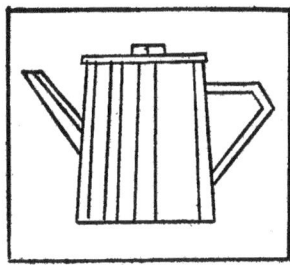

The D.I.D. was one of the R.A.S.C. units of the B.E.F. in France, 1939-40. It next saw service in the M.E.F. and formed part of 10 Corps in the Western Desert. The unit went ashore at Salerno on D Day and continued to serve with 10 Corps through the Italian campaign.

The appropriate unit sign was a teapot, to indicate one of the commodities supplied by the D.I.D.

No. 25 FIELD BAKERY.

This unit served in the Middle East, in the Western Desert and in Italy. The unit sign was the " cheerful baker."

★ ★ ★ ★ ★

Training Establishments and Administrative Units

BRITISH REINFORCEMENT TRAINING CENTRE (INDIA).

A white bulldog (the British Bulldog), set on a yellow star (the Star of India) on a red square background, was the badge of the organization set up for the training of British reinforcements in India.

ROYAL ARMOURED CORPS DEPOT (INDIA).

A black letter "D" on a square equally divided vertically, right half yellow, left half red, the Royal Armoured Corps colours.

B.A.O.R. TRAINING CENTRE.

The Rhine Army Training Centre, located at Paderborn in Westphalia, adopted as its badge the badge of 21st Army Group G.H.Q. and L. of C. troops, with the addition of the torch of learning (as used as a road sign in U.K. to denote a school) in yellow set on the vertical of the blue Crusader's cross on a red shield.

SPECIAL TRAINING CENTRE, LOCHAILORT.

A golden eagle on a black and white quartered shield set on a black background.

G.H.Q. 2nd ECHELON C.M.F.

Two rows of red rectangles set in echelon diagonally on a blue background was the badge of G.H.Q. 2nd Echelon C.M.F.

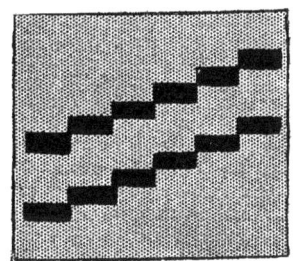

163rd INFANTRY O.C.T.U. (Artists Rifles).

This O.C.T.U. was formed in 1939 from the Artists Rifles, which had, in 1937, become an officer-producing unit of the Territorial Army. The Artists Rifles were raised in 1860 as the 38th Middlesex (Artists) Rifle Volunteers. In 1907 the Regiment was redesignated the 28th Bn. County of London Regiment (Artists Rifles), and during the 1914-18 war served in France and Flanders with the 47th (London) and 63rd (Royal Naval) Divisions. From formation the Artists wore the cap-badge designed by Wyon, Queen Victoria's Medallist, of the heads of Mars and Minerva, and the badge was retained by this O.C.T.U., the design being in white on a green background.

HOME GUARD UNITS

All Home Guard units wore the shoulder title—HOME GUARD —in yellow on a khaki background, and below this a khaki patch bearing distinguishing black letters to denote their county, *e.g.*, LON (London); BHM (Birmingham); BRX (Berkshire); EL (East Lancs); LEI (Leicester); WAR (Warwickshire); KT (Kent); SY (Surrey), etc., and below this the battalion number in black figures on khaki.

Few units of the Home Guard adopted any distinctive badges. There were, however, four exceptions: the Lincolnshire battalions, and the 8th, 9th and 10th Battalions of the Cornwall Home Guard.

In addition to these, the Home Guard A.A. units, which operated in Anti-Aircraft Command, manning Heavy A.A. Searchlight and Rocket Batteries, wore the distinguishing Anti-Aircraft Command badge, whilst the Northumberland battalions wore the badge of the Northumbrian District.

LINCOLNSHIRE HOME GUARD

The Lincoln Imp, in lincoln green, picked out in brown and set on a brown background, was the distinctive badge of the Lincolnshire Home Guard units.

8th BN. CORNWALL HOME GUARD

This was the battalion recruited in the Lizard area of Cornwall, which appropriately adopted as its badge a green lizard with black markings set on a black rectangle.

9th BN. CORNWALL HOME GUARD

This Battalion wore an adaptation of the shield of the arms of the Duchy of Cornwall (which is fifteen gold bezants on a black shield with a gold border). In the Home Guard badge the shield was outlined in white, the bezants in white and with a white figure "9" superimposed. The whole design set on a bright green background.

12th BN. CORNWALL HOME GUARD

Raised in the Land's End area of the Duchy, this Battalion adopted a badge which depicted in black the rugged coast and the Land's End lighthouse. This design was set on a scarlet background within a black border.

★ ★ ★ ★ ★

AMERICAN FORMATIONS

The wearing of formation badges was also adopted by the American Army. Coloured patches and badges were introduced in the American Expeditionary Force on the Western Front in 1918* and were reintroduced when the United States forces mobilized in 1941. Designated, in 1918, as "Shoulder Patches" and "Divisional Insignia," the official designation "Shoulder Sleeve Insignia" was subsequently adopted in the late war. Many of the badges of the U.S. formations became familiar in the U.K. with the arrival of the American forces. Over two hundred different "Shoulder Insignia" were adopted by the U.S. Army between 1941 and 1946. The following badges are, therefore, but a few of those which distinguished the American forces which saw action in the hard-fought battles in the Pacific, in North Africa, Italy, France and Germany. The majority of the badges now described belonged to formations which served in the U.K., or fought alongside British troops in North Africa, the Mediterranean and in North-Western Europe.

EUROPEAN THEATRE OF OPERATIONS.

An oval badge with a dark blue background; on it a fork of red lightning, picked out in yellow, pointing downwards, breaking a chain symbolic of occupied Europe, on the lightning the dark blue five-pointed star on a white background of the Army Service Forces. This was the insignia of the Administrative H.Q. of the American Forces in the U.K.— E.T.O.U.S.A. (European Theatre of Operations United States Army).

PERSIAN GULF SERVICE COMMAND.

The badge of the H.Q. of the U.S. forces in the Persian Gulf area which had as its primary task the movement of lease-lend supplies to Russia, was a red Arab dagger outlined in white, and a white seven-pointed star set on a light green shield with a dark green border.

---

* The first "shoulder patch" was approved for the 81st U.S. Division in October, 1918.

U.S. ARMY FORCES IN THE MIDDLE EAST.

On a background shaped like the entrance to a mosque, a white-five-pointed star on red, above two white and two blue wavy bands. This was the distinguishing shoulder insignia of the personnel of the United States Forces in the Middle East.

12th ARMY GROUP.

Composed of the First, Third and Ninth U.S. Armies, this formation served in the European Theatre of Operations—France and Germany. Its insignia was diamond-shaped, with the top point of the diamond squared off; within a black border the colouring was red and blue divided by a white band.

FIRST AMERICAN ARMY.

A black letter " A " on an olive drab background was the insignia of the First American Army which fought in Normandy, liberated Paris and was the first U.S. Army to cross the Rhine.

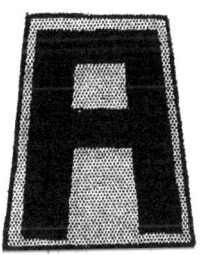

THIRD AMERICAN ARMY.

A white letter " A " within a red circle set on a blue circular background was the badge of the Third American Army which served in North-Western Europe, exploiting the break out of the Normandy beach-head and fighting through France and into Germany.

FIFTH AMERICAN ARMY.

A dark blue Moorish archway on a red background, the letter " A " and the figure " 5 " in white superimposed on the blue, was the 5th American Army's insignia. The 5th served in North Africa : it landed at Salerno, was the first formation to enter Rome when it fell to the Allies ; and as part of the 15th Army Group took part in the final operations in Northern Italy, ending in the German capitulation.

NINTH AMERICAN ARMY.

A white letter " A " surrounded by a white clover leaf design set on a red nonagonal background was the 9th Army's shoulder insignia. This formation landed in Normandy in June, 1944, captured Brest, after the break out of the beachhead, broke through the Siegfried Line to Aachen ; fought through the Northern Ruhr and advanced to the Elbe in the final stages of the campaign in North-West Europe.

XVIII AIRBORNE CORPS.

A blue dragon's head on white within a blue border was the badge of this Airborne Corps which landed in Normandy on D Day and later took part in the Airborne operations in the crossing of the Rhine.

17th AIRBORNE DIVISION.

A yellow eagle's claw on a black circular background, above the circle the word "Airborne" in yellow on a black background distinguished the 17th American Airborne Division, which saw action in the Ardennes and took part in the Airborne operations in the Rhine crossing.

82nd AIRBORNE DIVISION.

The white letters "A.A." in a dark blue circle on a red square surmounted by the word "Airborne" in white on a blue background was the badge of the 82nd U.S. Airborne Division which saw action in Sicily, Italy, in Normandy on D Day, at Nijmegen, and in the Ardennes.

101st AIRBORNE DIVISION.

Known as the "Screaming Eagle" Division. This formation badge was well known in England, where the Division was trained. It took part in the air invasion of Normandy and later won fame in its stubborn defence of Bastogne in the Ardennes. The Division insignia was an eagle's head in white with a yellow beak set on a black shield, above it the word "Airborne" in yellow on a black background.

1st DIVISION.

A red figure "1" on an olive drab shield-shaped background was the insignia of the 1st American Division which served in Algeria; Tunisia; in the invasion of Sicily; went ashore on "Omaha Beach" in Normandy on D_j Day; took part in the hard fighting in the Ardennes and in the advance into Germany.

2nd DIVISION.

Known as the "Indian Head" Division from its insignia, the head of a Red Indian with feathered head-dress set on a white five-pointed star on a black shield; this division served in England before taking part in the invasion of Normandy. The formation took part in the hard fighting in Normandy, in Brittany, in the "Battle of the Bulge" in the Ardennes, and the drive into Germany.

3rd DIVISION.

The 3rd U.S. Division insignia was a square evenly divided by dark blue and white diagonals. The Division took part in the invasion of Sicily and the hard fighting in the Salerno beach-head and at the crossing of the Volturno. It formed part of the force which landed in the South of France, driving northwards to Strassbourg and Colmar and deep into Germany, being the first U.S. troops to reach Munich and Berchtesgaden.

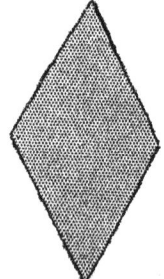

5th DIVISION.

A red diamond was the insignia of the 5th American Division. The formation served in Northern Ireland and took part in the invasion of North-Western Europe. The Division was present at hard fought battles in the Ardennes in January, 1945. It was part of the American force which liberated Luxembourg and then drove on into Germany.

28th DIVISION.

Known as the "Keystone" Division, the 28th Division wore as their insignia a red patch shaped like a key-stone. The Division served in Normandy, took part in the liberation of Paris and in the hard fighting in the Ardennes and in the Colmar pocket.

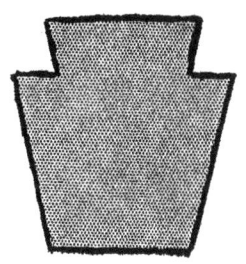

29th DIVISION.

This Division wore as its badge a circular design of dark blue and grey, the colours of the Union and Confederate armies. The formation took part in the D Day landings in Normandy and in the advance into Germany, seeing hard fighting at Aachen and in the Ruhr.

34th DIVISION.

This formation was known from its insignia as the "Red Bull" Division, its badge was a red bull's head on a black background. The Division served in Tunisia and in Italy, at Salerno, the Volturno, at Cassino and Anzio and in the final campaign in the Po Valley.

42nd DIVISION.

Known as the "Rainbow" Division, its insignia was a rainbow-shaped badge of red, yellow and blue. The Division served in North-West Europe and took part in the advance into Germany.

238

45th DIVISION.

Known as the "Thunderbird" Division from its badge, a yellow bird on a red background, this division served in Sicily and Italy, in the invasion of Southern France and the advance northwards into Germany.

66th DIVISION.

The black panther on a yellow circle within a red circle, the formation insignia, gave it the name of the "Black Panther" Division, which served in France, in Normandy and at Lorient and St. Nazaire.

75th DIVISION.

A blue "7" and a red "5" on a diagonally divided background of red, white and blue, was the 75th American Infantry Division insignia. The Division saw action in the "Battle of the Bulge" and in the drive into Germany.

85th DIVISION.

This formation was known as the "Custer Division" and its insignia was the letters "CD" in red on an olive drab circular. The Division served in Italy with the 15th Army Group, taking part in the liberation of Rome and in the Po Valley campaign.

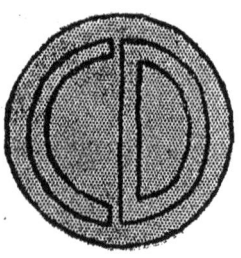

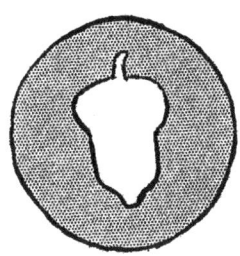

87th DIVISION.

A yellow acorn on a green circle was the insignia of the 87th Infantry Division which served in the Ardennes and in Germany.

THE AMERICAN ARMOURED DIVISIONS.

There were fourteen U.S. Armoured Divisions, each wearing the same shoulder insignia, a triangle evenly divided into three portions of yellow (at the top) and blue and red (at the base); superimposed on this background was a black tank, across it a flash of red lightning. The number of the Division was superimposed in black on the yellow portion of the badge. The insignia illustrated above is that of the 2nd ("Hell on Wheels") American Armoured Division which served in Tunisia, Sicily, Italy, Normandy, Belgium and Germany.

TANK DESTROYER UNITS.

These units were attached to all American Armoured and Infantry Divisions. Their distinctive insignia depicted a black panther crushing in its jaws a tank. The design was in black, red and white on a yellow circle with a black border.

ARMY SERVICE FORCES.

This badge was worn by the administrative personnel which provided the services and supplies for all U.S. Army units. It was a dark blue five-pointed star on a white background within a red scalloped border.

U.S. ARMY AIR FORCES

The insignia illustrated above was the Headquarters badge of the American Army Air Forces, a white five-pointed star, a red circle in the centre, and two golden wings, the design set on a blue circular background. This insignia formed the basis for all other U.S. Army Air Force badges.

EIGHTH U.S. AIR FORCE.

A golden "8," the white five-pointed star with central red circle, and golden wings set on a blue circular background was the insignia of the Eighth Air Force which was located in England, taking part in the bomber offensive against Germany and occupied Europe.

NINTH U.S. AIR FORCE.

Also stationed in England. The distinguishing insignia of the 9th Air Force was a red "9" on a golden circle below the white five-pointed star with central red circle flanked with white wings. The design was on a blue shield.

★ ★ ★ ★ ★

ALLIED CONTINGENTS AND FORMATIONS

Formation badges were also adopted by the Allied contingents which were raised and equipped in England and the Empire. The following are but a few of the many badges adopted by the Belgians, Free French Forces, Dutch, Czechoslovak, Greek, and Polish formations which served under British command during the operations which culminated in the liberation of their homelands.

Belgian Formations

1st INDEPENDENT BELGIAN BRIGADE GROUP.

This formation formed part of 21st Army Group and took part in the landings in Normandy and the liberation of its own homeland. The formation was raised, trained and equipped in the U.K.; its badge was a lion's head in yellow, set on a red inverted triangle with a black centre. The Belgian title of this formation was the *Brigade Piron*.

2nd INDEPENDENT BELGIAN BRIGADE GROUP.

The Belgian lion rampant in gold above a green shamrock* superimposed on a red letter "Y" within a black shield was this formation's badge.

4th BELGIAN INFANTRY BRIGADE.

A black shield; on it a yellow grenade picked out in black, a black letter "S" in the centre; in the right hand corner of the shield a small triangle equally divided into blue and red; in the left hand corner a small green shamrock.* This was the badge of the 4th (Steentraete) Infantry Brigade.

5th BELGIAN INFANTRY BRIGADE.

A dark green shield; on it a narrow inner border of yellow; two chevrons in yellow conjoined in the centre; superimposed on the lower part of the chevrons a white hunting bugle from which was suspended a green shamrock.* This badge was worn by the 5th (Merckem) Infantry Brigade.

---

* The shamrock appearing in these Belgian Army Badges links the formations with Northern Ireland where they were raised and trained.

6th BELGIAN INFANTRY BRIGADE.

The badge of the 6th (Deynze) Infantry Brigade may well be described as a truly allied badge. It was composed of a white shield with a red border. Within the shield was the rampant lion of Flanders in yellow, the white spearhead on a scarlet diamond of 1 Corps*; the badge of First Canadian Army, a horizontal diamond in red equally divided by a central dark blue band, and a green shamrock. This was one of the Belgian formations which served in Holland and Germany with the Canadian Army and with 1 Corps.

BELGIAN CONGO BRIGADE.

The yellow five-pointed star of the Congo, set on a square cobalt blue background, was the badge of the Belgian Colonial formation.

BELGIAN ARMY INFANTRY SCHOOL.

The badge of the Belgian Army Infantry School at Tervueren, near Brussels, was a red triangle— on it was the Belgian crown in yellow above two crossed rifles in black, set above a yellow rising sun.

* See 1 Corps, page 30.

Czechoslovakia

CZECH INDEPENDENT ARMOURED BRIGADE GROUP.

Formed and trained in England, this Czech formation took part in the operations in North-West Europe as part of 21st Army Group, landing in Normandy in June, 1944. It was the Czech Brigade which surrounded and held the German pocket of resistance at Dunkirk when the Nazi garrison was isolated by the swift coastal advance of the Canadian Army. The formation's badge was a red cross on a pale blue shield, with the white lion rampant of Bohemia superimposed on the cross.

★ ★ ★ ★ ★

France

FREE FRENCH FORCES.

A red cross of Lorraine, on a blue background, was the badge of the Free French Forces which fought alongside their British Allies in North Africa, in Libya at Bir Hakim, and in the invasion of North-West Europe and the liberation of France itself.

1st FRENCH ARMY.

The badge worn by all members of the First French Army, who fought in the operations in Germany and Austria, from the Rhine to the Danube, was a shield divided vertically into red and green, with a yellow mace superimposed thereon. At the base of the shield pale and dark blue wavy lines, to indicate the two rivers, Rhine and Danube, which appear in yellow letters on the dark blue background.

1st DIVISION.

The badge of the 1st Division of the French Army (1944-46) was a yellow shield, a black lion rampant thereon with red eye, tongue and claws.

4th MOROCCAN DIVISION.

This French Colonial formation, 4ème Division Marocaine de Montagne, was trained and equipped as a Mountain Division. Its badge (1943-46) was a double Moroccan Star in green on a red square.

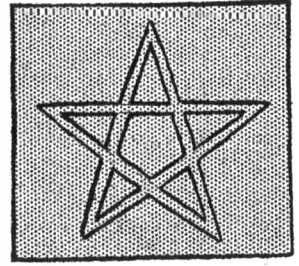

Greece

1st GREEK INDEPENDENT BRIGADE.
The head of Athena, in white, set on a blue circular background, was adopted by this Greek formation in the Middle East.

2nd GREEK INDEPENDENT BRIGADE.
The badge of this Brigade was identical with that of the 1st Greek Brigade except that it was set on a diamond-shaped background.

3rd (GREEK) MOUNTAIN BRIGADE.
The same badge was worn by this Brigade, but on a square background. The Brigade was formed and fought in Italy. It was known as the "Rimini Brigade" in commemoration of the part it played in the attack on that town.

★ ★ ★ ★ ★

The Netherlands

ROYAL NETHERLANDS BRIGADE.
The Royal Netherlands Brigade (Princess Irene's) wore as their badge the royal lion of the House of Orange above a scroll, on it the

word "NEDERLAND." This Brigade formed part of the Allied contingents of 21st Army Group and took part in the liberation of Holland. This badge was also worn by all Netherlands troops, in addition to other formation badges. When the Royal Netherlands Army was re-formed in Holland, the inscription "NEDERLAND" was replaced by the motto of the House of Orange, "JE MAINTIENDRAI."

1st NETHERLANDS DIVISION.

A white sword with yellow hilt set in the centre of a wreath of green leaves, the hilt flanked with the letters "E" and "M" in white, the whole design on a scarlet shield is the badge of the 1st Netherlands Division. The letters "E" and "M" stand for "Expeditionair Macht" (Expeditionary Force).

2nd NETHERLANDS DIVISION.

First Badge of Division   *Second Badge*

A shield divided vertically into five bars, red at the edges and in the centre, and two yellow between the red was the distinguishing badge of the Netherlands 2nd Division when it was raised in 1946. The badge was subsequently changed, the Division adopting a green palm tree on a dark blue shield—the coat of arms of Jan Pieterszoon Coen, one of the first Governors-General of the Netherlands East Indies (1617-1629).

ROYAL NETHERLANDS ARMY (GARRISON TROOPS) (OVERSEAS).

The distinguishing badge of the independent battalions and garrison troops serving in Java, Sumatra and other islands of the Netherlands East Indies was a dark green shield with a white sword flanked by the letters " BT " (Bewakings Troepen—Garrison Troops)—in red, with a spray of green leaves on either side of the hilt of the sword.

ROYAL NETHERLANDS ARMY (GARRISON TROOPS) (HOLLAND)

Garrison troops in Holland wore as a distinguishing badge a white archer, standing between two white frontier posts set on a red shield.

* * * * *

Polish Formations

H.Q. POLISH ARMIES IN THE MIDDLE EAST.

A grey mermaid with shield and upraised sword set on a red background was the badge of the Headquarters of the Polish Forces in the Middle East. This badge was based on the device of the arms of the City of Warsaw.*

POLISH L. of C. UNITS.

Three linked circles in black set on a rectangular background evenly divided, top half white and lower half red.

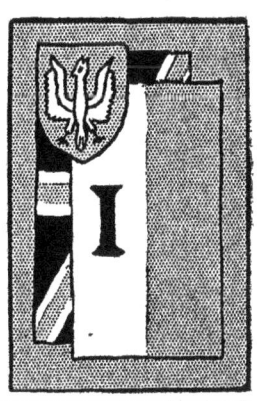

1st POLISH CORPS.

The red and white flag of Poland superimposed on the Union Jack, the figure "I" in black on the white half of the Polish flag and a red shield with a Polish eagle thereon superimposed on the corner of both flags. The badge was set on a khaki background.

---

* See also 2 Polish Corps, page 251.

2 POLISH CORPS.

The "Sirena" or Mermaid of the Arms of the City of Warsaw, in white, on a red shield with a white border was the badge of General Anders' 2nd Polish Corps which formed part of the Allied armies in the Middle East and in Italy.

This badge was, and still is, worn by a number of Household Cavalrymen. During the war, the Household Cavalry was formed into two regiments, the 1st and 2nd Household Cavalry Regiments, each having an equal complement of the Life Guards and Royal Horse Guards. The 1st Regiment served in the Middle East and in Italy. In July and August, 1944, the Regiment was placed under command of 2 Polish Corps, forming part of a Polish Armoured Car Brigade. In recognition of their services in action with this formation, General Anders gave permission for all serving members of the 1st Household Cavalry Regiment to wear the badge of the 2 Polish Corps. This did not apply to the members of the 2nd Household Cavalry Regiment, at that time serving with the Guards Armoured Division in Normandy and the badge is therefore only seen worn by a limited number of the Life Guards and The Blues. The badge is worn on the lower half of the battledress sleeve, above the cuff. This position had no particular significance, but in any other position it would have created difficulties with placing it among the regiment's own formation badge, shoulder titles, and N.C.O. chevrons.

POLISH ARMY CORPS.

A winged wheel in white on a black background.

1st POLISH ARMOURED DIVISION.

Raised, trained and equipped in Scotland, this formation formed part of 21st Army Group and took part in the invasion of Europe, landing in Normandy and taking part in the hard fighting which established the bridgehead. This badge, in black set on a yellow circle on a khaki rectangular background represented the helmet and falcon wings of the Polish cavalry which, under the leadership of King John Sobeike, defended Vienna against the Turks.

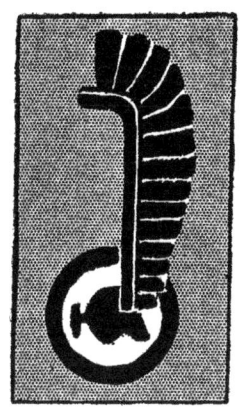

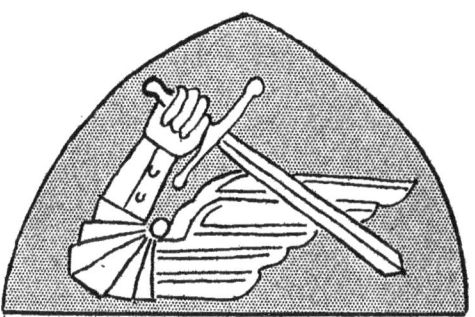

2nd POLISH ARMOURED DIVISION.

A mailed arm and hand grasping a raised sword with the traditional wings of the Polish Cavalry rising from the shoulder. This design was in black and white on a Gothic-window-shaped red background. This Division formed part of the 2 Polish Corps in Italy.

4th POLISH (GRENADIER) ARMOURED DIVISION.

A black and white grenade with red and white flames set on a khaki background.

3rd CARPATHIAN DIVISION.

This Division was raised at Qastina in Palestine in May, 1942. The formation joined the Eighth Army in Italy in 1942, taking part in the crossing of the Sangro, and the operations at Cassino, on the Adriatic coast, in the Apennines and at Bologna. The Divisional badge was a green fir tree on an equally divided background; top half white, and lower half red.

5th (KRESOWA) INFANTRY DIVISION.

Raised in Iraq in November, 1942, the Division trained in Paiforce and in Palestine. It landed in Italy in February, 1944, and formed part of the Eighth Army in the Italian campaign. A brown bison on a yellow shield with a brown border was the Division's badge. The bison was chosen as this beast lived in reservations in the Bialowieza Forest, on the Polish eastern border.

7th POLISH DIVISION.

A red griffin on a white background was the badge of this formation. The griffin was taken from the arms of the Province of Pomurce.

POLISH PARACHUTE BRIGADE.

A white diving eagle set on an azure blue background. Symbolic of the role of the Brigade.

6th (LWOW) POLISH INFANTRY BRIGADE.

A Polish lion rampant in white set on a shield, divided diagonally into red and blue. In the lion's fore-paws is a wheel within which is a mailed arm and upraised sword. This Brigade formed part of the 5th Polish Division and served with the 2 Polish Corps in Italy.

7th POLISH INFANTRY BRIGADE.

A red Polish griffin rampant with yellow beak set on a white shield within a blue border.

2nd POLISH ARMY TANK BRIGADE.

Of similar design to the badge of the 6th (LWOW) Polish Infantry Brigade. This badge had a square background and the colouring either side of the diagonal division varied. The top division was blue and the lower red.

2nd POLISH ARMOURED BRIGADE.

This Brigade retained the sign of the Armoured Corps of the pre-war Polish Army. An inverted isosceles triangle divided vertically into black and orange.

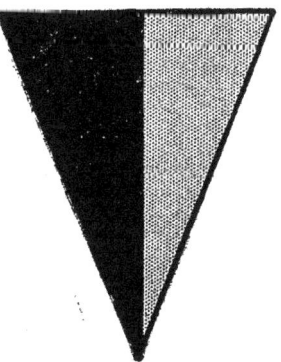

16th POLISH ARMOURED BRIGADE.

A black dragon, picked out in white and set on an orange oval, was this distinctive badge of this armoured formation.

* * * * *

Yugoslavia

ROYAL YUGOSLAV FORCES.

Yugoslav troops serving in the Middle East wore as a distinguishing badge the double-headed eagle of Serbia in white set on a royal blue shield.

* * * * *

Italian Formations

During the latter stages of the operations in the Italian campaign, Italian troops served with the Allied Armies under command of the 15th Army Group. Three Groups, the equivalent formations of Divisions, formed part of the Eighth Army. These were designated: The Cremona Group (under the command of 5 Corps), the Friuli Group (10 Corps), and the Folgore Group (13 Corps). These groups took part in the break out of the Apennines into the Po Valley; the liberation of Bologna; and the advance into Northern Italy which led to the German capitulation.

The Friuli Group

The Cremona Group

The Italian formations all wore as their badge a patch in the colours of the Italian flag, green, white and red, in each case a different emblem in bright blue set in the centre of the white portion. The Cremona Group an ear of wheat, the Friuli Group a castle gateway, and the Folgore Group a lightning flash. Other Groups serving with the Allied Armies included the Piceno Group a Roman arch, and Legnano Group (the representation of a statue from that in one of the main squares of the town from which the group took its name).

The Folgore Group

TYPES OF BADGES

THE EMBROIDERED BADGE, often privately purchased.

(1) 3rd Indian Division (The Chindits); (2) 1st Anti-Aircraft Division; (3) 55th (West Lancashire) Division.

THE "HOME-MADE" BADGE, made up under local arrangements when Ordnance issues were not immediately available.

(4) 50th (Northumbrian) Division, a hand-made badge worn in North Africa; (5) 7th Armoured Division, another hand-made badge of white canvas with an orange painted design; (6) The Eighth Army, a badge actually worn in the invasion of Sicily and made by a unit tailor.

THE PRINTED BADGE (the Ordnance issue).

(7) 22nd Beach Brigade; (8) 8th Indian Division; (9) Faeroe Islands Force.

The positioning of the formation badge on the battledress sleeve, that of a Lieutenant-Colonel of the Royal Engineers on the Headquarters Staff of 21st Army Group. The formation badge is worn below the shoulder title and above the arm of service stripe.

The badge of 30 Corps in use at a Corps Welfare Installation near Nienburg in Germany (1946).

The badge of 30 Corps, the boar, perpetuated outside the Corps Headquarters at Nienburg in Hanover. This statue was unveiled in December, 1945, by Lieut.-General Sir Brian Horrocks, the Corps Commander. The boar rests on a stone base on which are depicted the badges of the formations which composed the Corps. When the Corps H.Q. closed down in Nienburg, the statue was removed to Luneburg, where it stands today in a garden outside the British barracks.

The 30 Corps badge in use near Hanover, as a route directional sign.

[*Photo by Lieut.-Col. A. E. C. Bredin, D.S.O., M.C., The Dorsetshire Regiment.*]

The badge of the 50th (Northumbrian) Division in use as a directional sign. A scene from the Normandy beachhead. "40" was the serial number of the formation headquarters.

The formation badge of the 53rd (Welsh) Division as used as a vehicle marking on the left-hand wing of a staff car. The white "50" on the right-hand wing was set on a blue square denoting a vehicle of H.Q. R.E. 53 Division.

[*Crown Copyright Reserved.*

A truck of the 4th Bn. The Wiltshire Regiment in Valkenswaard (seven miles over the Dutch frontier), with the 43rd Division's Wessex Wyvern badge on the left-hand wing; the battalion vehicle marking, a white "56" on a dull red square, on the right wing; and on the bonnet the white five-pointed star within a white circle, the universal allied vehicle marking in North-West Europe.

[*Crown copyright reserved*

The formation badge as a directional sign. A scene from the Western Desert. Military police working in a "Sign Shop" painting directional signs of Tenth Corps. The signs, manufactured from the sides of petrol tins, were placed every two hundred yards along the desert tracks in the Corps area to enable drivers to keep to the route.

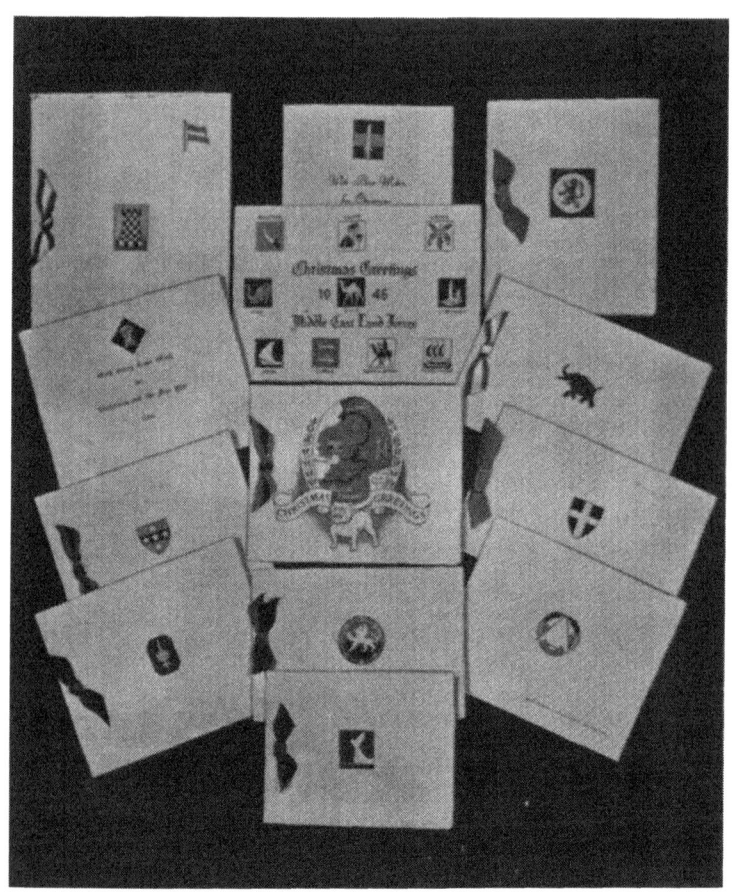

FORMATION BADGES USED ON GREETING CARDS

Regimental Christmas Cards gave way to some extent during the War to Brigade, Division, Corps and Command Greeting Cards, as such were not always confined to the personnel of the H.Q. concerned. Illustrated above are cards from Headquarters 11 Corps; 6th Armoured Division; Southern Command (U.K.); London District; 33rd Guards Brigade; G.H.Q., M.E.L.F.; H.Q. Eastern Command (U.K.); G.H.Q. Home Forces; Aldershot and Hants District; H.Q. 15th (Scottish) Division; 4 Corps; 38th (Welsh) Division and the 1st Infantry Division.

H.Q. 11 Corps' Card included a reproduction of the Corps H.Q. Flag, red, white, and red. G.H.Q. M.E.L.F. incorporated in their 1946 Christmas Card the badges of the Districts under command. H.Q. Eastern Command's 1946 Greeting Card depicted their Bulldog Badge and a map of the Command. H.Q. 1st Division added to their white triangle a portion of a laurel wreath, and scroll, on which was inscribed the motto *Primus Inter Pares* (First Among Equals).

A unique Christmas Card, produced after the war. The panorama is made up of the badges of the formations which made up Middle East Land Forces, including H.Q. M.E.L.F.; British Troops in Egypt; Cyprus District; Tripolitania District; Cyrenaica District; British Troops in Iraq; Aden District; Sudan Defence Force; British Troops in Palestine and Transjordan; British Troops in Greece; East Africa Command and Malta Force.

[Reproduced by permission of H.Q. M.E.L.F.

Formation badges used to decorate the covers of the Orders of Service of the Thanksgiving Services for the victories of the First, Second and Eighth Armies in North Africa, Italy and North West Europe.

Formation badges of the Eighth Army along the wall of the Central Supply Depot at Tobruk.

[Reproduced by permission of the Editor of the "R.A.S.C. Journal"]

The Reading Room of the Royal Military Academy Library at Sandhurst, in 1946-47, showing, around the walls, part of the collection of Formation Signs, presented by 161 (R.M.C.) O.C.T.U.

[*Photo by Gale & Polden Ltd.*]

The Display of Formation Badges emblazoned on banners carried in the grand finale of "Drums," the Army Pageant held in 1946 at the Royal Albert Hall.

Photo by Gale & Polden Ltd.

APPENDIX I

LIST OF ABBREVIATIONS

A.A.	Anti-Aircraft.
A.A.I.	Allied Armies in Italy.
A.C.A.	Allied Control Austria.
A.D.C.	Aide-de-Camp.
A.D.G.B.	Air Defence of Great Britain.
Adm.	Administration; Administrative.
A.F.H.Q.	Allied Force Headquarters (North Africa and Italy)
A.F.P.U.	Army Film and Photographic Unit(s).
A.F.V.	Armoured Fighting Vehicle.
A.G.R.A.	Army Group Royal Artillery.
A.L.F.S.E.A.	Allied Land Forces, South-East Asia.
A.M.D.C.	Army Mechanized Demonstration Column.
A.V.R.E.	Armoured Vehicle, Royal Engineers.
B.A.O.R.	British Army of the Rhine.
B.C.O.F.	British Commonwealth Occupational Force.
Bde.	Brigade.
B.E.F.	British Expeditionary Force.
B.F.I.G.	British Forces in Greece.
B.L.A.	British Liberation Army (21st Army Group).
Bn.	Battalion.
B.N.A.F.	British North Africa Force.
Brindiv	British/Indian Division (B.C.O.F.).
B.T.A.	British Troops in Austria.
B.T.B.	British Troops in Berlin.
B.T.E.	British Troops in Egypt.
B.T.L.C.	British Troops in the Low Countries.
B.T.N.I.	British Troops in Northern Ireland.
C.A.P.F.	Canadian Army Pacific Force.
C.B.	Companion of the Bath.
C.B.E.	Commander of the Order of the British Empire.
C.C.G.	Control Commission for Germany.
C.I.G.S.	Chief of the Imperial General Staff.
C.M.F.	Central Mediterranean Force.
C.M.P.	Corps of Military Police. (Now C.R.M.P.—Corps of Royal Military Police.)
C.O.H.Q.	Combined Operations Headquarters.
C.R.A.S.C.	Commander Royal Army Service Corps.
C.R.E.	Commander Royal Engineers.
C.V.O.	Commander of the Royal Victorian Order.
C.W.	Chemical Warfare.
D.E.M.S.	Defensively Equipped Merchant Shipping.
D.I.D.	Detail Issue Depot (R.A.S.C.).
D.L.I.	Durham Light Infantry.
D.M.I.	Director of Military Intelligence.
Div.	Division.
D.S.O.	Distinguished Service Order.
E.T.O.U.S.A.	European Theatre of Operations United States Army.
G.H.Q.	General Headquarters.
G.O.C.	General Officer Commanding.
G.R.E.F.	General Reserve Engineering Force.
H.Q.	Headquarters.

Ind.	Indian.
Indep.	Independent.
I.T.C.	Infantry Training Centre.
K.B.E.	Knight Commander of the Order of the British Empire.
K.C.B.	Knight Commander of the Order of the Bath.
K.D.	Khaki Drill.
K.R.R.C.	King's Royal Rifle Corps.
K.S.L.I.	King's Shropshire Light Infantry.
L. of C.	Lines of Communication.
L.F.A.	Land Forces Adriatic.
M.B.E.	Member of the Order of the British Empire.
M.C.	Military Cross.
M.E.F.	Middle East Forces.
M.E.L.F.	Middle East Land Forces.
M.T.	Mechanical Transport.
N.W.E.F.	North-Western Expeditionary Force.
N.Z.	New Zealand.
N.Z.E.F.	New Zealand Expeditionary Force.
O.B.E.	Officer of the Order of the British Empire.
O.C.T.U.	Officer Cadet Training Unit.
P.A.I.C.	Persia and Iraq Command.
Paiforce	Persia and Iraq Force.
P.T.C.	Primary Training Centre.
P.o.W.	Prisoner of War.
P.W.E.	Political Warfare Executive.
R.A.	Royal Artillery.
R.A.C.	Royal Armoured Corps.
R.A.F.	Royal Air Force.
R.A.M.C.	Royal Army Medical Corps.
R.A.S.C.	Royal Army Service Corps.
R.A.O.C.	Royal Army Ordnance Corps.
R.B.	Rifle Brigade.
R.E.	Royal Engineers.
R.E.M.E.	Royal Electrical and Mechanical Engineers.
R.T.R.	Royal Tank Regiment.
S. & T.	Supply and Transport.
S.A.	South Africa.
S.A.C.S.E.A.	Supreme Allied Commander, South-East Asia.
S.A.S.	Special Air Service.
S.D.F.	Sudan Defence Force.
S.E.A.C.	South-East Asia Command.
S.H.A.E.F.	Supreme Headquarters Allied Expeditionary Force.
S.O.R.E.	Staff Officer, Royal Engineers.
T.A.	Territorial Army.
T.D.	Territorial Decoration. (Efficiency Decoration (Territorial)).
T.F.	Territorial Force.
U.K.	United Kingdom.
U.S.	United States (of America).
VE Day	"Victory in Europe" Day (8th May, 1945).

★ ★ ★ ★ ★

APPENDIX II

ARM OF SERVICE STRIPS

Introduced in 1940. These strips of coloured cloth were two inches in length and were worn below the formation badge on the sleeves of the battledress blouse.

Arm of Service	Colours
Royal Armoured Corps.	Yellow—Red
Royal Artillery	Red—Blue
Royal Engineers	Blue—Red
Royal Signals	Blue—White
Infantry (except Rifle Regiments)	Scarlet
Infantry (Rifle Regiments)	Rifle Green
Royal Army Chaplains' Dept.	Purple
Royal Army Service Corps	Yellow—Blue
Royal Army Medical Corps	Dull Cherry

Arm of Service	Colours
Royal Army Ordnance Corps	Red—Blue—Red
Royal Electrical and Mechanical Engineers	Red—Yellow—Blue
Corps of Royal Military Police*	Red
Royal Army Pay Corps	Yellow
Royal Army Educational Corps*	Cambridge Blue
Royal Army Dental Corps*	Green—White
Royal Pioneer Corps*	Red—Green
Intelligence Corps	Green
Army Physical Training Corps	Black—Red—Black
Army Catering Corps	Grey—Yellow

* The distinction "Royal" was granted in November, 1946.

APPENDIX III

VEHICLE ARM OF SERVICE MARKINGS

Painted on front and rear mudguards and/or on tailboards of trucks and lorries.

Arm of Service	Colours
Headquarters of Formations	Black
Headquarters R.A. and R.A. Units	Red / Blue
Headquarters R.E. and R.E. Units	Cobalt Blue
Headquarters R. Sigs. and R. Sigs. Units	White / Dark Blue
Reconnaissance Regiments (R.A.C.).	Green / Blue

Arm of Service		Colours
Lorried Infantry Battalions		Green
Headquarters R.A.S.C. and R.A.S.C. Units		Red—Green
Headquarters R.A.O.C. and R.A.O.C. Units		Blue Red Blue
Headquarters R.E.M.E. and R.E.M.E. Units		Black Yellow Red

★ ★ ★ ★ ★

Allied Vehicle Marking

A white five-pointed star within a white circle; or the white star alone, was the universal Allied vehicle marking in the campaign in North-Western Europe.* This was painted on the top of all Allied vehicles to aid recognition by aircraft.

---

* See illustration page 261.

APPENDIX IV

DESCRIPTIVE INDEX OF BADGES

ANIMALS

Alligator

		Page
White alligator and a white palm tree on a black background	4th Australian Armoured Brigade	104

Buffalos

Water Buffalo in white above a white boomerang on a black background	12th Australian Division ...	103
Buffalo's head in white, with red horns, set on a blue square	{ 21st Indian Division ... { 268th Lorried Infantry Brigade	124 135
Buffalo, charging, in black, with red horns, hooves and eyes, set on a white circle below the inscription in black, "Laro aur Larte Raho"	44th Indian Armoured ... Division	127
Buffalo, charging, in black, with red horns, hooves and eyes, set on a blue triangle.	255th Indian Tank Brigade	131
Buffalo's head in white set between the arms of a white "V" on a red background.	Lushai Brigade	136

Bears

White polar bear on black background	{ 49th (West Riding) Division { Iceland Force	62 165
White polar bear on a circular background divided evenly into five diagonal stripes—blue, yellow, green, red and blue	M.N.B.D.O.	146
Koala bear in white on black background	3rd Australian Division ...	99

Bulls

Black bull, charging. Red horns, eyes and hooves on a yellow background	11th Armoured Division ...	44
Bull's head with black and white markings, red and brown nostrils and red-tipped horns, set on a yellow background in an inverted equilateral triangle with a black border	79th Armoured Division ...	45
Charging bull in black and white on a black rectangle	4th New Zealand Division	106

Boars

Black boar rampant in a white circle on a black square	30 Corps	37
Boar's head in white above a white boomerang on a black background	5th Australian Division ...	100

Camels

Camel, brown, on black square	G.H.Q., M.E.F.	9
Camel, gold, on black square	G.H.Q., M.E.F.	9
Camel and rider, in black silhouette on square white background	H.Q. Sudan and Eritrea ...	167

Caribou

		Page
Caribou's head in yellow (gold) on a red oval	Newfoundland Units, R.A.	214

Cats

Cat, black (Kilkenny), arched back, on orange square	9 Corps	34
Cat, black (Dick Whittington's), back view on red background	56th (London) Division ...	68
Cat, black, rear view, tail outlined in red, curled in shape of figure 9. Aircraft silhouette in red on cat's back	9th A.A. Division	81
Cat, black, side view, back arched, on khaki background	17th Indian Division ...	122

Deer, etc.

Stag's head in red on white background	22nd Armoured Brigade ...	196
White hart's head on a rectangle divided, top half red, lower half dark blue	303rd Infantry Brigade ...	209
Deer's head in yellow on a dark blue circle	Indian Field Broadcasting Units	212
Black head and antlers on a yellow circle or square	Trincomalee Fortress Area	188
Kudu, in white, on a black square	12th (African) Division ...	140
Springbok's head in light yellow, picked out in black and white, set on khaki	U.D.F. Repatriation Units	110

Dogs

Bulldog in white on black background	H.Q. Eastern Command ...	15
Bulldog in white, set above a white boomerang on a black background	1 Australian Corps ...	97
Greyhound in white, leaping over a boomerang in white, on a black background	{ 1st Australian Cavalry Division 1st Australian Motor Division	98 98
Dingo (Australian) dog in white, above a boomerang in white, on a black background	Australian Imperial Forces Base, M.E.F.	96
Head of a black Alsatian dog, open mouth showing bright red tongue, set on a pale green oval with a black border	Sussex District	159
Husky dog, white head, red ears and tongue, set on pale green circle	No. 1 District, C.M.F. ...	177
White bulldog, set on a yellow five-pointed star, on a red square background	British Reinforcement Training Centre (India)	229

Duck-Billed Platypus

Duck-billed platypus in white above a white boomerang set on a black rectangle	9th Australian Division ..	102

Elephants

Description	Formation	Page
Elephant's head, in yellow, on background evenly divided horizontally into red, black and red	Ceylon Army Command	21
Elephant's head in red, with white tusks, on blue background	{ Persia and Iraq Command { British Troops in Iraq	22 167
Elephant in red, charging (on its back a small red castle), set on a black circle	{ H.Q. Ninth Army and North Levant District	26 176
Elephant in black on red background	4 Corps	32
Elephant in black on green background	31st Indian Armoured Division	126
Elephant in white, trunk raised, on a black circular background	22nd (East African) Brigade	141
Elephant and palm tree in white on a black circle	Gold Coast Area	179
Elephant, rear view, in white on khaki background	253 L. of C. Sub-Area	184

Foxes

Description	Formation	Page
Fox's mask in red on a black (or yellow) circle	10th Armoured Division	44
Fox's mask in reddish brown on a yellow circle with a narrow brown border	8th Armoured Brigade	195

Gazelle

Description	Formation	Page
Red leaping gazelle on a white circle in a red diamond with a narrow white border	13 Corps	36

Goat

Description	Formation	Page
Leaping goat in red, set above three wavy blue lines, on a white or khaki background	{ Dodecanese Force { Force 281	166

Hog

Description	Formation	Page
Black Hampshire hog on a white rectangular or semi-circular background	Hampshire County Division	84

Hornet

Description	Formation	Page
Yellow hornet on a black background	2nd Indian Division	114

Horses

Description	Formation	Page
Horse's head, heraldic, with flowing mane, in white on a square black background	{ Eastern Command (India) { 21 Indian Corps	21 112
Horse in white, set above a boomerang in white on a black background	2nd Australian Army	96
Knight's charger's head, armour-clad, in white on black background	3rd Australian Army Tank	103
Horse's head in white, within narrow white circle, set on a dark green circular background	North Kent and Surrey District	159
Prancing white horse (the White Horse of Kent) on a dark green oval background	North Kent and Surrey District	159
White horse on bright green square or semi-circular background	9th Armoured Brigade	195
Knight's charger's armoured-clad head in white on a black background	20th Armoured Brigade	196

Kangaroo

		Page
White kangaroo leaping over a white boomerang set on a black background	6th Australian Division ...	100

Lions

Lion, heraldic, gold (or yellow) on circle divided top half dark blue, lower red	G.H.Q. Home Forces ...	9
Lion, rampant (heraldic, Scottish), in gold on background divided into three bands—red, black, red	H.Q. Scottish Command ...	16
Lion, rampant (heraldic, Scottish) in gold on red background	Scottish Command (other than H.Q.)	16
Lion, rampant (heraldic, Scottish) in gold on background divided into diagonals purple and green	North Highland District ...	162
Lion, rampant (heraldic, Scottish) in gold superimposed on white St. Andrew's Cross on red background	West Scotland District ...	161
Lion, rampant (heraldic, Scottish) in gold superimposed on white St. Andrew's Cross on dark green background	East Scotland District ...	161
Lion, Assyrian, in gold on black background, or in white on light blue background	H.Q. Tenth Army	27
Lion, Cyprus, in red on yellow background	25 Corps	37
Lion, rampant (heraldic, Scottish), in red in a yellow circle with a white border set on a black square	15th (Scottish) Division ...	53
Lion, Persian (scimitar in right paw), outlined in blue on yellow background	12th Indian Division ...	121
Lion and palm tree in yellow on black rectangle	Sierra Leone Area	180
Lions, heraldic, in gold, three on a red shield	Force 135	151
Lion, Cyprus, in yellow on green background	Cyprus District	176
Lion's head, heraldic, in black outlined in white on a khaki background	10th A.A. Division ...	81

Lizard

Pale green lizard on black rectangle	8th Bn. Cornwall Home Guard	231

Panda

Head of a giant panda in black and white	9th Armoured Division ...	43

Panther

Black leaping panther on a circle divided into three horizontal bands, red, white and red	34 Indian Corps	113

Porcupine

White porcupine above boomerang on black background	4th Australian Division ...	100

		Page
Rats		
Red desert rat (Jerboa) in a white circle on a red square	7th Armoured Division ...	42
Red rat picked out in white on a black background	7th Armoured Division ...	42
Black desert rat (Jerboa) on a white square	4th Armoured Brigade ...	193
Green rat on a white circle within a red ring	7th Armoured Brigade ...	194
Rhinoceros		
Standing rhino in white on a black oval	{ 1st Armoured Division ...	40
	2nd Armoured Brigade ...	193
Charging rhino in white on a black oval	1st Armoured Division ...	40
Black rhino on a white circle	East African Expeditionary Force	139
Rhino's head in grey, picked out in black, on a red circle, with inscription in black, "Laro aur Larte Raho"	42nd Indian Armoured Division	127
Rhino's head in black on a red circle	11th (East African) Division	141
Scorpions		
Black scorpion on a white background	Transjordan Frontier Force	171
White scorpion on a black background	2nd Australian Armoured Division	98
Salamander		
Green and black salamander passing through red and yellow flames	No. 1 Commando	145
Sea-horses		
Black sea-horse, picked out in white above a red bar, set on a khaki rectangle	North Caribbean Area ...	179
Yellow and white sea-horse set on a saxe blue shield	27th Armoured Brigade ...	198
Yellow sea-horse on a red circle on a royal blue inverted triangle	Royal Marines Training Establishment	149
Sea-lion		
Black sea-lion balancing a globe on its nose. Set on a yellow rectangle	12th Army	28
Spider		
Black tarantula spider on a yellow square or circle	81st (West African) Division	142
Tigers		
Tiger's head in black, white, yellow and red on khaki circle	H.Q. South-Eastern Command	16
Tiger, in natural colours, stepping out of a blue triangle set on a black triangular background	26th Indian Division ...	125
Tiger's head in black and yellow on square background	6th Indian Division ...	117
Tiger's head and shoulders in yellow and black on a red square	251st Indian Tank Brigade	130
Tiger's head in red on a white background	1st Armoured Brigade Group	193

BIRDS

Description	Unit	Page
Bird in white seated on a nest on a black bough on a green background	Northern Ireland District	162
Cock in red on a khaki or light yellow circle	23rd Indian Division	124
Crane bird with red head, neck and legs and a blue body	38th Indian Infantry Brigade	131
Crown bird in black on white rectangular background	Nigeria Area	180
Black displayed German Eagle, picked out in yellow, a scarlet arrow thrust upward through its breast, set on a khaki background	11th A.A. Division	82
Red eagle in flight, a red arrow through its breast, set on a bright blue background	1 A.A. Corps	76
Eagle in red in flight on a dark blue background	4th Indian Division	115
Eagle in gold, wings displayed, on a black background	East Riding and Lincs District	155
Golden eagle on a black and white quartered shield on a black shield	Special Training Centre, Lochailort	230
Eaglet in white on a red square	Rawalpindi District	185
Double-headed eagle in white on royal blue shield	Royal Jugoslav Forces	255
Emu in white above a white boomerang, set on a black background	8th Australian Division	102
Falcon's head, in white, on a red square	Arab Legion	171
Kiwi in white on black background	{ 3rd New Zealand Division { 6th New Zealand Division	106 107
Kea's head in black and white on black background	5th New Zealand Division	107
Kookaburra in brown and white seated on a white boomerang on a black background	7th Australian Division	101
Liver bird in black on white square or circle	23rd Armoured Brigade	197
Macaw in blue on a red diamond with a dark blue oval	48th (South Midland) Division	61
Magpie on a black background	3 Australian Corps	97
Oyster catcher (Tjaldur), in black and white, standing on a black rock against background of dark blue sea and light blue sky	Faero Islands Force	165
Paddy bird in white on a red square	404th (East Bengal) L. of C. Area	184
Pelican in white on a black shield	Bahawalpur State Forces, India	138
Parakeet's head in white above a white boomerang on a black background	{ 2nd Australian Corps { New Guinea Force	97 166
Partridge, black, Francolin, in flight on a white oval	{ 8th Corps { South-Western District	33 158
Penguin above a white boomerang on a black background	2nd Australian Division	99
Penguin in black and white on a khaki background	22nd Beach Brigade	145
Peewit (plover) in black and white on a light blue diamond with a narrow red border	Political Warfare Executive M.E.F.	213

		Page
Stork in flight on green rectangular background	South Burma District ...	188
Sussex martlet in black on a green circle	Canadian Corps District ...	159
Swan in white above a white boomerang on a black background	First Australian Army ...	96

FISH

Dogfish in white above three wavy white lines on a red square	Kohat District	186
Dolphin in blue on a square black background	No. 15 Area M.E.F. ...	175
Two blue-grey fish set on a red circle	Unit Provinces Area ...	187
Red salmon on background of three wavy blue bands on a white background with a narrow red border	2 Corps	31

FLOWERS

White Tudor rose on blue (or green) background	23rd Division	54
Red (Lancashire) rose with green stalk and leaves on a khaki circle or square	55th (West Lancashire) Division	67
Red (Lancashire) rose set in a yellow entwined border on a dark green square	{ Lancs and Border District { North-Western District ...	156 156
Red (Lancashire) rose and white (Yorkshire) rose on a black rectangle	71st Independent Infantry Brigade	205
Thistle flower on a stalk with two leaves in white (or silver) on a dark blue background	9th (Scottish) Division ...	51
Thistle flower on a stalk with two leaves in which, flanked either side, is the letter "A" in white. Set on a square blue background	3rd A.A. Division	78
Tulip in red, with light green leaves, set on white rectangle	{ Lincolnshire County Division { 212th Independent Infantry { Brigade	85 207
White daisy, with pale green centre, stalk and leaf set on black rectangle	32nd Army Tank Brigade ...	198

FRUIT

Green apple on a royal blue diamond	Northern Command ...	15

LEAVES

Three four-leafed clover leaves and stems in yellow on a dull red background	8th Indian Division ...	118
Fig leaf in green on white square	{ 3 Corps ... ... { H.Q. Land Forces, Greece { H.Q. British Forces in { Greece	31 168 168
Fern leaf in white on black circle or square	2nd New Zealand Division	105
Maple leaf in gold (or yellow) on black circle with gold (or yellow) border	Canadian Military Headquarters	86
Shamrock leaf in green	38th Infantry Brigade ...	203

NUTS

		Page
Acorn in brown on a white square	40th Division	56
Cob nut, green shell, yellow nut on a khaki background	36th Independent Infantry Brigade	203

TREES

Green oak tree (Sherwood oak), black branches and trunk, outlined in white on black square	46th (North Midland) Division	59
Black palm tree on white background	West African Command ...	23
Palm tree in white on black background	11th Australian Division ...	103
Palm tree in yellow, outlined in black set above a yellow scroll with the black initials "R.W.A.F.F." on a green circle	West African Expeditionary Force	139
Palm tree in yellow on a red square	109 (Bangalore) L. of C. Area	183
Three trees (oak, ash and thorn), green, with black trunks on white oval set on a black rectangle	12 Corps	36
Yellow palm tree on black square	Madras Defended Port Area	187

AEROPLANES

Black aircraft in silhouette, pierced by a red sword, on a light blue background with a black edge	1st A.A. Division	77
Black aircraft in silhouette, nose downwards, five red flames rising upwards from the wings and fuselage, the whole on a khaki background	5th A.A. Division	79
Black aircraft in silhouette, nose downwards, a red eight-pointed star superimposed on the fuselage, the whole on a sky blue square	8th A.A. Division	80
Red aircraft in silhouette below a red five-pointed star set on a diamond divided right half dark blue, left half white	Indian Air Formation Signals	222
Yellow aircraft on a royal blue square	Air Despatch Group, R.A.S.C.	224

ANCHORS

Naval fouled anchor in red on a pale blue circle with a red border	Beach Groups	144
Anchor, a tommy-gun, and an albatross in red on a dark blue background	Combined Operations Headquarters	143
Naval fouled anchor in red, set on dark blue shield, with yellow grenade superimposed on the anchor	Royal Marine Engineers ...	149
Naval fouled anchor in yellow on a red circle set in the centre of a yellow eight-pointed star	117th (Royal Marine) Infantry Brigade	148
Naval fouled anchor in red on a Navy blue background	Orkney and Shetland Defences	163
Black anchor, with a red figure 2 entwined, set on a blue circular background, with a black border	No. 2 Area S.E.A.C. (Singapore)	189

		Page
Anchor in black, suspended by two links from the horizontal blade of a black sword, set on a red background	No. 2 District, C.M.F. ...	178
Naval fouled anchor in red, with white rope set on a black background, the letters "A.A." (or "R.A.") in white, set either side of the anchor	Maritime Anti-Aircraft Artillery	215
Naval fouled anchor in yellow, set on an inverted red equilateral triangle with a narrow yellow edge on two sides, superimposed on a dark blue shield	Amphibian Support Regiment, Royal Marines	148

ARMOUR

White knight in armour on white charger, lance at the point, set on a scarlet background	8 Corps	33
Knight's helmet, plumed, in white on a red square	2nd Armoured Division ...	41
Mailed fist in white on a black square	6th Armoured Division ...	41
Mailed hand and arm raised, holding aloft a sword in pale blue on a red background	2 A.A. Corps	76
White knight in armour on a white horse on a black square	3rd Australian Armoured Division	98

WEAPONS

Arrows, Spears, etc.

Two spears in black crossed over a native carrier's head-band in black on a yellow shield	82nd (West African) Division	142
Black arrow, representing a Naga spear, pointing upwards through a blue wavy line on a white circle with a black border	202nd (Assam) L. of C. Area	183
White spearhead on a red diamond	1 Corps	30
White spearhead on a red diamond, with two dark blue diagonal bands	1 Corps Troops, R.E. ...	220
Gold arrow on a black square	7th Indian Division ...	117
Black bow and arrow, held by a black arm and hand, set on a red square	Anti-Aircraft Command ...	75
White arrow, pointing upwards, on red shield with central black band	Northern Command (India)	21
Red arrow piercing the centre of a black and white target set on a black square	6th A.A. Division	80

Daggers, Knives, etc.

Two white daggers crossed on a red background	Waziristan District ...	186
Arab dagger, white curved blade, black hilt, set on a square red background	H.Q. Palestine and Transjordan	166
Arab sheathed knife in black, set on white jagged-edged background, set on dark green square	Iraq Base and L. of C. Area	176
Commando dagger in silver (white), hilt uppermost, the letters "S.S." set on either side of the hilt	No. 2 Commando	145

Description	Unit	Page
Crossed daggers in white, the blades forming a "V"—and a letter "V" superimposed on the hilts which rests on a croll bearing the word "Force." All set on a light green circle	"V" Force	150
Two silver (white) Commando daggers set horizontally on a black rectangle. The hilt of each dagger in the shape of letter "S"	H.Q. Special Service Brigade	146
Dagger in yellow, held by a yellow hand and forearm, set on a red square	19th Indian Division	123
Dagger, unsheathed, point uppermost on a black background	Commando Brigades	145
Kris, Malayan dagger, with wavy-shaped blade in yellow on a dark green background	Malaya Command	23
Kukris, a pair, crossed, in white on a dark green background	43rd Indian Lorried Infantry Brigade	132
Panga upright, white blade and black handle, set on a red shield with a black border	28th (East African) Brigade	141
Pangas, a pair, crossed left over right, silver (white) blades, black handles, set on a green background or on a red circle with a black border	East Africa Command	23

Other Weapons

Description	Unit	Page
Battleaxe, in yellow, on a black circle or square	78th Division	71
Battleaxe in white, held aloft by an armour-clad hand and arm on a black background	1st Australian Armoured Division	97
Battleaxe in white on a black background	1st New Zealand Division	105
Battleaxe in yellow on a royal blue rectangle	116th Indian Infantry Brigade	134
Bayonet, vertical, point uppermost, in yellow set on a black shield	150th Indian Infantry Brigade	134
Lances with red and white pennants. A pair crossed below a stringed bugle horn in white on a black background	60th Indian Infantry Brigade	133
Crossed lances in white behind a white tank set on a blue cross on a red shield	R.A.C. Training Centre, B.A.O.R.	223
Spiked mace, held aloft by a mailed fist on a red shield, divided diagonally by a yellow band	34th Armoured Brigade	199
Seaxes, three in white, on a red shield or red square	Essex County Division	84
Two seaxes, with blue blades and yellow hilts, set on a black shield within a yellow border	2 Corps District	160
Three seaxes in blue set on a red square	223rd Independent Infantry Brigade	208
Sword bayonet, point uppermost, set on a rectangle divided horizontally into three bands, blue, red and blue	33rd Guards Brigade	203

Swords

Description	Unit	Page
Crossed Cavalry swords and an upright pike set behind a Cromwellian helmet, all in black and white on a red background	East Central District	161
	Central Midland District	161

		Page
Crossed swords, hilts uppermost, in yellow on a blue cross on a red shield	H.Q. 21st Army Group ...	14
	H.Q. British Army of the Rhine	190
Red sword, held aloft by a white hand and arm rising from three wavy blue lines, set on a black rectangle	77th Division	71
Red sword, point uppermost, blade passing through a yellow crown, set on a dark blue background	London District	153
Rapier and cutlass in black, crossed on a yellow background	South Caribbean Area ...	179
Small white sword, point uppermost, on a black shield set on a red cross on a white background	No. 21 Area M.E.F. ...	177
Sword, white blade, yellow hilt, set on a blue cross on a white shield	Second Army	25
Sword, white blade, yellow hilt, set on a red cross on a white shield	First Army	24
Two black (Mahratta) swords, crossed above a circular black shield on a red background	110th (Poona) Area ...	183
White sword, point uppermost, red flames leaping from the blade, set on a black shield, the upper portion of which is occupied by a sky blue band and narrow bands of rainbow colours	Supreme Headquarters Allied Expeditionary Force (S.H.A.E.F.)	8
White sword, with curled hilt, set on a red shield, a black band set across the centre bearing the Roman figures "XIV" in white	Fourteenth Army ...	29
White sword, with the letters "B.T." set on either side of the blade in red and a spray of green leaves on either side of the hilt, the whole on a dark green shield	Royal Netherlands Army Garrison Troops (Overseas)	249
White sword (tulwar), raised aloft by a white hand and arm on a black background	20th Indian Division ...	123
White sword, held aloft by a brown hand, set on a green circle	39th Indian Division ...	126

Guns

Black cannon on a red rectangle	Lahore District	186
Two crossed cannons in dark blue set above a dark blue cannon ball on a red square	301st Infantry Brigade ...	209
Muzzle-loading gun and a stack of cannon balls on a circle divided into red and blue	Coast Artillery Units ...	214

LETTERS

"A.A." in white, the letters overlapping, set on an evenly divided rectangle, top half red, lower half dark blue	Anti-Aircraft and Coast Units, R.A. (C.M.F.)	214
"AA" in white, set on either side of a red anchor with a white rope on a black square	Maritime A.A. Artillery ...	215

		Page
"AF" in white on a saxe blue circle with a red border	Allied Force Headquarters	10
"G.F." in dark green in the centre of a yellow five-pointed star on a dark green circle	General Reserve Engineering Force	152
"GO" in black on a green circle on a square black background	8th Armoured Division ...	43
"HD" conjoined in red within a red circle on a blue square	51st (Highland) Division ...	64
"JP" conjoined in blue on a red circle	54th (East Anglian) Division	66
	162nd Independent Infantry Brigade	206
"NM" conjoined in black on a khaki rectangle	148th Independent Infantry Brigade	206
"P" in white on a black square	G.Q.H. Liaison Regiment	211
"R" in white on a black shield	"R" Force	150
"RA" in white, set either side of a red anchor, with a white rope on a black square	Maritime Anti-Aircraft Artillery	215
"T" in red	Tunnelling Companies, R.E.	218
"TT" in red on a black square	50th (Northumbrian) Division	63
Three black "V"s on a red background	15 Indian Corps	111
"W" set on a base line in red on a khaki background	53rd (Welsh) Division ...	66
"Y" in white on a khaki square	5th Division	49
"Y" in white on a black circle	5th Division	49

GEOMETRICAL

Circle, divided in centre, top half yellow, lower half dark green	2nd South African Division	109
Circle in red on a black square	5th Indian Division ...	116
Red circle, one quadrant displaced, set on a white square	4th Division	48
Black circle with red border	British Troops in Berlin ...	190
White circle above a white rectangle, set on a green square	10 Corps	35
A quarter of a circle in red	4th Division	48
Diagonal bands of red (or pink) and blue forming a cross on a black square	10th Indian Division ...	120
Diamond, divided in centre, top half yellow, lower half green	1st South African Division	108
White diamond	12th Division	52
Red diamond on a blue square	61st Division	69
Diamond, horizontal, in red, with a central dark blue band	First Canadian Army ...	86
Diamond, horizontal, scarlet	1 Canadian Corps ...	88
Diamond, horizontal, dark blue	2 Canadian Corps ...	88
Diamond, horizontal, in black, with a central red band	1st Canadian Armoured Brigade	92
Diamond, horizontal, in black, with a central dark blue band	2nd Canadian Armoured Brigade	92

		Page
Small white equal-sided diamond superimposed on a larger red equal-sided diamond	42nd Armoured Division ...	45
	42nd (East Lancashire) Division	57
Hexagon, with six equal segments—red, blue, French grey, green, maroon and black	Candian Army Pacific Force	93
Oval, scarlet	44th (Home Counties) Division	58
Oval, scarlet, with narrow white border	44th (Home Counties) Division	58
Pyramid, composed of three inner triangles, grey, salmon buff and green, within a blue border	204th Independent Infantry Brigade	206
Rectangle, red	1st Canadian Division ...	89
Rectangle, royal blue	2nd Canadian Division ...	90
Rectangle, French grey	3rd Canadian Division ...	91
Rectangle, dark green	4th Canadian Armoured Division	91
Rectangle, maroon	5th Canadian Armoured Division	91
Red ring on a black square	72nd Indian Brigade ...	205
Ring in white on a black background	29th Independent Brigade Group	202
White ring linked with a red ring on a black background	36th Division	55
Red ring on a black equal-sided diamond	Central Command (India)	20
Black square, set on the centre of a black cross on a yellow background	18th Division	54
Square, divided in centre, top half yellow, lower half green	3rd South African Division	109
Square, quartered, top quarters red and green, the lower green and red	Colombo Sub-Area ...	188
Equilateral triangle in white	1st Division	46
Small red inverted equilateral triangle set on a black equilateral triangle	3rd Division	47
Triangle, equilateral, in yellow, in the centre of a larger dark green triangle	6th South African Armoured Division	110
Two equilateral triangles, one inverted above the other, top triangle green, lower black	33rd Armoured Brigade ...	198
Equilateral triangle, divided horizontally into three equal bands, light blue, yellow, and light blue	66th Division	69

STARS

Four red stars with white edges on a square black background	New Zealand Expeditionary Force	105
Red four-pointed star on a white square	6th Division	50
	70th Division	70
Royal Blue nine-pointed star on a black circle	9th Indian Division ...	119
Five white stars (conventional representation of the constellation of the Southern Cross) on a shield. Field of the shield varying in colours (eighteen different variations)	Southern Command (U.K.)	17

		Page
White five-pointed star on a rectangle, divided evenly, top half light blue/grey, lower half dark blue	Military Adviser-in-Chief, Indian State Forces	137
Four yellow stars on a square background, evenly divided into three horizontal bands, red, black and red	Southern Army (India) ...	111
Yellow five-pointed star, set on a rectangle or a shield evenly divided, top half red, lower half dark blue	G.H.Q., India	10
Yellow (gold) five-pointed star set on a dark blue background	Indian Units, B.C.O.F. ...	137
Star, nine-pointed, in royal blue on a black circle	9th Indian Division ...	119
Star, eight-pointed, composed of eight diamonds, four red and four blue, in alternate colours	32nd Independent Guards Brigade	202

BUILDINGS, MONUMENTS, etc.

Castle gateway in white on a square, divided evenly into red, black and red horizontal bands	North-Western Army (India) ...	111
Frontier fort in white (Jamrud Fort, Khyber Pass) on a red background	Peshawar District	185
The Great Cromlech of Stonehenge in red, set on a yellow background on a green grass base within a black and red circle	Salisbury Plain District ...	157
Indian triumphal arch (the Gateway of India, Bombay) in black and white on red background	108 (Bombay) L. of C. Area	182
Mosque (the Mohamed Ali Mosque in Cairo) in black on a white background	No. 17 Area, M.E.F. ...	175
Martello Tower in black and white on a black diamond	11 Corps	35
A pyramid in red, and two palm trees in red on a white background	British Troops in Egypt ...	169
Land's End lighthouse and rocky coast in black on red background with narrow black border	12th Bn. Cornwall Home Guard	232

TORCHES

Black torch, red flames, set on a white shield with three blue wavy lines in the lower portion	H.Q. Central Mediterranean Force	11
Black torch, red flames held in a white hand, set on a buff or yellow background	No. 56 Area, C.M.F. ...	179
Yellow torch, red flames, on a black diamond	218th Independent Infantry Brigade	207
Yellow torch on a blue cross set on a red shield	B.A.O.R. Training Centre	229

KEYS

Crossed keys in white on black square	{ 2nd Division	47
	{ 5th Infantry Brigade ...	201
Yellow key on a red rectangle	Gibraltar Garrison ...	164
Yellow key set on a rectangle divided diagonally into red and dark blue	R.A. Units, Gibraltar ...	271

HORSESHOES

		Page
Black horseshoe on a red square	13th Division	52
Red horseshoe on a black circle	3rd Indian Motor Brigade	129
Two white interlocked horseshoes on a black rectangle	H.Q. Park Transport Group R.A.S.C.	225

BELLS

A pair of red bells, suspended from a red bow, set on a dark blue background	47th (London) Division ...	60
Yellow bell on a blue shield	South Midland District ...	158

CARDS

Black Ace of Spades on a green square	25th Indian Division ...	125
Black Ace of Clubs on a white square	11th (African) Division ...	140

GATES

Red three-barred gate on a black background	British Troops in Northern Ireland	163
White three-barred gate on a light green background	Northern Ireland District	162

MUSICAL INSTRUMENTS

Trumpet in white on a black background	9 Corps	34
Side drum in yellow, red bands top and base, white cords (Drake's Drum), set on a khaki background	45th (Wessex) Division ...	59
Stringed bugle horn in white, superimposed by a crown and the figures "95" superimposed on the cords, set on a square divided diagonally into green and black	61st Independent Infantry Brigade	204

DOMINO

Dark blue and white domino on a horizontal diamond in red	12th A.A. Division ...	82

SHEARS

Pair of sheep shears in yellow on a dark green background	Durham and North Riding County Division	83

FEATHERS

Prince of Wales's feathers in red on a dark green circle	North Wales District ...	155
	Midland West District ...	155

DRAGONS

Burmese dragon (Chinthe, pagoda custodian) in yellow and white, set on a square divided into three bands—red, yellow, red, the Roman figures "XII" in white on the lower red portion	12th Army	28
Burmese dragon in gold (yellow) on a dark blue circle	3rd Indian Division ...	114

		Page
Red (Welsh) dragon on a green background	South Wales District ...	155
White dragon on black square	4th New Zealand Armoured Brigade	107
Wyvern (dragon) in yellow on dark blue square	43rd (Wessex) Division ...	57
Yellow (Chinese) dragon, set on a red rectangle with a central black band	H.Q. Land Forces, Hong Kong	168

PHŒNIX

Head of a white Phœnix rising from red flames, in its beak a white torch with red flames, set on a dark blue circle with a white border	219th Independent Infantry Brigade	208
Head of a blue Phœnix rising from red flames, in its beak a torch, set on a white oval	British Military Headquarters in the Balkans	212
Phœnix in blue, rising from red flames on white circle with blue border	Supreme H.Q. South-East Asia	11
Yellow Phœnix, wings outspread, arising from red flames surmounted by a red seven-pointed corona, set on a black square	Madras District, 105 (Madras) L. of C. Area	181

IMPS, DEVILS, etc.

Green imp, set on brown rectangle	Lincolnshire Home Guard	231
Red devil behind a dark blue diabolo, set on a yellow circle	16th Armoured Brigade ...	196

SHIPS, BOATS, etc.

Arab dhow in full sail in white, set on a light blue diagonal on a yellow square	No. 18 (Suez Canal) Area M.E.F.	175
Arab dhow in full sail in white on a black background	H.Q. British Troops in Aden	167
Barbary pirate's galley in black, set on a square background, blue sea and white sky	Tripolitania District ...	174
Egyptian caique in white on a black sea and dark blue sky	No. 16 Area, M.E.F. ...	175
A liner in red on a light blue sea, yellow sky set in a light blue border	80th Division	72
Norfolk wherry in full sail in red on a dark blue square	76th Division	70
Sampan in full sail in yellow on a dark blue sea with a red sky	11th Army Group ...	12
Vikings' galley in white, red cross on sail, on a black background	5 Corps	32
Vikings' galley in white above three wavy white lines, to denote sea, and a white rising sun, set on a pale blue square	British Troops in Norway	169
Native craft in full sail in white on a maroon background	Sind District	185

www.ingramcontent.com/pod-product-compliance
Ingram Content Group UK Ltd.
Pitfield, Milton Keynes, MK11 3LW, UK
UKHW022122230426
12048UKWH00011BA/654